Feminist Community Engagement

COMMUNITY ENGAGEMENT IN HIGHER EDUCATION

Edited by Dan W. Butin

This series examines the limits and possibilities of the theory and practice of community engagement in higher education. It is grounded in the desire to critically, thoughtfully, and thoroughly examine how to support efforts in higher education such that community engagement—a wide yet interrelated set of practices and philosophies such as service-learning, civic engagement, experiential education, public scholarship, participatory action research, and community-based research—is meaningful, sustainable, and impactful to its multiple constituencies. The series is by its nature cross-disciplinary and sees its readership across the breadth of higher education, both within student and academic affairs.

Dan W. Butin is an associate professor and founding dean of the School of Education at Merrimack College and the executive director of the Center for Engaged Democracy. He is the author and editor of more than 70 academic publications, including the books *Service-Learning in Theory and Practice: The Future of Community Engagement in Higher Education* (2010), which won the 2010 Critics Choice Book Award of the American Educational Studies Association; *Service-Learning and Social Justice Education* (2008); *Teaching Social Foundations of Education* (2005); and, most recently with Scott Seider, *The Engaged Campus: Majors and Minors as the New Community Engagement* (2012). Dr Butin's research focuses on issues of educator preparation and policy, and community engagement. Prior to working in higher education, Dr Butin was a middle-school math and science teacher and the chief financial officer of Teach For America. More about Dr Butin's work can be found at http://danbutin.org/.

The Engaged Campus: Majors, Minors and Certificates as the New Community Engagement
   Edited by Dan W. Butin and Scott Seider

Engaged Learning in the Academy: Challenges and Possibilities
   By David Thornton Moore

Deepening Community Engagement in Higher Education: Forging New Pathways
   Edited by Ariane Hoy and Mathew Johnson

Turning Teaching Inside Out: A Pedagogy of Transformation for Community-Based Education
   Edited by Simone Weil Davis and Barbara Sherr Roswell

Service-Learning at the American Community College: Theoretical and Empirical Perspectives
   Edited by Amy E. Traver and Perel Zivah Katz

Feminist Community Engagement: Achieving Praxis
   Edited By Susan Van Deventer Iverson and Jennifer Hauver James

Feminist Community Engagement

Achieving Praxis

Edited by
*Susan Van Deventer Iverson and
Jennifer Hauver James*

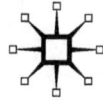

FEMINIST COMMUNITY ENGAGEMENT
Copyright © Susan Van Deventer Iverson and Jennifer Hauver James, 2014.

All rights reserved.

First published in 2014 by
PALGRAVE MACMILLAN®
in the United States—a division of St. Martin's Press LLC,
175 Fifth Avenue, New York, NY 10010.

Where this book is distributed in the UK, Europe and the rest of the world, this is by Palgrave Macmillan, a division of Macmillan Publishers Limited, registered in England, company number 785998, of Houndmills, Basingstoke, Hampshire RG21 6XS.

Palgrave Macmillan is the global academic imprint of the above companies and has companies and representatives throughout the world.

Palgrave® and Macmillan® are registered trademarks in the United States, the United Kingdom, Europe and other countries.

ISBN: 978–1–137–44109–6

Library of Congress Cataloging-in-Publication Data is available from the Library of Congress.

A catalogue record of the book is available from the British Library.

Design by Newgen Knowledge Works (P) Ltd., Chennai, India.

First edition: December 2014

10 9 8 7 6 5 4 3 2 1

Transferred to Digital Printing in 2015

Contents

Series Editor's Preface   vii
Dan Butin

Acknowledgments   xi

Chapter 1   Introduction   1
Susan Van Deventer Iverson and Jennifer Hauver James

Chapter 2   Feminism and Community Engagement:
An Overview   9
Susan Van Deventer Iverson and Jennifer Hauver James

Part I   Theoretical Considerations

Chapter 3   Conversations from Within: Critical Race
Feminism and the Roots/Routes of Change   31
Begum Verjee and Shauna Butterwick

Chapter 4   Role Modeling Community Engagement for
College Students: Narratives from Women
Faculty and Staff of Color   53
Jasmine Mena and Annemarie Vaccaro

Chapter 5   Social Media for Social Justice: Cyberfeminism in
the Digital Village   75
Carolyn M. Cunningham and Heather M. Crandall

Chapter 6   Transgressing *Intellectual* Boundaries Begins with
Transgressing *Physical* Ones: Feminist Community
Engagement as Activist-Apprentice Pedagogy   93
Dana Bisignani

Part II Feminist Applications

Chapter 7	Feminist Student Philanthropy: Possibilities and Poignancies of a Service-Learning and Student Philanthropy Initiative *Christin L. Seher*	115
Chapter 8	The Personal Is the Political: Community Engagement with Men as Feminist Border Crossing *Lamea "Elle" Shaaban-Magaña and Melanie L. Miller*	135
Chapter 9	Moving from Theory to Practice: The Rocxxy Summer Internship in Feminist Activism and Leadership *Angela Clark-Taylor, Quinlan Mitchell, and KaeLyn Rich*	155
Chapter 10	Developing Sustainable Community Engagement by Repositioning Programs into Communities *Jana Noel*	175
Chapter 11	Conclusions: Re-visioning Community Engagement as Feminist Praxis *Jennifer Hauver James and Susan Van Deventer Iverson*	193

List of Contributors 205

Index 211

Series Editor's Preface

Dan Butin

It has been 40-some years since the rise of women's studies courses and programs brought feminist theory and practice into higher education. This intellectual movement attempted to rethink and remake the academy—from the curriculum to its pedagogy to its entire mode of power relations—in a non-male-centered mode of being. It is a model eloquently captured by Adrienne Rich (1979) in her essay "Towards a Woman-Centered University" where, she pointed out, "What we have at present is a man-centered university, a breeding ground not of humanism, but of masculine privilege" (p. 127).

Rich laid out a series of arguments that showed—clearly and bluntly—how the academy exploited, controlled, and shaped women at all levels of the system, from students to staff to faculty. And she painted a picture of how it could be otherwise, from the conceptual reimagining of what constitutes knowledge to the deeply practical and central need for adequate childcare. But at its core, she argued, such change had to do with community:

> Ideally, I imagine a very indistinct line between "university" and "community" instead of the familiar city-on-a-hill frowning down on its neighbors...What I am really suggesting is that it [the university] change its focus...a university responsive to women's needs would serve the needs of the human, visible community in which it sits...In a sense the solution I am proposing is anarchistic: that the university should address itself to the microcosms of national problems and issues that exist locally, and that it should do so with the greatest possible sense that it will not simply be giving, but be receiving...(p. 152)

It is with these words resonating in my head that I welcome and embrace this book by Susan Van Deventer Iverson and Jennifer Hauver James. It is, in fact, shocking and surprising—given Rich's eloquent and clear conjoining of feminist praxis and community engagement—that it has taken these 40-some years before such an important book was conceived and produced. But finally, with this book, we have the beginnings of a deeply needed dialogue within and across the fields of women's studies and service-learning on feminist modes and models of community-based teaching, learning, and research.

It is sorely needed. Community engagement—the umbrella term I use for the philosophical orientations and pedagogical practices such as service-learning, community-based research, and civic engagement—is an incredibly powerful model of teaching, learning, and research. But it is also, for better and worse, saturated with gendered norms and notions that impact how students, faculty, administrators, and the larger public view and engage with it.

It is no coincidence, I would suggest, that service-learning is enacted primarily within the so-called soft and applied fields in higher education (e.g., Education, Social Work, Communications) (Becher & Trowler, 2001; Butin, 2006); that it is done disproportionately by female faculty and by faculty of color and those not on the tenure-track (Antonio et al., 2000; Jaeger & Thornton, 2006); and that "service"—whether within or outside the academy's walls—is all too often deemed "women's work" which has no alignment to faculty rewards or advancement (Acker & Armenti, 2004; Acker & Feuerverger, 1996; Misra et al., 2011).

This book offers an entry point for such discussions as it attempts to both advance and question the field of service-learning. For a feminist lens, I would argue, has deep resonance and alignment with the key precepts within the service-learning field. As Rich noted elsewhere in her essay, higher education should "organize its resources around problems specific to its community; for example, adult literacy; public health... And the nature of much research (and its usefulness) might be improved if it were conceived as research *for*, rather than *on*, human beings" (pp. 152–153). This is at the heart of the "four Rs" that I (Butin, 2010) speak of—relevance, respect, reciprocity, and reflection—that should undergird all aspects of community engagement. And this is exactly what this book offers.

Iverson and James have brought together a wonderful mix of scholars and practitioners from across diverse disciplines to engage with the difficult questions of meaningful and sustainable community engagement. Above and beyond their own extremely helpful summation and synthesis of how feminist theory and practice can inform (and disturb) service-learning, their contributors offer distinct chapters for ways of thinking and engaging in community-based teaching, learning, and research that support powerful practices.

I was especially taken by the varied pedagogical models found throughout the book. From a "pay it forward" model of feminist student philanthropy to placing students in apprenticeships with nonprofit leaders to moving the center of service-learning fully into the community, the authors demonstrated how we can indeed begin to reimagine what teaching in higher education might look like. All of these examples embrace the activist turn that Iverson and James clearly place at the heart of feminist praxis, whereby "our challenge," they suggest, is "to erase the void between theory and action" (p. 21).

This is an especially appealing model because it allows all of us—students and faculty, insiders and outsiders to such a feminist praxis—the chance to develop and define an identity of ourselves and our relationships to the larger world. As one of the authors aptly stated of her research findings, "Community engagement was not merely something they [women faculty and staff of color] *did*, it was a central part of who they *were* as people" (p. 61). Indeed, it is a minimal step from the feminist rallying cry that the "personal is political" to the realization that community engagement allows and forces us to acknowledge that our education is not some kind of disinterested product, but a deeply interesting and important real-world process.

It is my hope that this book thus offers numerous opportunities for dialogue and debate about how to institutionalize an engaged and powerful model of community-based teaching, learning, and research that is not beholden to calcified and traditional models in higher education. Through this book, Iverson and James offer an important space and place that begins to make good on Rich's desire to foster a "breeding ground" of humanism that intersects feminist thought and community engagement in the academy. It's about time.

References

Acker, S., & Armenti, C. (2004). Sleepless in academia. *Gender and Education*, *16*(1), 3–24.

Acker, S., & Feuerverger, G. (1996). Doing good and feeling bad: The work of women university teachers. *Cambridge Journal of Education*, *26*(3), 401–422.

Antonio, A. L., Astin, H. S., & Cress, C. M. (2000). Community service in higher education: A look at the nation's faculty. *The Review of Higher Education*, *23*(4), 373–397.

Becher, T., & Trowler, P. (2001). *Academic tribes and territories: Intellectual enquiry and the culture of disciplines*. New York: McGraw-Hill International.

Butin, D. (2006). The limits of service-learning in higher education. *The Review of Higher Education, 29*(4), 473–498.
Butin, D. (2010). *Service-learning in theory and practice: The future of community engagement in higher education.* New York: Palgrave Macmillan.
Jaeger, A. J., & Thornton, C. H. (2006). Neither honor nor compensation: Faculty and public service. *Educational Policy, 20*(2), 345–366.
Misra, J., Lundquist, J. H., Holmes, E., & Agiomavritis, S. (2011). The ivory ceiling of service work. *Academe, 97*(1), 22–26.
Rich, A. C. (1979). Toward a woman-centered university. In *On lies, secrets, and silence: Selected prose, 1966–1978* (pp. 125–155). New York: Norton.

Acknowledgments

Like any volume of this nature, it took the contributions of many to bring it to fruition. Most obviously, this book is the result of a close collaboration between the coeditors, Susan and Jennifer, and the contributors. We are incredibly grateful to have had the opportunity to work with such a smart, passionate group of authors. We are grateful to you for your patience with and attentiveness to our requests and for your timely responses. We would also like to thank many people who have helped us in big or small ways. Specifically, we were inspired by those whose work urged us to think differently and critically about community engagement, such as Jennifer Baumgardner, Donna Bickford, Dan Butin, Judith Butler, Carol Gilligan, Rebecca Ropers-Huilman, Lynn O'Brien, Andrea O'Reilly, and Amy Richards. As well, the volume benefited greatly from the encouraging feedback we received from reviewers. Our contacts at Palgrave, Mara Berkoff and Sarah Nathan, and series editor, Dan Butin, have been supportive in turning this idea into a reality. Finally, we acknowledge Brenda McKenzie, a doctoral student in the higher education administration program at Kent State University, whose competent assistance and patience with the editing process for this book was invaluable.

Individually, Susan extends appreciation to colleagues at both Kent State University and University of Maine. In both places, my thinking has been enriched by faculty, staff, and students who enrich and expand each other's ideas. In particular, I am thankful for mentors who provided early inspiration for thinking about the intersections of feminism and service-learning. In my first-year teaching in my doctoral program, Elizabeth Allan handed me a graduate class to teach for which she had secured funds to incorporate a service-learning component. That teaching experience led me to wrestle with advantages and limitations of experiential education and community engagement, and inspired my thinking about civic action, more than service.

Mazie Hough provided counsel and imaginative space as I taught introductory women's studies and incorporated feminist activism into the course, when colleagues were telling me I could not assign activism. Both these feminist mentors supported my evolving thinking about feminist community engagement. As well, I am indebted to Susan Marine who facilitated the connection with Dan Butin and the invitation to write this book. Susan participated in a roundtable on service-learning in the women's studies curriculum. It was that session, of which I was a participant with Elizabeth Colwill, Coralynn Davis, Jennifer Musial, Leandra Preston, Ivy Schweitzer, Leseliey Rose Welch, and Jamie Huber, at the 2011 National Women's Studies Association annual conference that sparked the thinking for this volume. I extend my deepest gratitude to Jennifer, my coeditor, for her collaboration on this volume. From our early days in the Kent State archives, thinking about how the events of May 4, 1970 influenced our teaching of a first-year seminar about citizenship, to our current collaborations—you have modeled and inspired deep critical thinking about teaching, learning, and pedagogy. I am often reminded of Ken Teitelbaum's observation of our unlikely cross-disciplinary connection and wonderment at if we had not met as new faculty. I cannot imagine my professional, and personal, life without your presence, influence, and friendship. Finally, to Yale and Mia, my allies in social change, I extend gratefulness for your daily support, love, and patience.

Jennifer would first and foremost like to say thank you to Susan, whose commitment to keeping critical feminist discourses alive is an inspiration. You have been a powerful presence in my life both personally and professionally as we have traversed this academic journey together—sometimes from down the hall, more recently across the miles. You are one of the smartest women I know and I am honored to have been able to learn alongside you (again!) on this project. To Linda Valli and Jeremy Price, with whom I had the privilege to work at the University of Maryland, you were among the first to challenge my understandings of gender and sexuality, pushing me always to interrogate the taken-for-granted. Your work and your mentorship will always serve as models I aspire to emulate. Linda once said to me, "Stay bold." I think of this advice often, remembering to trust my inner voice and speak with confidence. To Jamie Huff Sisson, a former doctoral student whose intellect and compassion I have come to greatly admire. I am grateful for all I have learned from you as we have sought to understand and address the impact of gendered discourses at work within the field of early childhood education. To my cousin, Lizzy Hull Barnes, and my aunt, Kay Melby, who have long served as role models of strength and beauty; perhaps without even knowing it, you have taught me to love myself and to choose a life in which I can be more fully me. To my mother, Jane Curzio and my brother, Chris Hauver, thank you for many years of listening to my rants; your patience and love have made me strong. Finally, I'd like to thank the three people who play the leading roles in my life: to Bruce, whose love fills my every day, and to my daughters, Sarah and Grace, for whom this book is actually written. I love you.

CHAPTER 1

Introduction

*Susan Van Deventer Iverson
and Jennifer Hauver James*

Higher education has always been inextricably linked to its communities; yet, it has varied in the degree to which it has engaged and fostered relationships with those communities. Just being present is not synonymous with enacting civic responsibility. Those of us within the academy ought to, we believe, make the most of the opportunities afforded us to be a positive force in our communities, working alongside our partners to take up and address persistent issues of equity and access. This is not easily done. As Hurwitz noted, "Civic engagement in inevitable, but thoughtful and principled political engagement is harder" to facilitate and enact (in Harward, 2012, p. xii).

More and more, universities are calling on faculty to incorporate service-learning, community-based and field experiences in their courses—both as a means of growing students' civic identities and as a way to have a presence in the local community. Approaches to community engagement (CE) are varied; however, educators grapple with how to design experiential opportunities, develop students' civic consciousness, cultivate action-taking skills, and facilitate the creativity needed to imagine new solutions to old (and new) sociopolitical problems. Ample debate circulates about what to do and why. These questions are inherently related, as our methods are shaped by the commitments we hold. For those of us who wish for our students to have a "thick sense of justice necessary for the conscious (re)production of an ideal society" (Wheeler-Bell, 2014, p. 464), we are challenged to go beyond isolated, "feel good" acts of charity, the sort that constitute the bulk of CE efforts in the academy (Westheimer & Kahne, 2004).

Our limited thinking about community engagement (reduced to volunteerism) has, not surprisingly, yielded limited outcomes. Students' participation in volunteerism is up, but young adults lack civic (i.e., political) knowledge (Galston, 2007). Students *feel good* about their individual contribution(s) but fail to consider themselves in relation to a larger whole (Galston, 2007). Thus, we argue that we must move beyond charitable approaches to social problems to an examination of root causes. What is needed to shift our perspective from "How am I doing?" (and answering, "I feel good about helping them") to asking "How are we doing?" (Galston, 2007, p. 638)?

Much theorizing about CE (e.g., Barber & Battistoni, 1994; Butin, 2010) has emerged, in part, as a response to concerns over perceived weakening of civil society and disengagement from democracy (Colby, Ehrlich, Beaumont, & Stephens, 2003). Some question the role of higher education in working toward the common good and CE efforts (Kezar, Chambers, & Burkhardt, 2005). Though the literature on students' civic learning outcomes is growing (Eyler & Giles, 1999; Lichtenstein, Tombari, Thorme, & Cutforth, 2011), more scholars are beginning to ask what students are *not* learning (e.g., activism, resistance, capacity to question, participation in social movements) (e.g., Costa & Leong, 2012; Hurtado & DeAngelo, 2012; Wheeler-Bell, 2014). A response to these questions about learning outcomes may be found in critical and feminist perspectives on CE.

This volume aims to pick up this critical conversation by asking (and answering) the question: "What might be gained by bringing a feminist lens to the work of community engagement?" Many educators have brought a feminist lens to bear on their work within communities; these efforts, however, have largely been situated in feminist-identified communities and women's studies programs. We see the potential for feminist activism to reach beyond women's studies. We thought the time was ripe to bring a feminist perspective into a broader discussion of CE.

This volume has its origins in a roundtable discussion at the 2011 National Women's Studies Association annual conference. The panelists at the roundtable represented various disciplinary perspectives, but were seated at a women's studies conference, talking about "moving beyond the walls of women's studies with service-learning." With full appreciation and recognition for this disciplinary history, we want this volume to pollinate beyond the boundaries of women's studies, to connect with an audience who may (or may not) be affiliated with women's studies and may (or may not) be steeped in feminist thinking.

We extended our call for chapter proposals to insiders and outsiders of various circles: those within and outside of women's studies and community engagement. In response, we received proposals from a varied and interesting group of contributors, illuminating the diversity of "who" does CE work. As we molded the volume, we sought to ensure this collection would be intentionally multidisciplinary, in an effort to appeal to a broad audience. Our contributors hail from education, administration, communication, psychology, nutrition, counseling, and women's studies, among other disciplines. Our chapters chiefly concern community engagement in the United States, although we do include some perspectives from Canada. Our chapters draw primarily on work by White feminists (as we are), although chapters from other perspectives (e.g., the hybridity of feminism with critical race theory) deliberately challenge conventional thinking. Most of our contributors are full-time faculty; however, we also have contributors who are staff, administrators, community partners, and students. All chapters are authored by individuals who hold affiliation with higher education; however, most of our contributors are writing about, and their work is deeply embedded in, their communities. By definition, their community engagement interacts with and honors the work of their partners. Finally, our collection concentrates on issues and activities that are contemporary, but we are cognizant of historical points of reference on which and against which these current concerns and practices can be assessed.

Taken together, the essays in this volume illuminate successes and challenges of feminist community engagement. We have arranged these in two broad categories. Part I includes chapters that provide theoretical considerations, expand our understandings, and cross some (presumed) boundaries in the field of community engagement. Part II describes feminist community engagement as applied and experienced. While we have made this arbitrary division to the chapters, it should be noted that all chapters could arguably be assigned to either section. They are all rooted theoretically in feminism and many offer practical applications for our CE work.

Part I begins with a chapter by Verjee and Butterwick reflecting on their personal encounters with CE work within their institution. Using an autobiographical approach, they "illustrate the interconnection of racism, sexism and classism and how these underpin the dominant charity model of CE" (p. 31). Drawing upon critical race feminist theory and Whiteness Studies, their counter-stories call us to ask questions about who is doing CE work and to consider the differentiated risks in doing this work for women of color versus White women. In Chapter 4, Mena and Vaccaro extend the preceding narrative with their critical ethnographic study of how women of color role model CE. They illustrate the rich learning that can occur when college students observe women of color role models and emulate their community engagement actions. However, their findings also expand our dominant conceptions of community (to include family, religious groups, and neighbors or "fictive kin"). They reveal how CE is an important aspect of identity for women of color and used strategically to promote group survival.

Cunningham and Crandall, in their chapter on social media for social justice, move us away from the embodied experiences of women of color, to "the digital village." Rooted in their teaching, they draw upon a cyberfeminist lens to critically analyze gender inequities in nonprofits. Specifically, they present two vignettes from their experiences designing and teaching a graduate class, in order to highlight tensions (e.g., the politics of race and gender) involved in engaging CE work with students. In Chapter 6, Bisignani echoes points raised by Cunningham and Crandall, providing a critique of pedagogical models that merely send students into the community as uncritical and temporary volunteers. She advocates instead for an activist-apprentice model of service-learning that crosses not only intellectual borders (meaning to disrupt students' charitable thinking about their service), but also physical boundaries that separate the classroom within the academy from the surrounding community.

In Part II, authors describe and reflect on their practice. Seher, in the first chapter in this section, is a self-admitted novice to feminist pedagogy. She reflects on her incorporation of Pay It Forward (PIF), a service-learning and student philanthropy initiative, into a senior-level undergraduate community nutrition course. Acknowledging limitations in students learning outcomes, she considers how a feminist lens might push students' critical consciousness. Moving to the co-curricular, Shaaban-Magaña and Miller describe how one women's center engaged men in activism campaigns against interpersonal violence. Rooted in the feminist rallying cry of "the personal is political," these authors describe challenges, tensions, and successes in involving men in CE work through their women's center.

In Chapter 9, coauthored by a faculty member, student, and community partner, Clark-Taylor, Mitchell, and Rich describe the development of a summer internship in feminist activism. They highlight their successes and challenges as they purposefully shifted an internship in women's and gender studies from service to activist CE work. Finally, Noel, echoing some points introduced by Bisignani, challenges those involved with CE work to (re) position efforts into communities. She critiques how CE efforts have come to be "located on a university campus, set apart from communities," and, as such, she argues "they run the risk of overlooking or misunderstanding the challenges communities face as they struggle toward social, economic, cultural, and racial justice" (p. 175). She advances a three-pronged approach that can be utilized to develop sustainable CE programs, and she illuminates this approach with several exemplars.

Readers might recognize several salient themes that undergird this collection. First, this volume aims to *cross boundaries* or borders that have framed the work of feminism and community engagement. When we consider where this work might happen, we are situated not only in "bricks and mortar" classrooms or the "streets" of our communities, but also in virtual/cyber spaces. Cunningham and Crandall, in their chapter on "social media for social justice," describe how cyberfeminism can be used to critically analyze gender inequities in nonprofits. Our contributors also move beyond "classrooms," whether traditional or virtual spaces, to co-curricular places. For instance, the project described by Magaña and Miller is situated in the women's center; however, it crosses identity boundaries too, by engaging men's activism. Initial efforts involving men in campaigns against violence evolved into young men's leadership and mentoring. Finally, Bisignani's chapter pushes us beyond the classroom and into the community. She argues we must physically transgress boundaries in order to move into more complex ways of thinking and being.

Another theme that cuts across several chapters is that feminist community engagement is *relational*. It is through observation of and engagement with others that individuals "hone their knowledge and skill, creating an environment of constant renewal of praxis" (Ollis, 216). Bisignani's chapter describes an activist-apprentice model that engages students with community partners, providing students with practical organizing and activist skills. Mena and Vaccaro too describe the importance of role modeling CE, specifically for women of color. Their work resonates with Magaña and Miller; both demonstrating how critical models, mentors, and authentic relationships are to learning and developing the skills needed for CE, and for collective action.

Consciousness-raising is central to feminism, which demands that we become personal with our subject—whether material studied in class, the communities in which we engage, or ourselves. Several of our contributors reflect on their changing awareness, and the critical importance of this *reflexivity* to their practice. Reflexivity, the third theme, is a process of reflection in which one examines oneself, her assumptions and preconceptions, and how these affect decisions, experience, and actions (Hertz, 1997; Warren, 2011). The contribution by Verjee and Butterwick illustrates this process through their critical narrative, in which they draw upon critical race feminist theory to illuminate the politics of privilege and exclusion in dominant (charitable) approaches to community engagement. Seher, in her reflexive chapter on her use of PIF, a service-learning and student philanthropy program, considers how a feminist lens could help her to achieve pedagogical goals that move students beyond volunteerism toward social action.

Most, if not all, chapters in this volume illustrate the final theme: *disruptive pedagogy*. We align with those scholars who assert that community engagement must move beyond its charitable orientation to instead cultivate activist-oriented attitudes, knowledge, and skills. Some feminists, concerned that community engagement has devolved into solely charity service, have abandoned such efforts, concerned they reinforce "the very power inequalities that feminists have worked so diligently to expose and challenge" (Costa & Leong, 2012, p. 171). Yet others are reclaiming and disrupting this field. Bringing an explicitly critical perspective, educators are deploying pedagogical and engagement strategies that "apprentice" activist work (Bisignani, Chapter 6). For instance, Clark-Taylor, Mitchell, and Rich, describing a summer internship offered through the University of Rochester's Gender and Women's Studies program, explicitly designed to develop students' skills in feminist leadership and activism. Others argue for or model through their practices, how to (re)design spaces that can develop activist orientations and are, in turn, disrupting normative assumptions about their communities (e.g., Magaña & Miller, Chapter 8) and practices (e.g., Seher, Chapter 7). Noel (Chapter 10) argues that we must disrupt university-driven (and university-serving) agendas that sustain community engagement efforts in and on campuses. She advocates instead for CE efforts to reposition themselves in the community; in this way CE efforts will attend to issues of power; ensure authentic reciprocity; and empower deeper collective action.

In sum, these themes—boundary-crossing, relational, reflexive, and disruptive—are at the core of what we hope feminist CE has to offer readers. We anticipate faculty will pick up this volume to disrupt their pedagogical practices, and to reflect on how a feminist lens shapes the design of a course, the learning objectives, and the types of CE that students conduct. Administrators and staff in postsecondary institutions can draw from this volume to (re)imagine their CE practices. As institutions increasingly adopt experiential learning requirements in their curriculum, more courses will incorporate experiential approaches, partner with community agencies, and use service-learning. Thus, scholars, educators, and students across disciplines who are interested in experiential learning, service-learning, activism, civic engagement will find value in this text. Finally, having chapters that are coauthored by individuals who are within and outside the academy (i.e., a faculty member and a community partner) and across academic disciplines and administrative units (i.e., a faculty member with campus service unit), suggests this text could be used to spur campus/community, and interdisciplinary and cross-departmental, dialogues. The literature on CE is growing; this volume is unique, however, in its goal to bring a feminist lens to mainstream practices. We hope that your reading will spark fruitful dialogue and intentional action whether you are experienced or new to CE.

References

Battistoni, R. (1997). Service learning and democratic citizenship. *Theory into Practice, 36*(3), 150–156.
Butin, D. W. (2010). *Service-learning in theory and practice: The future of community engagement in higher education.* New York: Palgrave.
Costa, L. M., & Leong, K. J. (2012). Introduction critical community engagement: Feminist pedagogy metes civic engagement. *Feminist Teacher, 22*(3), 171–180.
Eyler, J., & Giles, Jr., D. E. (1999). *Where's the learning in service-learning?* San Francisco, CA: Jossey-Bass.
Galston, W. A. (2007). Civic knowledge, civic education, and civic engagement: A summary of recent research. *International Journal of Public Administration, 30,* 623–642.
Hertz, R. (Ed.). (1997). *Reflexivity and voice.* Thousand Oaks, CA: Sage Publications.
Hurtado, S., & DeAngelo, L. (2012). Linking diversity and civic-minded practices with student outcomes: New evidence from national surveys. *Liberal Education, 98*(2), 14–23.
Hurwitz, E. (2012). On civic education: Make sure we link the local with the international. In D. W. Harward (Ed.), *Civic provocations* (pp. xii–xiii). Washington, DC: Bringing Theory to Practice.
Kezar, A. J., Chambers, T. C., & Burkhardt, J. (2005). *Higher education for the public good: Emerging voices from a national movement.* San Francisco, CA: Jossey-Bass.
Lichtenstein, G., Tombari, M., Thorme, T., & Cutforth, N. (2011). Development of a national survey to assess student learning outcomes of community-based research. *Journal of Higher Education Outreach and Engagement, 15*(2), 7–34.
Warren, J. T. (2011). Reflexive teaching: Toward critical autoethnographic practices of/in/on pedagogy. *Cultural Studies <=> Critical Methodologies, 11*(2): 139–144.
Wheeler-Bell, Q. (2014). Educating the spirit of activism: A "critical" civic education. *Educational Policy, 28*(3), 463–486.

CHAPTER 2

Feminism and Community Engagement: An Overview

*Susan Van Deventer Iverson
and Jennifer Hauver James*

In this chapter, we provide a closer examination of feminism and its relevance and application to community engagement (CE). Feminism is not new to CE. The "disciplining" of feminism (Butin, 2010) in the academy, having taken root in women's studies, actually preceded the CE movement (Costa & Leong, 2012b). That feminist work has, over time, only occasionally intersected with scholarly conversations of CE speaks to the deep suspicion many feminists hold of the charitable orientation of most CE work (Naples & Bojar, 2002). To date, feminist approaches to and conversations about CE have remained largely within the field of women's studies where political action is a shared aim. In this volume, we ask the question, "What might be gained by bringing a feminist lens to the work of CE?" Our aim is to move this feminist perspective beyond the disciplinary bounds of women's studies and illustrate the transformative potential for merging feminist theory with social action (Bubriski & Semaan, 2009).

This chapter provides an overview of perspectives on feminism and community engagement, so that readers will have a conceptual orientation for the chapters that follow. Readers with a more sophisticated understanding of community engagement and/or feminism will likely find this chapter review of familiar ground. We begin with a discussion of feminism, inclusive of an examination of why some feminists adopt approaches seemingly outside the

CE movement. Next, we offer an elaboration and critique of community engagement; and finally, we explicate how feminism can serve as a theoretical strategy for combining activist engagement with democratic concerns for social justice and equality (Gilbert, 2010; Holt, 2000; Rhoads, 1997).

Feminism(s)

Feminism is a movement striving for the political, social, and educational equality of women with men. Much confusion seems to exist around who or what or when to credit for feminism's origins (Kaminer, 1993). Yet, its basic assumptions are that gender is central to the structure and organization of society; gender inequality exists; and gender inequality should be eliminated (Allan, 2008).

Feminism, while often treated as a unitary category, is not a monolithic ideology. Numerous branches of feminist thought each offer a distinctive view and explanations for women's oppression (Flax, 1990; Tong, 1998). Here, we discuss a few perspectives in order to illustrate distinctions and theoretical tensions (for a comprehensive review, see Tong, 1998), and how they may impact approaches to conceptions of community engagement.

Liberal Feminism

Grounded in the values of individual autonomy and self-fulfillment, the main thrust of liberal feminism is that "female subordination is rooted in a set of customary and legal constraints blocking women's entrance to and success in the so-called public world" (Tong, 1998, p. 2). Liberal feminists, who "do not see hierarchy and bureaucracy as intrinsically antifeminist" (Martin, 1990, p. 184), have fought in the legal and political arenas for not only access but equity, and to obtain the same opportunities and benefits that are given to men. Evidence of twentieth-century liberal feminist action can be seen in the passage of the Equal Pay Act and Title IX, among other legislative milestones (Tong, 1998).

Liberal feminism has been criticized for focusing more on the needs of the White, middle-class woman, paying no substantive attention to race, ethnicity, or class differences among women (Tisdell, 1998). An example—of both a liberal feminist civic engagement and the critiques levied—can be found in the battered women's movement. Liberal feminist activists in the battered women's movement tend to align with legal and political systems—at times, as Kendrick (1998) notes, "in response to pressures by funding agencies...and law enforcement" (p. 152). Reliance on government

Feminism and Community Engagement • 11

funding, and the adoption of bureaucratic processes and professionalization, provide stability and security (Kendrick, 1998; Martin, 1990). Yet, critics observe the development of stable ties with institutional structures contributes to an erosion of commitment to feminist goals (Garber, 2012; Phillips, 1992; Warren, 1987). Further, a dominant discourse on domestic violence emerges that constructs "battered women" as low-income, heterosexual, and non-Euro-American (Kendrick, 1998; Pleck, 1987). Thus, efforts to describe and address the concerns of "others" (e.g., racial minorities, lesbians, low-income women, Third World women) risk being perceived as a projection of what is culturally right or normal onto others in need of rescue (Gilman, 1999). Additionally, Third Wave feminists have levied criticism that liberal feminists—specifically "White women"—striving for equality with White men, have become so focused on individual achievement that they became "wholehearted supporters of the very structures we most wanted to contest" (Heywood & Drake, 1997, p. 12).

Radical Feminism

In contrast, radical (or structural) feminists are primarily concerned with structured power relations and systems of oppression and privilege based on gender, race, class, and so on (Tisdell, 1998). Radical feminists identify various systems of oppression (embedded in capitalism and patriarchy) as "connected inseparably" (Jaggar, 1983, p. 313), and assert that "every issue is a women's issue, just as every issue has race and class implications" (p. 321). Fundamentally, radical feminists insist that the sex/gender system is the cause of women's oppression, and to eliminate sexism (and heterosexism and patriarchy), we must advance women's ways of knowing and being (Alcoff, 1988; Firestone, 1971; Jaggar, 1983). Further, social change will be realized with new "tools;" as Audre Lorde states, "the master's tools will never dismantle the master's house."

An illustration of radical feminism can be found in feminist collectives: They emerged as an alternative to bureaucratic power and hierarchical relations, and focused on process and the equal distribution of power among members (Bordt, 1997). Further, they endorsed separatism, as illustrated by the philosophy of the Columbus Women's Action Collection: "the work of the women's movement must be done by women" (Taylor & Rupp, 1998, p. 66). This feminist collective emerged in 1970 at Ohio State University (OSU); they sponsored consciousness-raising groups, antirape activism, and fueled the establishment of the women's studies program (Taylor & Rupp, 1998). Yet, it is this institutional intersection (e.g., with OSU) that troubles the sustainability of radical efforts, who philosophically are reluctant to accept organizational ties and government funding, for fear of cooptation (Martin, 1990). Further, radical feminism can be criticized for its overemphasis on structures, which underplays or ignores an individual's capacity for agency (Tisdell, 1998).

While some radical feminists emphasize the values and virtues culturally associated with women (e.g., emotion, sharing, interdependence), others offer androgyny as "the proper paradigm" for gender (Tong, 1998, p. 47). Yet such perspectives—emphasizing an essential nature of women—have been criticized for rendering difference invisible (Rothenberg, 2004).

Multicultural Feminism

Multicultural feminists[1] maintain that all women are not created or constructed equal. They express dissatisfaction with "white"[2] (and Western) feminism that tends to conflate "the condition of 'women' with that of white, middle-class, Christian women" (Spelman, 1988, p. 156). They are critical of "the guise of value-free descriptions" that "smuggle in normative considerations that carry with them the stigma of inferiority" (Rothenberg, 1990, p. 43).

Black feminists, among the first to challenge these assumptions of unity, adopted the concept of womanism to reject gender-based dichotomies that lead to a false homogenizing of women (Higginbotham, 1992, p. 273). Collins (1990), with her description of the Black woman's standpoint, suggested that Black women have a distinctive set of experiences, and interpretations of those experiences, that offer a different view of reality. Collins identifies key themes in Black feminist thought—experience as a criterion of meaning, the use of dialogue in assessing knowledge claims, the ethic of caring, and the ethic of personal accountability. These themes are shared by many other feminists (e.g., Cook & Fonow, 1990; Westkott, 1990) but Collins supports her arguments for Black feminist thought with examples from the Afro-American culture identifying the notion of sisterhood[3] as an important part of Black women's culture, as well as Black women's role and relationship in their family, with their children, and in their communities.

Critical race feminism (CRF), a corresponding field of multicultural feminist thought, is also antiessentialist in nature, and puts power relations at the center. Begum Verjee (2012), by example, draws upon CRF to draw attention to how power operates in the institutionalization of service-learning at one university. Through counter-storytelling (a hallmark of critical race methodology), Verjee gives voice to women of color experiencing social oppression, and in turn calls for institutional recognition of (and accountability for) how institutionalized Eurocentric values can cause harm to people (and in particular women) of color.

Poststructural Feminism

Poststructural feminists, like multicultural feminists, hail from the postmodern era, and share a view of the self as fragmented (Tong, 1998). Poststructural feminists, building on the ideas of Derrida, Foucault, and others, acknowledge, reject, and seek to disrupt binaries (i.e., male/female, public/private, White/Black, thought/emotion) as a main categorizing force in society, and advocate a move away from "disabling vestiges of essentialism" (McNay, 1992, p. 120; see also Allan, Iverson, & Ropers-Huilman, 2010; Flax, 1990; Lather, 1991; Weedon, 1997). Meaning—constantly in play, always already in motion, and historically contextualized—arises out of difference (Bacchi, 1999).

Sawicki (1991) contends difference—contingent and discursively constituted—can be more effectively understood as a product of power operating at the micro-levels of society. Simultaneously inhabiting and inscribed with identity discourses, women are "both victims and agents within systems of domination" (Sawicki, p. 10). Being a woman, then, is to "take up" a position within a constantly shifting context and to be able "to choose what we make of this position and how we alter this context" (Alcoff, p. 435).

While critiqued for being "too theoretical and esoteric to be of much practical use" (Allan, in Allan et al., 2010, p. 11), poststructural feminist thought has (perhaps underutilized) potential for contesting, disrupting, and illuminating programs, policies, and pedagogies about civic engagement (and gender) in higher education (Butin, 2003; Le Grange, 2007). Tisdell (1998), in her articulation of the contribution for poststructural feminist pedagogies to the field of adult education, provides an analogous example. These pedagogies, she argues, highlight issues of positionality, problematize the notion of "Truth," sustain an emphasis on resistance, and deconstruct categories and binaries. As such, this theoretical perspective (and pedagogies) can enable deconstruction of binaries such as the public/private divide; it can also unveil issues of positionality, such as how identity (one's race, gender, class, sexuality, among other dimensions of identity) has "an influence on teaching and learning, on instructors' and students' construction of knowledge, and on classroom dynamics" (Tisdell, 1998, p. 147) in service-learning pedagogies. Further, poststructural feminist perspectives can illuminate what Gore (1993) refers to as "institutionalized pedagogy as regulation" (p. 142) and how these pose limitations (and possibilities) for learning and an emancipatory agenda in education (Tisdell, 1998).

Cyberfeminism

Also within the postmodern turn, cyberfeminism describes the work of feminists interested in theorizing and critiquing about gender and the Internet, technology, and new media (Consalvo, 2003; Hawthorne & Klein, 1999; Kenway & Nixon, 1999; Rosser, 2005). Kenway and Nixon (1999) observe that cyberfeminism is best understood as "feminist politics in, about, and around women's relations to digitized, networked, and increasingly converging information and communication technologies" (p. 458). An aim of cyberfeminism is to utilize the Internet as vehicle for the dissolution of sex and gender (Wajcman, 2006); yet, some critique this as a utopian view, observing that cyberspace is a "significant public political space to which differently located women have unequal access" (Kenway & Nixon, 1999, p. 458).

Concurrent with the growth in online education, scholar/educators are exploring the intersections of cyberspace and community engagement (Crabill & Butin, 2014). Eudey (2012), drawing from her experience teaching women's studies courses online, illuminates how "the social justice aims of civic engagement can readily be achieved within online courses" (p. 233). Through cyber-pedagogies, the authority of the instructor is decentered contributing to increased student-to-student interactions, which have the potential, Schweitzer (2001) observes, to "actualize some of the basic goals of feminism and feminist pedagogy" (p. 188). Eudey adds that by incorporating cyberactivism, educators can cultivate a shift from "weak" uses (p. 240) of online activism (i.e., clicking a "like" button or sharing a link) to a realization of the power of social media for consciousness-raising and mobilizing (online and offline) action. Kenway and Nixon (1999) advance that such "feminist cyber-civics" as a "butt-kicking tool of empowerment" has considerable implications for citizenship, including the potential to "change the power dynamics of the public sphere of cyberspace" (p. 460).

In sum, feminism has many names and is taken up in a number of ways. There exist, however, threads across feminist thinking and practice that serve as core tenets of this volume. First and foremost, a feminist perspective, when overlaid on conversations of community engagement, pushes us to ask critical questions about the communities in which we work and the aims we ascribe to the work we do: "Whose voices are heard and whose are silenced? Who makes the decisions and by what criteria? Who benefits from such decisions and who loses?" (Butin, 2003, p. 1682). Such a perspective brings explicit attention to power relationships at work in the discursive, institutional, and sociocultural contexts in which community engagement takes place.

Further, feminism places emphasis on consciousness-raising. Consciousness-raising (CR) groups, which blossomed in the late 1960s and early 1970s, are an essential part of feminism: they are a mechanism by which to gain awareness and a means through which to organize, strategize, and act (Keating, 2005). Different from the incorporation of reflection-on-action, a hallmark in service-learning pedagogy (and broadly experiential learning, see Kolb, 1984), CR transcends the binary of awareness or action, and "moves to *both* awareness *and* action" (Bickford & Reynolds, 2002, p. 240, emphasis in original). It facilitates an understanding of self as an agent of change; CR contributes to commitment and the internalization of a sense of responsibility to dismantle causes of inequality (Rosenberger, 2000).

Finally, feminism is rooted in activism; Scanlon argues that for feminist pedagogy to be truly feminist it must emphasize action and prepare students to be change-agents. This is different from service-learning or community engagement through which students may get "into the streets." Feminist (and critical) scholar-educators argue that service learning and community engagement do not place sufficient emphasis on larger social issues and social responsibility and that few students understand their service as a contribution to structural change (Bickford & Reynolds, 2002; Naples & Bojar, 2002; Rhoads, 1997). Feminist activism enables individuals to develop a deeper understanding of feminist issues and promotes the development of skills necessary to work toward feminist social change (Naples & Bojar, 2002).

In what follows, we draw on the elements of feminist thought outlined here to situate ourselves within these larger scholarly conversations regarding conceptions of "community" and "engagement."

Community Engagement

The Carnegie Foundation for the Advancement of Teaching classification of "community engagement" defines the term as "the collaboration between institutions of higher education and their larger communities (local, regional/state, national, global) for the mutually beneficial exchange of knowledge and resources in a context of partnership and reciprocity" (Driscoll, 2008, p. 39). Further elaboration on the Carnegie Foundation website indicates,

> The purpose of community engagement is the partnership of college and university knowledge and resources with those of the public and private sectors to enrich scholarship, research, and creative activity; enhance curriculum, teaching and learning; prepare educated, engaged citizens; strengthen

democratic values and civic responsibility; address critical societal issues; and contribute to the public good. (Saltmarsh & Driscoll, n.d., ¶4)

Despite the rhetorical clarity of this statement, there exists a significant lack of consensus about the meaning of the phrase "community engagement" and about many other concepts used synonymously (e.g., civic engagement, democratic engagement, community service) (Costa & Leong, 2012a). In this section, we unpack and problematize "community" and then "engagement," returning to the umbrella term of "community engagement" and its use for our purposes here.

Community

What do we mean by "community"? Who makes up a community? How do communities relate to one another? What does it mean to engage in one's community? And to what ends would we do so? Critical questions like these are too seldom brought to bear on CE practices.

Conversations of service-learning and other engaged learning practices typically underscore the notion of community as both context and outcome of students' learning without asking or trying to answer these critical questions. Donahue (2000), for instance, describes service-learning as that which "integrates academic learning with meeting *community needs* to the benefit of both students and *the community*" (p. 429, italics added). Despite a fairly consistent coupling of the word "community" with "engagement," scholars rarely elaborate on what they mean by "community" in ways that facilitate deep thinking about the structures and contexts that shape the learning that can take place off campus. A feminist lens demands a more critical read of the word "community."

Occasionally in an effort to define one's community, scholars will use qualifiers such as "local," "home," "urban," "campus," "virtual," or "global." "Civic" is a term often used interchangeably with and alongside community (e.g., civic engagement as synonymous with community engagement). The civic (community) is typically understood as that which happens in a public sphere and so here community takes on a public character. In the "service" of civic (or community) interests, individuals (citizens) are expected to set aside private matters and interests. In this way, family (one's private sphere) is less likely to be a site for "community service." While the word "civic" may serve to bound "community," it may also serve to reinscribe gendered notions of community.

Feminist scholars have argued that the public/private divide has been instrumental in the gendering of communities (Aisenberg & Harrington,

1988; Lee, 2007; Yuval-Davis & Anthias, 1989). The public (masculine) domain is typically associated with governmental, political affairs, whereas the private (feminine) domain is associated with domestic, family, and kinship matters (Lee, 2007; Yuval-Davis, 1997). Feminists have illuminated how (previously deemed) "private" matters, such as domestic violence, are a public concern warranting political, policy, and legal responses (Dobash & Dobash, 1992; Kendrick, in Naples, 1998; Walker, 1984). As captured in the now axiomatic feminist phrase, *the personal is political*, bell hooks (1984) reminds us that "broader perspectives can only emerge as we examine both the personal that is political, the politics of society as a whole, and global revolutionary politics" (p. 28). Thus, it is important not only to define our communities, but also to think carefully about the assumptions embedded in those definitions.

Use of the phrase "community," in so far as it is often coupled with charity and service work, also has lingering connotations about women's work that feminists rightly resist. In the context of higher education, engaging in community outreach or service is often seen as "doing the university's housework" (Masse & Hogan, 2010, p. 7). Friedman (1992) adds that the concept of community harbors "social roles and structures which have been highly oppressive for women" (p. 103). Still others are critical of "the ideal of community" (Young, 1995, p. 234) as a "warmly persuasive word" (Williams, in Schofield, 2002, p. 664) that advances an idealized, and seemingly exclusively positive, notion of community. The "romance of community" (Joseph, 2002) provides a "form of affective compensation—that you feel good, that you enjoy being part of something larger than yourself, that you are doing good work" (Boyd & Sandell, 2012, p. 258). Such conceptions, because they are embedded in the contexts in which we work, must be unpacked and reshaped. For feminism and CE to work together, CE will need to be much more thoughtful about how it conceptualizes, engages, and reports on the communities in which engagement takes place. Failure to engage in these critical practices can undermine efforts to build coalitions; fail to make visible power relations that are operating in communities; and marginalize (activist) efforts that may seek to disrupt the status quo.

The reader may note that, in this section, we have been complicit with that about which we are critical: We have not offered a firm definition of community. Our intent here is to problematize the term community and stir others to interrogate taken-for-granted assumptions "that consensus will be reached and that the nature of community is real, concrete, and shared" (Tierney, 1993, p. 24). In a volume where feminist thought meets CE, it is important to keep critical questions alive and at the fore. We continue this interrogation by unpacking "engagement" in the next section.

Engagement

Communities are the locations where individuals enact their social roles. As Lister (1997) observed, "citizenship as a practice" flows from our membership in communities (p. 29). Scholars across the fields of civic education, service-learning, and women's studies have theorized about the power of community *engagement* to facilitate students' civic learning. Like the term "community," however, meanings of the term "engagement" hinge on the assumptions one holds about what constitutes appropriate and meaningful citizenship. What sorts of skills, knowledge, and dispositions contribute to civic maturity? How do our ideas about civic maturity inform our pedagogical approaches? In this section, we situate ourselves within conversations about the aims of civic engagement.

Though many typologies exist, there is a general tendency to distinguish between more personally responsible and legalistic forms of citizenship and more critical forms of citizenship that seek to bring about social change. Often, scholars privilege one type of citizenship over another. Banks (2008), for example, delineates a hierarchy of four levels of engagement. *Legal citizenship*, what Oldfield (1990) referred to as citizenship as status, is "the most superficial level," embodying certain rights and responsibilities to the nation-state but not involving any meaningful participation in the political system (Banks, p. 136). The next level, *minimal citizenship*, is typically enacted through voting. Beyond voting, *active citizenship* involves civic participation and involvement, but "the actions of active citizens are designed to support and maintain—but not to challenge—existing social and political structures" (p. 136). In the final level, *transformative citizenship*, individuals take action to promote social justice.

Westheimer and Kahne (2004) offer a similar framework that moves from citizenship as *personally responsible* or *participatory* in nature to citizenship that is *justice-oriented*. Educators focused on citizenship as being personally responsible emphasize character education and individual responsibility for leading a moral life and contributing to the community in cooperative and positive ways (i.e., volunteering at a soup kitchen, picking up trash). Proponents of participatory citizenship focus on "preparing students to engage in collective, community-based efforts" in an effort to teach students about government (p. 243). By contrast, educators who are *justice-oriented* seek "to prepare students to improve society by critically analyzing and addressing social issues and injustices" (Westheimer & Kahne, 2004, p. 242).

Because of its grounding in the field of service-learning, Butin's framework is particularly useful for thinking about the power of engagement for civic learning. Butin (2010, 2003) delineates four perspectives of engagement: *technical, cultural, political,* and *antifoundational* that each reflect a specific philosophical or pedagogical intent. Though these perspectives can "overlap" and "blend," they each have "distinctive and divergent goals" (Butin, 2010, p. 8). The *technical* perspective explicitly focuses on facilitating student outcomes—whether cognitive, affective, personal, or social. This view, "a major strand with the service-learning scholarship," is seen by many educators as a proven, innovative, pedagogical technique to more fully engage students (Butin, 2010, p. 8). Here, attention is given to the quality and design of the service-learning experience—the length of time students spend engaged in the process, the frequency and degree to which they reflect on their experience, and the level of interaction they have with other participants and the ways these variables impact student learning outcomes.

A *cultural* perspective, Butin (2010) notes, "emphasizes individuals' meaning-making"—how we make sense of "who we are with respect to both local and global communities" (p. 9). At the macro-level, this perspective fosters democratic renewal; it enhances one's "sense of community and belongingness to something greater" than oneself (p. 10). At a micro-level, it can facilitate multicultural/intercultural competence in students (Boyle-Baise, 2002; O'Grady, 2000). For instance, through participation in service-learning experiences, students reduce negative stereotypes of others and develop an increased tolerance for diversity (Einfeld & Collins, 2008).

Butin (2003) observes that the technical and cultural perspectives are often intertwined and undergird the "educating for democracy" movement in US higher education that aims to civic-minded, global citizens. Yet, he critiques that these perspectives fall short in their attention to power imbalances and silenced perspectives, which are embodied in the *political* (the third) perspective. This perspective challenges and questions normative assumptions: "Whose voices are heard and whose are silenced? Who makes the decisions and by what criteria? Who benefits from such decisions and who loses? To what extent is the innovation a repetition, a reinforcement, or a revocation of the status quo?" (Butin, 2010, p. 11). This perspective aligns with others that might be viewed as critical or transformative approaches—it aims to transgress traditional hierarchical structures, and rejects "banking" methods of teaching, wherein students passively "receive" prescriptive curricula that teachers "deliver"; rather, this perspective favors a constructivist approach to teaching and learning (Barr & Tagg, 1995; Butin, 2010; Freire, 1970; hooks, 1994).

Finally, Butin's (2010) *antifoundational* perspective (referred to as *poststructuralist* in his earlier work, 2003) argues "there is no neutral, objective, or contentless 'foundation' by which we can ever know the 'truth' unmediated by our particular condition" (p. 12). Butin (2003) asks, "Does service-learning perpetuate or disrupt our notions of who the teacher is and who the learner is? Who then served is and who is doing the serving? Moreover, how does service-learning help to construct students' notions of themselves and others and gendered, racial, and status-bound individuals?" (p. 1683). Such questions can appear similar to those raised under the political perspective. However, the key distinction is in the disruption of binaries: Wherein the political perspective asked who benefits and who loses, the antifoundational perspective complicates a (potentially taken-for-granted) assumption of who is served (one who is disadvantaged) and who is serving (one who is privileged). Butin (2010) notes we "cannot simply default into an either/or binary," but instead "knowledge and meaning become fragmented and partial" (p. 13). This perspective can facilitate "border crossings" between groups, and is an opportunity to deconstruct the very notion of borders themselves; it enables justice-oriented approaches "from a position of doubt rather than certainty" (Butin, 2010, pp. 13–14).

It is this last form of citizenship that we believe is made possible through feminist approaches to community engagement. While all forms of engagement make contributions to society, the outcomes for individuals and society, as Westheimer and Kahne (2004) argue, will vary depending on the aims we have in mind. Citizenship as personally responsible, for example, which Westheimer and Kahne identify as the dominant conception undergirding the character education and community-service movements, "obscures the need for collective and public sector initiatives... [and] distracts attention from analysis of the causes of social problems and from systemic solutions.... [V]olunteerism and kindness are put forward as ways of avoiding politics and policy" (p. 243). Civic education limited to the concept of personally responsible citizenship, they argue, risks teaching students that "citizenship does not require democratic governments, politics, or even collective endeavors," working against the sorts of critical reflection and action "essential in a democratic society" (p. 244). Similarly, civic republican and liberal citizenship discourses, Abowitz and Harnish (2006) observe, emphasize loyalty and individual action, leading to civic education (in K-12) "as civic republican literacy (factual consumption of American history, geography, and government), combined with varying degrees of patriotic identity and the liberal virtue of tolerance for difference" (p. 680). Alternatives, which they termed "critical discourses" (e.g., feminist perspectives) challenge dominant conceptualizations of citizenship, offering transformative ways for students to practice citizenship that "rely heavily on the values and skills associated with social justice activism" (p. 671).

In this volume, we seek to understand how individuals (and through what pedagogies individuals might) transition from the "patronizing role of charity" (Eyler & Giles, 1999, p. 47) to "a more systemic view of social problems and a greater sense of the importance of political action to obtain social justice" (p. 135). A critical, feminist approach to engagement demands attention to "the very epistemologies that underlie civic engagement discourses and projects as well as the pedagogical processes by which they are instantiated" (Costa & Leong 2012a, p. 171). It is our understanding that feminist pedagogy values "many of the same ideals put forth by scholars of civic engagement, including critical analysis, self-reflectivity, and active participation to accomplish the social good" (Costa & Leong, 2012a, p. 172). Unfortunately, the political, activist nature of feminist pedagogy is too often seen as "troublemaking" (Pudup, 2012, p. 127). Thus, another aim of this collection is to explore various pedagogical and theoretical approaches that help us to understand and grow comfortable embracing the political aims and practices of (feminist) community engagement.

Praxis: Feminism Meets Communities of Engagement

Feminism is foremost (and *essentially*)[4] about action; it is inextricably linked to social change, advocacy, and activism. Yet, as feminism became institutionalized (e.g., through women's studies programs in colleges and universities), debate developed (and continues) about a chasm between feminist theory (and the feminist classroom as the site for theorizing) and social activism. Some claim that social activism—engagement with social, cultural, and political organizations and their activities—is separate from formal study and should be pursued according to individual inclinations, while others, citing the origins of women's studies in political activism, see the academic world and the activist world as commingled (Demaske, 2002; Naples, 1998; Naples & Bojar, 2002). Feminists like Smith criticize "the abstract forms of knowledge production that rendered invisible the experiential dimensions of knowing" (in Naples & Bojar 2002, p. 9). We argue, along with others, that our challenge is to achieve *praxis*: to erase the void between theory and action (Bignell, 1996; hooks, 1994; Stanley, 1990).

Praxis, put simply, is the enactment of a field of thought; it is the nexus of theory and practice. Thus, feminist praxis exists when, as hooks (1984) states, feminist theories get "into the streets" (p. 110). Pedagogically, it is when the content and ideas circulating in the classroom move into communities. Some argue that feminism in the academy (e.g., women's studies programs) is disproportionately about theory. Many classes (not exclusive to women's studies) engage students in ideas (i.e., analyzing sexist oppression) that might (and will hopefully) fuel commitment—what Eyler and Giles (1999) describe as the "urgency to do something" (p. 162)—but do not require students to act on that commitment or practice/develop skills enabling them to act (now or in the future) on that commitment. It is, in large part, this shortcoming to which the community engagement movement (and service-learning pedagogy in particular) can respond.

As explored here, our participation in communities exists along a continuum. While community engagement continues to be dominated by charitable-oriented approaches, ample recognition has been given for the need to shift our community engagement efforts to justice-oriented approaches. Feminism, in theory and as a field, provides a conceptual framework for (further) facilitating the needed shift. A feminist perspective also calls to question learning outcomes. What are the implications for students' learning, when community engagement incorporates feminist, activist-oriented pedagogy? Toward what sorts of civic engagement? Gilbert (2010) notes that research on the ways in which students experience "activist-oriented feminist pedagogy...is very limited and sparse" (p. 11). What happens when feminist pedagogical principles are applied to service-learning initiatives (e.g., Bickford & Reynolds, 2002; DeMuth, 2011; Robinson, 2011; Stake & Rose, 1994)? Further, what possibilities exist for feminist praxis in developing community partnerships and for reciprocal outcomes in campus-community relationships (e.g., Gilbert & Masucci, 2004; Webb, Cole, & Skeen, 2007)? These and other questions have catalyzed the scholarship featured in the remaining chapters of this volume.

Notes

1   This strand of feminist thinking has evolved in ideological complexity, with corresponding fields of thought (e.g., critical race feminism, postcolonial feminism, Third World feminism, transnational feminism, among others); see Narayan (1997) for further elaboration.
2   Notably, any reference to all White women is a danger of viewing White identity as a monolithic phenomenon. Stanfield (1993, p. 23) observed that phrases such as *White people* beg the question, *which White people*? We acknowledge that we adopt, while concurrently being critical of, unitary categories.
3   The notion of sisterhood has been adopted in other branches of feminism, for example Third Wave feminism (see Heywood & Drake, 1997).
4   We intend all that is embedded in our use of this word: that action is the *essence* of feminism.

References

Abowitz, K. K., & Harnish, J. (2006). Contemporary discourses of citizenship. *Review of Educational Research, 76*(4), 653–690.

Aisenberg, N., & Harrington, M. (1988). *Women of academe: Outsiders in the sacred grove*. Amherst, MA: University of Massachusetts Press.

Alcoff, L. (1988). Cultural feminism versus post-structuralism: The identity crisis in feminist theory. *Signs: Journal of Women and Culture, 13*(3), 405–436.
Allan, E. J. (2008). *Policy discourses, gender, and education: Constructing women's status.* New York: Routledge.
Allan, E. J., Iverson, S. V., & Ropers-Huilman, R. (Eds.) (2010). *Reconstructing policy in higher education: Feminist poststructural perspectives.* New York: Routledge.
Bacchi, C. L. (1999). *Women, policy and politics: The construction of policy problems.* Thousand Oaks, CA: Sage.
Banks, J. A. (2008). Diversity, group identity, and citizenship education in a global age. *Educational Researcher, 37*(3), 129–139.
Barr, R. B., & Tagg, J. (1995). From teaching to learning: A new paradigm for undergraduate education. *Change: The Magazine of Higher Learning, 27*(6), 12–26.
Bickford, D. M., & Reynolds, N. (2002). Activism and service-learning: Reframing volunteerism as acts of dissent. *Pedagogy: Critical Approaches to Teaching Literature, Language, Composition, and Culture, 2*(2), 229–252.
Bignell, K. C. (1996). Building feminist praxis out of feminist pedagogy: The importance of students' perspectives. *Women's Studies International Forum, 19*(3), 315–25.
Bordt, R. L. (1997). How alternative ideas become institutions: The case of feminist collectives. *Nonprofit and Voluntary Sector Quarterly, 26*(2), 132–155.
Boyd, N. A., & Sandell, J. (2012). Unpaid and critically engaged: Feminist interns in the nonprofit industrial complex. *Feminist Teacher, 22*(3), 251–265.
Boyle-Baise, M. (2002). *Multicultural service learning: Educating teachers in diverse communities.* New York: Teachers College Press.
Brookey, R. A., & Miller, D. H. (2001). Changing signs: The political pragmatism of poststructuralism. *International Journal of Sexuality and Gender Studies, 6*(1/2), 139–153.
Bubriski, A., & Semaan, I. (2009). Activist learning vs. service learning in a women's studies classroom. *Human Architecture: Journal of the Sociology of Self-Knowledge, 7*(3), 91–98.
Butin, D. W. (2003). Of what use is it? Multiple conceptualizations of service learning within education. *Teachers College Record, 105,* 1674–1692.
——— (2010). *Service-learning in theory and practice: The future of community engagement in higher education.* New York: Palgrave.
Collins, P. H. (1990). *Black feminist thought: Knowledge, consciousness, and the politics of empowerment.* Boston: Unwin Hyman.
Consalvo, M. (2003). Cyberfeminism. In S. Jones (Ed.), *The encyclopedia of new media* (p. 1987). Thousand Oaks, CA: SAGE Publications.
Cook, J. A., & Fonow, M. M. (1990). Knowledge and women's interests: Issues in epistemology and methodology in feminist sociological research. In J. M. Nielson (Ed.), *Feminist research methods* (pp. 69–93). Boulder, CO: Westview Press.
Costa, L. M., & Leong, K. J. (2012a). Introduction critical community engagement: Feminist pedagogy meets civic engagement. *Feminist Teacher, 22*(3), 171–180.
——— (2012b). Critical and feminist civic engagements: A review. *Feminist Teacher, 22*(3), 266–276.

Crabill, S. L., & Butin, D. (Eds.). (2014). *Community engagement 2.0? Dialogues on the future of the civic in the disrupted university.* New York: Palgrave.
Demaske, C. (2002). Feminist scholarship and activism: An on-going debate. *Feminist Con/text.* Retrieved from http://www.icahdq.org/divisions/feminist/context/2002Fall/femScholarship.htm.
DeMuth, D. M. (2011). Doing feminist and activist learning outcomes: What should students be able to do as a result of this women's and gender studies project/course/curriculum? *Atlantis, 35*(2), 86–95.
Dobash, R. E., & Dobash, R. P. (1992). *Women, violence and social change.* New York: Routledge.
Donahue, D. M. (2000). Charity basket or revolution: Beliefs, experiences, and context in preservice teachers' service learning. *Curriculum Inquiry, 30*(4), 429–450.
Driscoll, A. (2008, January/February). Carnegie's community-engagement classification: Intentions and insights. *Change,* pp. 38–41.
Einfeld, A., & Collins, D. (2008). The relationships between service-learning, social justice, multicultural competence, and civic engagement. *Journal of College Student Development, 49*(2), 95–109.
Eudey, B. (2012). Civic engagement, cyberfeminism, and online learning: Activism and service learning in women's and gender studies courses. *Feminist Teacher, 22*(3), 233–250.
Eyler, J., & Giles, Jr., D. E. (1999). *Where's the learning in service-learning?* San Francisco, CA: Jossey-Bass.
Firestone, S. (1971). *The dialectic of sex.* New York: Bantam Books.
Flax, J. (1990). *Thinking fragments: Psychoanalysis, feminism, and postmodernism in contemporary West.* Berkeley, CA: University of California Press.
Freire, P. (1970/2000). *Pedagogy of the oppressed.* New York: Continuum International Publishing Group.
Friedman, M. (1992). Feminism and modern friendship: Dislocating the community. In S. Avineri & A. de-Shalit (Eds.), *Communitarianism and individualism* (pp. 101–119). Toronto, ON: Oxford University Press.
Garber, J. (2012). Defining feminist community. In J. DeLilippis, & S. Saegert (Eds.), *The community development reader* (2nd ed., pp. 338–346). New York: Routledge.
Gilbert, M. K. (2010). *Educated in agency: A feminist service-learning pedagogy for community border crossings.* Doctoral dissertation, Boston College. UMI/ProQuest database #3418869.
Gilbert, M., & Masucci, M. (2004). Feminist praxis in university-community partnerships. In D. Fuller & R. Kitchin (Eds.), *Radical theory/critical praxis: Making a difference beyond the academy?* (pp. 147–158). Victoria, BC: Praxis (e)Press.
Gilman, S. L. (1999). "Barbaric" rituals? In J. Cohen, M. Howard, & M. C. Nussbaum (Eds.), *Is multiculturalism bad for women?* (pp. 53–58). Princeton, NJ: Princeton University Press.
Gore, J. (1993). *The struggle for pedagogies: Critical and feminist discourses as regimes of truth.* New York: Routledge.

Hawthorne, S., & Klein, R. (Eds.). (1999). *CyberFeminism: Connectivity, critique and creativity*. North Melbourne, Victoria, Australia: Spinifex Press.
Heywood, L., & Drake, J. (Eds.). (1997). *Third wave agenda: Being feminist, doing feminism*. Minneapolis, MN: University of Minnesota Press.
Higginbotham, E. B. (1992). African-American women's history and the metalanguage of race. *Signs: Journal of Women in Culture and Society, 17*(2), 251–274.
Holt, S. (2000). Survivor-activists in the movement against sexual violence. In J. Gold & S. Villari (Eds.), *Just sex: Students rewrite the rules on sex, violence, activism and equality* (pp. 17–29). New York: Rowman and Littlefield Publishers.
hooks, b. (1984). *Feminist theory: From margin to center*. Boston, MA: South End.
——— (1994). *Teaching to transgress: Education as the practice of freedom*. New York: Routledge.
Jaggar, A. (1983). The politics of socialist feminism. In *Feminist politics and human nature* (pp. 299–324). Totowa, NJ: Rowman and Littlefield Publishers.
Joseph, M. (2002). *Against the romance of community*. Minneapolis, MN: University of Minnesota Press.
Kaminer, W. (1993, October). Feminism's identity crisis. *The Atlantic Monthly*, pp. 51–68.
Keating, C. (2005). Building coalitional consciousness. *NWSA Journal, 17*(2), 86–103.
Kendrick, K. (1998). Producing the battered woman: Shelter politics and the power of the feminist voice. In N. A. Naples (Ed.), *Community activism and feminist politics: Organizing across race, class, and gender* (pp. 151–173). New York: Routledge.
Kenway, J., & Nixon, H. (1999). Cyberfeminisms, cyberliteracies, and educational cyberspheres. *Educational Theory, 49*(4), 457–474.
Kolb (1984). *Experiential learning: Experience as the source of learning and development*. Englewood Cliffs, NJ: Prentice-Hall.
Lather, P. (1991). *Getting smart: Feminist research and pedagogy with/in the postmodern*. New York: Routledge.
Lee, T. M. L. (2007). Rethinking the personal and the political: Feminist activism and civic engagement. *Hypatia, 22*(4), 163–179.
Le Grange, L. (2007). The "theoretical foundations" of community service-learning: From taproots to rhizomes. *Education as Change, 11*(3), 3–13.
Lister, R. (1997, Autumn). Citizenship: Towards a feminist synthesis. *Feminist Review, 57*, 28–48.
Martin, P. Y. (1990). Rethinking feminist organizations. *Gender & Society, 4*(2), 182–206.
Masse, A. M., & Hogan, K. J. (Eds.). (2010). *Over ten million served: Gendered service in language and literature workplaces*. Albany, NY: SUNY Press.
McNay, L. (1992). *Foucault and feminism: power, gender and the self*. Boston, MA: Northeastern University Press.
Naples, N. A. (Ed.). (1998). *Community activism and feminist politics: Organizing across race, class, and gender*. New York: Routledge.
Naples, N. A., & Bojar, K. (Eds.). (2002). *Teaching feminist activism: Strategies from the field*. New York, NY: Routledge.

Narayan, U. (1997). *Dislocating cultures: Identities, traditions, and Third-World feminism*. New York: Routledge.
Novek, E. M. (1999). Service-learning is a feminist issue: Transforming communication pedagogy. *Women's Studies in Communication, 22*(2), 230–240.
O'Grady, C. R. (Ed.) (2000). *Integrating service-learning and multicultural education in colleges and universities*. Mahwah, NJ: Lawrence Erlbaum Associates.
Oldfield, A. (1990). *Citizenship and community: Civic republicanism and the modern world*. New York: Routledge.
Phillips, A. (1992). Must feminists give up on liberal democracy? *Political Studies, 40*(s1), 68–82.
Pleck, E. (1987). *Domestic tyranny: The making of social policy against family violence from colonial times to the present*. New York: Oxford University Press.
Pudup, M. B. (2012). The politics of engagement. In D. Butin & S. Seider (Eds.), *The engaged campus: Certificates, minors, and majors as the new community engagement* (pp. 109–129). New York, NY: Palgrave.
Rhoads, R. A. (1997). *Community service and higher learning: Explorations of the caring self*. Albany, NY: SUNY Press.
Robinson, T. C. (2011). *Teaching activist intelligence: Feminism, the educational experience & the Applied Women's Studies Department at CGU*. Theses & Dissertations. Paper 7. http://scholarship.claremont.edu/cgu_etd/7
Rosenberger, C. (2000). Beyond empathy: Developing critical consciousness through service-learning. In C. O'Grady (Ed.), *Integrating service-learning and multicultural education in colleges and universities* (pp. 23–43). Mahwah, NJ: Lawrence Erlbaum Associates.
Rosser, S. V. (2005). Through the lenses of feminist theory: Focus on women and information technology. *Frontiers: A Journal of Women Studies, 26*(1), 1–23.
Rothenberg, P. S. (1990). The construction, deconstruction, and reconstruction of difference. *Hypatia, 5*(1), pp. 42–57.
Rothenberg, P. S. (Ed.). (2004). *Race, class and gender in the United States: An integrated study* (6th ed.). New York: Worth Publishers.
Saltmarsh, J., & Driscoll, A. (n.d.). *Classification description: Community engagement elective classification*. Stanford, CA: Carnegie Foundation for the Advancement of Teaching. Retrieved from http://classifications.carnegiefoundation.org/descriptions/community_engagement.php
Sawicki, J. (1991). *Disciplining Foucault: Feminism, power, and the body*. New York: Routledge.
Schofield, B. (2002). Partners in power: Governing the self-sustaining community. *Sociology, 36*(3), 663–683.
Schweitzer, I. (2001). Women's studies online: Cyberfeminism or cyberhype? *Women's Studies Quarterly, 29*(3–4), 187–217.
Spelman, E. (1988). *Inessential woman*. Boston: Beacon University Press.
Stake, J. E., & Rose, S. (1994). The long-term impact of women's studies on students' personal lives and political activism. *Psychology of Women Quarterly, 18*(3), 403–412.

Stanley, L. (1990). *Feminist praxis*. London: Routledge.
Taylor, V., & Rupp, L. J. (1998). Women's culture and lesbian feminist activism. In N. A. Naples (Ed.), *Community activism and feminist politics: Organizing across race, class, and gender* (pp. 57–97). New York: Routledge.
Tierney, W. G. (1993). *Building communities of difference: Higher education in the twenty-first century*. Westport, CT: Bergin & Garvey.
Tisdell, E. J. (1998). Poststructural feminist pedagogies: The possibilities and limitations of feminist emancipatory adult learning theory and practice. *Adult Education Quarterly, 48*(3), 139–156.
Tong, R. P. (1998). *Feminist thought: A more comprehensive introduction* (2nd ed.). Boulder, CO: Westview Press.
Verjee, B. (2012). Critical race feminism: A transformative vision for service-learning engagement. *Journal of Community Engagement and Scholarship, 5*(1), 57–69.
Wajcman, J. (2006). TechnoCapitalism meets TechnoFeminism: Women and technology in a wireless world. *Labor and Industry, 13*(3), 12.
Walker, L. (1984). *The battered woman syndrome*. New York: Springer Publishing.
Warren, K. J. (1987). Feminism and ecology: Making connections. *Environmental Ethics, 9*(1), 3–20.
Webb, P., Cole, K., & Skeen, T. (2007). Feminist social projects: Building bridges between communities and universities. *College English, 69*(3), 238–259.
Weedon, C. (1997). *Feminist practice and poststructuralist theory* (2nd ed.). Oxford, England: Blackwell Publishers.
Westheimer, J., & Kahne, J. (2004). What kind of citizen? The politics of educating for democracy. *American Educational Research Journal, 41*(2), 237–269.
Westkott, M. (1990). Feminist criticism of the social sciences. In J. M. Nielson (Ed.), *Feminist research methods* (pp. 58–68). Boulder, CO: Westview Press.
Young, I. M. (1995). The ideal of community and the politics of difference. In P. A. Weiss & M. Friedman (Eds.), *Feminism and community* (pp. 232–257). Philadelphia, PA: Temple University Press.
Yuval-Davis, N. (1997). Women, citizenship, and difference. *Feminist Review, 57*, 4–27.
Yuval-Davis, N., & Anthias, F. (Eds.). (1989). *Woman-Nation-State*. New York: Macmillan.

PART I

Theoretical Considerations

CHAPTER 3

Conversations from Within: Critical Race Feminism and the Roots/Routes of Change

Begum Verjee and Shauna Butterwick

Introduction

This chapter explores our personal encounters with community-university engagement (CE). Using Critical Race Feminist Theory (CRFT) and Critical Whiteness Studies, we seek to illustrate the interconnection of racism, sexism, and classism and how these underpin the dominant charity model of CE. An autobiographical approach informs this discussion, a method of counter-storytelling which legitimizes the voices of women of color and White feminist allies speaking about social injustice. As a racialized administrative staff member and doctoral student, and a White professor in a University in Canada, we offer our narratives and critical reflections of the politics of privilege and exclusion. We conclude that the reproduction of the dominant charity model is closely associated with the Whiteness of higher education institutions which also creates barriers to bringing an antiracist and anticolonial approach to CE.

We begin by introducing ourselves. Begum is a racialized Muslim heterosexual able-bodied woman, an immigrant to this land of First Peoples. She met Shauna when she was an administrative staff member involved with multiple social justice projects and Shauna became her doctoral supervisor. She now works at another institution of higher education in Canada.

Shauna is a White, able-bodied, middle-class heterosexual woman, a member of the dominant settler society, who has been involved with community engagement throughout her academic career. It is important to locate ourselves and the institutions within which we work and to make the point that universities continue to be sites in which racism, sexism, and other forms of social oppression are produced, reproduced, and maintained. Despite claims of access, inclusion, and equity, academia remains a bastion of White privilege (Henry & Tator, 2010). For these reasons, we suggest that without significant recognition of these forms of racist, sexist, and classist oppressions operating in higher education institutions, CE would likely fall short in its goals of social and political activism. We argue that without institutional transformation, higher education institutions may continue to support charity-based partnerships that maintain the status quo, that is, hierarchies of privilege and penalty. Part of this transformation requires antiracist and anticolonial analyses of CE practices.

In writing these stories, particularly using the lenses of CRFT and Whiteness Studies, our own learning and understanding of our experiences has deepened. We invite others involved with CE to engage in dialogical explorations of their CE work using these theoretical resources to inform conversations across differences, in particular with respect to race. These are difficult discussions, but, we argue, they are essential to working toward an antiracist feminist social justice orientation of community-university engagement.

Critical Race Feminist Engagement

Many scholars are critical of CE for falling short in its emphasis on social and political action and appearing more like charitable work and its association with colonization (Westheimer & Kahne, 2004). Further, some argue that CE fails to place sufficient emphasis on larger social issues, and collective engagement toward eradicating social injustice (O'Grady, 2000). A social justice orientation to CE, with roots in activism, is emerging from the dominant discourses on CE as an action-oriented strategy for combining social analysis and activist engagement for social change (Butterwick & Gurstein, 2010; Kahne, Westheimer, & Rogers, 2000; Stoecker & Tryon, 2009; Verjee, 2012).

Feminists working in the CE movement purposefully advocate an activist orientation (Naples & Bojar, 2002). However, a feminist lens exploring how gender operates in the CE movement is limiting as it pays little attention to race or class hierarchies among women. It is well established that the dominant culture of universities is premised on ideologies of Whiteness, patriarchy, and classism; socially stratified in an intersectional hierarchical arrangement which functions to colonize, marginalize, and silence racialized people working at such institutions (Bannerji, 2000; Henry & Tator, 2010; hooks, 2003; Razack, 1998; Schick, 2000). Adding "critical race" to our feminist lens of CE provides us with an analysis of the ways in which universities disenfranchise and marginalize women of color. This chapter critiques feminist CE with the purpose of highlighting the inequities and injustices that women of color face in the academy, and therefore in CE organizing.

CRFT is grounded in critical race theory (CRT), a framework developed by critical legal scholars as a way to foreground how racism is a key dimension of oppressive societal, social, and institutional structures (such as the legal system and education) (Delgado & Stefancic, 2000; Vargas, 2003). CRT, in addition to offering a critique, also identifies counter-narrative as an important mechanism for challenging hegemonies based on hierarchies of race, gender, and class and through these processes outlines avenues for social change (Ladson-Billings & Tate, 1995). A CRFT lens necessitates an intersectional analysis of inequities that exist in society in understanding gender, racial, and class stratification. From a CRFT standpoint, a model of CE would be underpinned by accountability to racial, gender, and class equity, and therefore social justice. Such a model calls for transformation of social, political, and economic systems, particularly within educational settings (Closson, 2010; Verjee, 2012).

Nelson and Prilleltensky (2010) and Verjee (2012) suggest that structural and systemic change is the only way in which meaningful and substantive long-term relationships can be secured in any type of CE effort. CRFT helps to outline an ethic of the scholarship of engagement and collaboration with communities that addresses the root causes of inequality. Such a project must be *led* by racialized communities affected by systemic discrimination and exclusion in their desire for social change (Verjee, 2012). This requires addressing ideologies of White privilege within academe, and committing to institutional transformation. Universities, therefore, would need to invest in understanding the histories, social relations, and conditions that structure groups unequally (Razack, 1998), as much of critical CE involves working with marginalized communities to remedy and alleviate multiple sites and spaces of oppression.

Razack (1998) suggests that this requires institutional accountability, "a process that begins with recognition that we are each implicated in systems of oppression that profoundly structure our understanding of one another. That is, we come to know and perform ourselves in ways that reproduce social hierarchies" (p. 10). Mohanty (1997) further suggests that any collaboration between institutions and communities, must involve a critique of hegemony. The long-term preparedness of Universities to develop lasting partnerships with marginalized communities, partnerships that are mutually beneficial and reciprocal, requires universities to be willing and able to change (Maurrasse, 2001). The process of moving toward an equal two-way exchange involves "deliberate attention to language, leadership behaviors, [and] organizational structures" (Weerts & Sandmann, 2008, p. 86). CRFT offers a framework for analysis that contributes to understanding and reorganizing institutions in order to further their capacity to create authentic CE partnerships that work collectively to solve local, national, and global injustices.

Whiteness Studies, a subcategory of CRFT, brings focused attention to the interpretation of race. As McIntyre (1997) notes "white people's lack of consciousness about their racial identities has grave consequences in that it not only denies white people the experience of seeing themselves as benefiting from racism, but in doing so, frees them from taking responsibility for eradicating it" (p. 16). In Endres and Gould's (2009, p. 425) study of Whiteness and community service learning (CSL) they outlined the challenges of shifting away from "viewing race as a static biological characteristic, to attending to Whiteness as a set of cultural constructions imbued with privilege and power." As a cultural construction, Whiteness is not static; rather, it is a social activity constantly being recreated. An important consideration attended to in Whiteness Studies is an understanding of how moral agency underpins the ideology of Whiteness. Alcoff (1991–1992) spoke to the problem of speaking for others and Ahmed (2007) explores how this desire to act is associated with White privilege and White ignorance of the complexity and politics of social problems. Given that taking action on social problems is core to most CE projects, an important link should be explored with respect to how Whiteness is linked with the charity model which dominates CE.

Autobiographical Method

We have employed an autobiographical approach as a form of counter-narrative to the dominant CE discourse that rarely talks about conflicts and struggles within the academy. Autobiographical accounts play a significant role in transformation praxis as they provide a form of "antithetical knowledge" which Said (1997) described as "writing in opposition to the prevailing orthodoxy" (p. 157), and as Mirza (1999) asserts, autobiographical narratives offer "alternative accounts of social reality which challenge prevailing orthodoxies" (p. 111).

We write about our personal experiences, acknowledging we face different levels of risk. As a racialized woman, Begum must confront the possibility of fallout that may arise from sharing her experiences around CE and service-learning. As Razack (1998) and Dei, Karumanchery, and Karumanchery-Luik (2004) have noted, there are significant risks when racialized people raise questions about race and racism; therefore the risks must be carefully calculated. However, as Harris (1997) suggests, accepting and embracing such risks is a central part of our work as social justice activists working for social transformation. CRFT is a useful lens for engaging with that risk as it helps us to theorize our personal experiences and see how our different levels of risk are directly linked to gender, race, and class hierarchies within the academy. Following Begum's story, Shauna explores some of her CE experiences, noting how her privileged position as a White scholar afforded her more freedom and less risk, compared with Begum.

Begum's Counter-story; Prior Doctoral Student

In the spring of 2001, a group of university administrators interested in the development of service-learning efforts came together to share ideas and engage in conversations. After indicating a strong interest, I was invited to participate in these discussions. At that time, I was enrolled in a doctoral program, the focus of which was to critically investigate our own practice in educational settings. Participating in conversations of CE and service-learning became the site of critical engagement for my doctoral work.

All the participants of the CSL working group were women administrators, and the majority were White. I brought to our meetings articles, models, and research reports that I had been gathering on service-learning for my doctoral work, and regularly took minutes, prepared agendas, and sent out notices for future meetings. My involvement with this informal group was voluntary; it was not part of any paid employment. I played a leadership role with this group and held some of the evening meetings at my home, as part of a rotation. We continued to meet as a group for about two years.

As we engaged the conversation, I became increasingly concerned that we needed a more critical perspective of service-learning, one that challenged the dominant charity model which emphasized "helping" the disadvantaged. A critical lens, I argued, would focus on the root causes of inequities, by centering the experiences and knowledges of communities impacted by social injustice that challenge dominant ideologies, power and privilege and social stratification. I also called for an approach that emphasized working in partnership with our local communities to explore and analyze social issues, and work for social, economic, and political transformation. At this time, reading and theorizing about these issues within the working group seemed acceptable.

As noted above, my engagement with the CE group was being informed by my own doctoral research and my use of CRFT as a powerful lens through which hegemonic systems and practices, particularly around race and racism could be examined. The idea of counter-narrative that is central to CRT, informed my conversations about CE where I attempted to interrupt the dominant charity model approach. I also used counter-narrative as my doctoral methodology, interviewing students, staff, and community members of color about their experiences. Based on their experiences and my analysis, my dissertation outlined the need for a CRFT vision of CE and service-learning (that vision is summarized in the implications section of this chapter).

While I felt that my initial contributions to the CSL group had been welcomed in those early conversations, the more CSL became institutionalized and formalized, the more I encountered resistance to my critical approach and restrictions to my participation. A key moment came a few years after participating in the initial working group. Our university was hosting a national CSL conference, and I eagerly submitted my registration. I was informed that I could not attend the opening session; there was limited space and only those with formal CSL roles could attend. I learned from other colleagues that most of the attendees at that opening event were women, and all were White. Had there been only men in attendance at this conference, I suspect women would have been quick to point out the systemic sexism at play, and would have insisted on the situation being remedied. However, at no time was the White dominance noticed or problematized. There is color blindness in the academy that often sweeps race and racism outside the door, where lack of representation and inclusion are less likely to be addressed. This is primarily because White women as administrators hold positions of privilege and power, and many are color-blind to racism as everyday praxis.

Masse and Hogan (2010) state that women are disproportionately involved in service work in the academy in "doing the university's housework" (p. 7). This, however, begs the question—which women? Razack (1998) and Bannerji (2000) point out that the lower echelons of the labour market are highly racialized and gendered in Canada. Systemic exclusion is embedded, supported and reinforced by our educational, political, and social institutions (Aylward, 1999; Dei, 1996). The continued denial of access to employment and the erection of job ceiling barriers particularly into management positions, serve as obstacles to political, social, and economic equity for women of color, and provide evidence that systemic racism is deeply entrenched within education and society. It is primarily White women who are involved in service-work as faculty and as administrative managers in the academy.

I also learned from others who attended that event, that the charity model of service learning dominated the discussions, with much attention given to getting as many students as possible involved with "doing good" and helping those less fortunate. During discussions about the emerging field of research on CE in Canada, my substantive knowledge of the area and my doctoral research (well-known to the representatives at this event) were never mentioned. I attended the second day of the conference, and along with others, noted that all keynote and panel speakers, and conference facilitators, were White and some described the Aboriginal communities with which they were engaged as "dysfunctional" based on racist normative assumptions. This pathological view of communities being served by CSL dominated the conference discussions; there was no recognition of the legacy and ongoing practices of colonialism and systemic discrimination that keep such families marginalized. As Battiste (2000), Monture-Angus (2003), and Vargas (2003) state, understanding how histories, systems, and practices subordinate Aboriginal students and families is crucial to resisting approaches that blame the lack of parental involvement on dysfunctional family environments. Without a critical understanding of the histories of genocide, exclusion, and discrimination that inform contemporary social relations, such beliefs continue to perpetuate negative stereotypes and maintain hierarchies of race stratification. Appalled by the tenor of discussions, I did not attend the third day of this conference.

As DePass and Qureshi, (2002) state, women of color may be admitted into the house of the academy, but are often relegated to cook and eat in the kitchen, not in the dining room with those who "belong" in the academy. I can only assume that my exclusion was related to a deep discomfort around my challenges to hegemonic Whiteness and the promotion of a charity paradigm of CSL, informed by a deficit view of community. Despite being one of the few Canadian scholars engaged in service-learning research, through the rules of engagement I was disenfranchised. In my work as an unpaid volunteer, I was invited into the CSL kitchen, but my approach in using "critical ethnic spices" were not welcomed. Such practices of exclusion is what Razack (1998) identifies as "border control," as encounters between the powerful and the powerless, between the dominant and subordinate, where the powerful are mostly White in the academy, and powerless nearly always racialized (p. 88). In these spaces, the racialized are either not allowed in, or are made invisible for fear that they may disrupt the status quo.

Following this conference, a colleague sent me news about a new Canadian service-learning list serve. One of the goals of the conference was to build a network. I assumed that all participants' names and contact information of conference participants had been collected to that end. Obviously not all of the participants were informed. I also learned from my colleague that a national coalition was being formed as well as a steering committee. I joined the list serve and indicated my interest in serving on the steering committee but received no response. A while later, a draft for the vision and mission of the organization were sent out with the terms of reference for representation on the steering committee. Only staff members with formal CSL roles were eligible to serve; students were not permitted to participate for a period of five years. After contacting the chair, it was confirmed that given the rules of participation and representation, I could not participate. As Williams (1994) suggests, North America no longer uses state troops to block entry to education and other public institutions, rather, racist, sexist, and classist systems are relied upon to exclude and maintain the status quo.

I learned further lessons about marginalization when I sought CSL-related employment. I made my interests known and despite the rapid development of CSL, I was informed there was no budget for new positions. When positions were eventually advertised, I applied to all of them, including entry-level positions, but never got an interview. I made inquiries to HR and was informed that some of these positions were "contract positions" which had been promised to individuals already working on temporary assignments with the newly developing service-learning initiative. Most of those hired were White, except for a few racialized support and clerical staff. It is documented that as temporary job vacancies came up, people who are known and viewed as a good "fit," usually White, are hired (Verjee, 2012). As Calliste (2000) states, gaining employment and promotion through institutional ranks is often not based on merit. One must be a member of the dominant and privileged group to be perceived as suitable and supportive of the status quo.

I continued to apply for administrative positions over several years under the service-learning initiatives, but was never invited to an interview although a few colleagues that I referred to these positions were interviewed and hired. I also began to attend and speak at conferences, outlining a vision for institutional transformation and the inclusion of marginalized voices, particularly racialized voices, in planning and decision-making around CE. After completing my doctorate, I made one more attempt to apply for a position with the service-learning initiative. In speaking with those involved with hiring, I learned that my critical views of CSL development at this institution had been noted; the end result was that I was not considered for this position. I made several attempts by phone and email to have a dialogue with a senior CSL administrator around my "critique of CSL," but all my requests went unanswered, which confirmed that I was no longer welcome to participate in this endeavor at this University.

From my perspective, the White women involved in CE were unable to see how racism was being played out through "normal ways of operating," that is, through the structural dimensions of institutionalizing Whiteness within CE. Bannerji (2000) speaks to these practices of racist exclusion which is so much part of our daily currency and ways of being that they are not even visible. Racist domination and oppression become a normal way of seeing and being. Racialized students, staff, and faculty in Canadian institutions of higher education have acknowledged that such institutions are toxic, hostile, and unwelcoming (Henry & Tator 2010; Verjee, 2012). For bell hooks (1994), higher education is seen as a political and educational site where power relations and social inequality are produced and reproduced. Collins (2013) suggests that for racism to exist, state-sanctioned institutional mechanisms must maintain racial and "othered" hierarchies. Experiences of a "chilly" climate are common on university campuses in Canada, where women of color experience barriers that decrease their visibility, power, and voice as they encounter sexism, racism, and classism (Mayuzumi & Shahjahan 2008). Despite claims of access, inclusion, and equity, institutions of higher education remain a landscape of White privilege (Ahmed & Swan, 2006).

My experience with exclusion and lack of awareness of racism were not limited to the institutionalization of CSL. Racism is structured by the ideologies and practices of White supremacy, where classrooms and daily interactions in education mirror the everyday world (Razack, 1998). hooks (2000) and James (2010) state that the impact of racism, and the values, attitudes, and ideas expressed are not a result of encounters between people, but are structured by the ideologies and practices of institutions and society.

At the time that I was experiencing these daily micro-aggressions against me, students and staff organizing grassroots antiracism activism were also encountering barriers. As the ground swell of activity increased, so did the scrutiny by senior administrators. At one student-led antiracist dialogue event, White women administrators attended, sat silently without participating, and reported back to senior administrators. It was obvious that their attendance at this event was to scrutinize and police, as comments made by senior administrators later spoke to the discomfort that "some people felt" during this event. Such grassroots organizing were subsequently crushed. Organizers were questioned around who or which department was in charge, and staff were shuffled and repositioned into different departments at the University thereby making it difficult for them to continue participating. Other staff were "let go" with claims of lack of "fit" in their positions. At another student-led antiracism event, senior members of the administration were invited to attend and upon hearing the stories of racism on campus, a senior administrator claimed she did not realize racism existed at the university. When a person in the most senior position at a university makes such a disclosure, it speaks to the praxis of race inclusion and equity within the academy.

Women of color in the academy often speak of navigating and surviving daily micro-aggressions (Bannerji, 2000; hooks, 2003; Razack, 1998). The day-to-day reality involves overcoming hurdles, mediating confrontations, and just fighting to survive. When women of color address the White supremacy at play as part of their everyday realities, they are constructed as angry, troubled, and problematic, which leaves them feeling invisible, silenced, and delegitimized. Blamed for their problematic character flaws and perceived as inferior, they are often asked to take anger management courses, reprimanded and relegated to the margins as penalty, thereby making it difficult for them to contribute fully and meaningfully to the development of the academy.

Colonialism operates in Canadian society today as part of an ideology of social stratification and differentiation sustained by the political, economic, and social domination of White supremacy (James, 2010). As Shome (2000) suggests, "Whiteness is not just about bodies and skin color, but rather more about the discursive practices" that sustain White supremacy (p. 108). At this institution, mostly White women were involved in the development of service-learning and CE. Many identified as feminists organizing for the purpose of collaborating with communities for change. In my opinion, their practices in the academy around participation and inclusion were part of a White supremacist praxis informing feminist community engagement.

While my experiences and knowledge as a racialized scholar and activist were, it seemed, too risky and dangerous, my critical view and perspective have been valued elsewhere and I have had opportunities to make contributions at other institutions of higher education. After my employment, I was invited to take a position as founding director for an MA program in Community Psychology and had the privilege of developing this program from a social change and anticolonial feminist lens. I recently moved to Ontario where I am an instructor at a college teaching courses on global citizenship. In this position I continue to bring my CRFT lens to support the underpinnings of this course where students examine the social problems of our world, and utilize a critical lens in determining the root causes of social issues with a focus on action and social change. As I continue with my work in the academy, I am contemplating a career in public service where I might be able to make more of a difference in civic life.

Shauna's Counter-story; Faculty Member

Begum's story sheds light on the challenges and risks she faced as a racialized scholar and activist naming the injustices and hegemonic practices, often legitimized through the "normal" rules of participation within higher education. As a White feminist scholar, my privileged position within the academy is a particular place from which to take up a critical social justice approach to CE and CSL; it has allowed me, to a certain extent, more freedom and less risk, compared with Begum. My privilege as a White faculty member, however, is also a liability when it comes to awareness of racism. I see how in many ways, I was "dysconscious" King (1991) of racism; I had an impaired consciousness, rather than a lack of consciousness.

As Begum's story illustrates, CSL and CE initiatives are based on a deficit and often racist understanding of communities. Such views are strongly associated with the Whiteness of universities, and the paradigm of volunteerism and helping others that informs dominant approaches to CE. To be frank, I have reached this understanding only through sustained dialogue with Begum and through further reading into CRFT, decolonizing, and Critical Whiteness Studies. Understanding how CE is enacted in Canadian universities requires acknowledgment of how charity is implicated in Canada's history as a nation; its existence is founded on the colonization of Indigenous peoples by White European settlers. What is poorly understood and acknowledged is the violence of this colonial relationship, which continues today. As Regan (2010) notes: "Many Canadians still believe that Indigenous peoples have been the fortunate beneficiaries of our altruism" (p. 84). Studies of historical documents reveal a language of paternalism and how charity, informed by racism, was at the core of colonizing practices (Haig-Brown, 2006). Other studies (Jacob, 2009) have focused on maternalism and how White women were implicated in this colonial charity model, specifically with respect to the removal of Indigenous children.

When Begum shared with me her various experiences of exclusion, I associated those actions with privileged individuals who were "color blind." The notion of the university as a "white supremacist institution," a characterization that Begum used in her dissertation, was initially shocking. In my "racial dysconsciousness" (King, 1991), White supremacy was a notion I tended to link to blatant racist actions of groups who believe in the superiority of the White "race" and the inferiority of all others. The *coherence* of Begum's story has connected the dots for me and provided a map illustrating not a random collection of moments, but a sustained politics of exclusion based on Whiteness.

Using the lenses of CRFT and Critical Whiteness Studies I have reconsidered my understanding of redistribution, reciprocity, and mutuality, key concepts that have informed my social justice orientation to CE. Ernest Boyer (1996), considered a key leader in the CE movement, emphasizes the importance of using "the rich resources of the university to [address] our most pressing social, civic and ethical problems" (p. 32). From a transformative perspective of CE, this orientation is limited and underlies the dominant charity discourse; without addressing the fundamental power differences operating to create unequal access to resources, the status quo persists. Redistribution is also, for the most part, a one-way relationship; the resources of the university are used to "help" solve communities' problems which are perceived as rooted in community's deficit of resources and capacity. In this view, communities do not have knowledge, wisdom, nor vision.

Reciprocity and mutuality are dimensions of CE I have endeavored to embrace in my CE practice and they are also concepts found in the critical CE literature (e.g., Franz, 2009; Grusky, 2000). While Weerts and Sandmann (2008) are moving in the right direction in their attention to reciprocity and mutuality addressed in their argument for a two-way engagement between communities and universities, their work could be deepened with a CRFT antiracist perspective. They identified the important role of "boundary spanners," individuals who "act as knowledge and power brokers between university and external partners" (p. 86), but the racial dimensions of those positions were not problematized. Begum was, in many respects, a "boundary spanner," working to transform CE informed by CRFT, trying to bring the experiences of communities and individuals of color into the CE conversation. Using a CRFT framework brings attention to how reciprocity and mutuality cannot be fully achieved without endeavoring to "unsettle and change the power relations, structures and mechanisms of the social world" (Maguire, 2001, p. 65).

Bringing a CRFT, decolonizing, and Critical Whiteness Studies lens to my teaching and supervision of graduate students' guides me move toward a transformative approach. I have introduced students to the charity-social justice paradigm of CSL (Marullo & Edwards, 2000) and various critiques of CSL (e.g., Bickford & Reynolds, 2002; Blouin & Perry, 2009; Bruce & Brown, 2010; Butin, 2003; Cooks, Scharrer, & Castaneda, 2004; Crabtree, 2008; Daigre, 2000; Densmore, 2000; Endres & Gould, 2009; Ferrari & Worrall, 2000; Keith, 2005; McCabe, 2004; Mitchell, 2007; Mitchell & Humphries, 2007; Sleeter, 2000; Verjee, 2010) including Ivan Illich's *The Hell with Good Intentions* (1968). CRFT, decolonizing, and Critical Whiteness Studies can bring more sustained attention to formations of exclusion, but articulating an alternative to the deficit orientation is of equal importance. The notion of "community cultural wealth" outlined by Yosso (2005, p. 69) can support a vision of an alternative approach by "focus[ing] on and learn[ing] from the array of cultural knowledge, skills, abilities and contacts possessed by socially marginalized groups that often go unrecognized and unacknowledged."

CRFT, decolonizing, and Critical Whiteness Studies can help to sharpen the edges of classroom discussions. For example, one of my students, a student of color, born in Canada, with extensive professional experience, was assumed by other volunteers at the agency where she did her CSL placement (a literacy program), to be a new immigrant with limited ESL abilities. A White student, placed at the same agency, did not encounter such stereotyping. While we debriefed these experiences, more attention should have been given to how racist stereotypes and Whiteness were operating.

These critical perspectives help to deepen a transformative vision of my CE research. My current collaborative research project with Filipino activists grew out of a longer-term partnership that began several years ago. At that time, I was invited by these activists to serve as an external evaluator for a project focused on building a national Filipino movement. A key aspect of the project was multiple participatory action research (PAR) projects taking place within different communities across Canada that explored racism, sexism, and classism plaguing the Filipino community, particularly the discrimination and intergenerational poverty experienced by more recent immigrants (see Philippine Women's Centre of BC 1996, 1997a, 1997b, 1997c, 2000). We negotiated my role and considered funders' accountability requirements. Given my knowledge of adult education and popular education processes, I was invited to also comment on their pedagogic processes, which I did at their national meetings. While in many respects I was an ally and my reports to the funder emphasized the impressive and creative work that was taking place, during annual consultations, I missed opportunities to further challenge funders' deficit view of this community and to also raise questions about the need for and role of an external evaluator. I could have also pushed the boundaries of my role and engaged even more in a collaborative evaluation process.

My current research grew out of that three-year engagement and my intrigue with how these Filipino activists used various art forms (theater, music, visuals, dance) to organize, educate, and politicize. The group agreed the research would be useful in documenting their successes, would support further reflection on their praxis, and might inform future arts-based projects. This partnership is one among others this group has had with academic researchers (e.g., Pratt, 2009; Zaman, Diocson, & West, 2007). We were successful in securing funds and I hired a member of that group as the co-investigator; she has been instrumental in gathering data and contacting members of the wider community. She is a member of the Filipino community and a woman of color; our engagements are dialogic and collaborative, but the structures of academic research at the university have reproduced a racialized hierarchy where I am positioned as her supervisor. Pushing back on this status hierarchy requires constant vigilance.

We are working on creating a collaborative analysis process that will include other activists, but face challenges as many of them continue to work in low-waged service positions, holding down several jobs in order to make a living wage. On their rare days off, they are devoted to advocacy work. As members of a feminist organization, they have faced federal policy changes that have cut funding to civil society organizations; what funding is available is denied to groups if they are involved in advocacy. Paradoxically, while their funding has been cut, federal funding for research now requires partnership research. Given these significant challenges, we are exploring ways to be collaborative. I am aware that my assumptions about their limited capacity to engage in the project need to be spoken and discussed directly with those involved. I must sustain my awareness of the insidious ways that the deficit-oriented charity model enters into my consciousness and actions.

I conclude this section by reviewing what it means to be a "White Ally." Park (2013) sees this as a problematic position because it "presume[s] that struggles against injustice are the responsibility of someone else...the idea of white allies also reinscribes the idea that Whites have a choice as to whether to fight racism, to fight White supremacy" (p. 5). This cautionary note brings into view my inactions and my hesitations to speak out and rock the boat. Fear of backlash prevents White allies like me from taking risks of speaking out, but in the struggle against racism and colonization, we need to work on equalizing the risk taking. As Applebaum (2008) argues, "Whites must be willing to risk engaging in the difficult listening that leaves one open and vulnerable" (p. 298). Speaking out and naming racism; confronting procedures that maintain exclusions, bringing in a CRFT lens to analyze institutional structures, policies, and actions must be part of the practice of White Allies.

Lessons Learned and Implications: Who's Doing the Work, Taking the Risk?

We have thought long and hard about writing a section on implications. Begum has been telling her story for a very long time and very little has changed. Women of color are invited into the kitchen to cook, into the formal dining room to service, and back into the kitchen to clean up. Then they are asked to create menus for tomorrow, knowing full well that White women will take a look at these menus, decide what to pick and leave out, maybe change the ingredients ever so slightly, and again place women of color to work in the kitchen in preparation for these meals. We would like to see White women, working as allies, taking up this cause. With that in mind, below we outline some measures that we believe would aid in the transformation of CE in universities from a charity and colonial model to a transformative or social justice framework.

We have organized our discussion of implications using Nancy Fraser's (2001) framework of the three interlocking dimensions of social justice: recognition, redistribution, and representation. Redistribution of resources is one dimension which addresses unequal access, but this must be linked to recognition (respect for differences) and representation (the creation of mechanisms for equal political voice). Taking action on the mechanisms of exclusion requires that there be an alignment of systems and practices throughout the academy; changing only one thing will not achieve the transformation that is required. We need a vision of antiracist and anticolonial praxis informing CE practice based on recognition of color blindness and "racial dysconsciousness" (King, 1991). A critical review of projects, staffing, and community outcomes is needed. We need to hear more from other racialized feminists, which requires we create conditions for that telling and listening (Minh-ha, 1989). In that process, we must be vigilant and interrupt repositioning White people as experts (Lopes & Thomas, 2006, p. 224). Adopting clear antiracism and anticolonial policies with respect to hiring and promotion of racialized people in the academy is essential, particularly around CE efforts. Part of this politics of recognition process is an understanding that diversity and equity policies have primarily benefited White women, and have done little to advance women of color. Another practice that can create a vision is through formal representation. Universities could establish standing committees made up of community representatives. Communities have knowledge, wisdoms, and perspectives that universities need to invite, welcome, and listen to, and one way to create access is to bring Indigenous and racialized women from community organizations to work within the academy in CE efforts. Such a committee must be informed by an antiracist affirmative action lens.

Preparing students for their CSL and CE experiences must include antioppression training (Curry-Stevens, 2007; Freire, 1970) informed by CRFT, decolonizing, and Whiteness Studies. Professional development of CSL and CE faculty and administrators would be similarly framed, creating spaces for "deep dialogue" around the structures of race and racism within the academy, as a microcosm of society, and how that plays out in various settings within the academy. Creating spaces within feminist publications, like this one, that sheds light on the limitations of White feminist theorizing and praxis in CE are important aspects of raising awareness regarding the interconnection between Whiteness, racism, and the charity model of CE.

Taking Off Our Bullet Proof Vests?

In this chapter, we brought CRFT and Critical Whiteness Studies to frame our personal encounters with CE in the academy. In coauthoring this discussion of racism and Whiteness, we have endeavored to move toward more equal risk-taking. At the heart of our recommendations is that we must engage in difficult conversations about racism, colonialism, and Whiteness in the academy and how they inform CE practices and the charity model. Building coalitions informed by CRFT and Whiteness Studies requires that we engage with differences, and the historical and political history of how those differences have been created through mechanisms of exploitation and injustice. Building coalitions that transform institutions of higher education and their CE practices involves others also sharing their counter-narratives. Applebaum (2008) reminds us further that this dialogue must also be about complicity: "Acknowledging rather than denying complicity is the first step in creating a shared language and a condition of dialogue" (p. 298).

References

Ahmed, S. (2007). The phenomenology of Whiteness. *Feminist Theory, 8*(2), 149–168.
Ahmed, S., & Swan, E. (2006). Doing diversity. *Policy Futures in Education, 4*(2), 96–100.
Alcoff, L. (1991–1992). The problem of speaking for others. *Cultural Critique, 20*, 5–32.
Applebaum, B. (2008).White privilege/White complicity: Connecting "benefiting from" to "contributing to." In R. Glass (Ed.), *Philosophy of education yearbook* (pp. 292–300). Philosophy of Education Society.
Aylward, C. A. (1999). *Canadian critical race theory: Racism and the law.* Halifax, NS: Fernwood Publishing.
Bannerji, H. (2000). *The dark side of the nation: Essays on multiculturalism, nationalism and gender.* Toronto: Canadian Scholars' Press Inc.
Battiste, M. (2000). Maintaining Aboriginal identity, language, and culture in modern society. In M. Battiste (Ed.), *Reclaiming indigenous voice and vision* (pp. 192–208). Vancouver: UBC Press.

Bickford, D. M., & Reynolds, N. (2002). Activism and service-learning: Reframing volunteerism as acts of dissent. *Pedagogy: Critical Approaches to Teaching Literature, Language, Composition and Culture, 2*(2), 229–252.

Blouin, D. D., & Perry, E. M. (2009). Whom does service learning really serve? Community based organizations' perspectives on service learning, *Teaching Sociology, 37*, 120–135.

Boyer, E. (1996). The scholarship of engagement. *Bulletin of the American Academy of Arts and Sciences, 49*(7), 18–33.

Bruce, J., & Brown, S. (2010). Conceptualising service-learning in global times. *Critical Literacy: Theories and Practices, 4*(1), 6–15.

Butin, Dan W. (2003). Of what use is it? Multiple conceptualizations of service learning within education. *Teachers College Record, 105*(9), 1674–1692.

Butterwick, S., & Gurstein, P. (2010). Community-based action research as community engagement: Tales from the field. In H. Schutze & P. Inman (Eds.), *The community engagement and service mission of universities* (pp. 213–230). Leicester, UK: National Institute for Adult and Continuing Education.

Calliste, A. (2000). Anti-racist organizing and resistance in academia. In G. J. S. Dei & A. Calliste (Eds.), *Power, knowledge and anti-racism education* (pp. 141–161). Halifax, NS: Fernwood Publishers.

Closson, R. (2010). An exploration of critical race theory. In V. Sheared, J. Johnson-Bailey, S. A. J. Collin III, E. Peterson, & S. Brookfield (Eds.), *The handbook of race and adult education* (pp. 173–186). San Francisco, CA: John Wiley & Sons.

Collins, P. H. (2013). Prisons for our bodies, closets for our minds. In M. L. Anderson & P. H. Collins (Eds.), *Race, class & gender: An anthology* (pp. 224–230). Belmont, CA: Wadsworth, Cengage Learning.

Cooks, L., Scharrer, E., & Castaneda Paredes, M. (2004). Toward a social approach to learning in community service learning. *Michigan Journal of Community Service Learning*, 44–56.

Crabtree, R. D. (2008). Theoretical foundations for international service-learning. *Michigan Journal of Community Service Learning, 15*(1), 18–36.

Crenshaw, C. (1997). Resisting Whiteness' rhetorical silence. *Western Journal of Communication, 61*, 253–278.

Curry-Stevens, A. (2007). New forms of transformative education: Pedagogy for the privileged. *Journal of Transformative Education, 5*(1), 33–58.

Daigre, E. (2000, Winter). Toward a critical service-learning pedagogy: A Freirean approach to civic literacy. *Academic Exchange*, 6–14.

Dei, G. J. S. (1996). *Anti-racism education: Theory and practice*. Halifax, NS: Fernwood Publishing.

Dei, G. J. S., Karumanchery, L. L., & Karumanchery-Luik, N. (2004). *Playing the race card: Exposing white power and privilege*. New York: Peter Lang Publishing.

Delgado, R., & Stefancic, J. (2000). Introduction. In R. Delgado & J. Stefancic (Eds.), *Critical race theory: The cutting edge* (pp. xv–xix). Philadelphia: Temple University Press.

Densmore, K. (2000). Service learning and multicultural education: Suspect or transformative? In C. O'Grady (Ed.), *Integrating service learning and multicultural education in colleges and universities* (pp. 45–58). New Jersey: Lawrence Erlbaum Associates.

DePass, C., & Qureshi, S. (2002). Paradoxes, contradictions, and ironies of democratic citizenship education. In Y. M. Hebert (Ed.), *Citizenship in transformation in Canada* (pp. 175–190). Toronto: University of Toronto Press.

Endres, D., & Gould, M. (2009). I am also in the position to use my whiteness to help them out: The communication of whiteness in service learning. *Western Journal of Communication, 73*(4), 418–436

Eyler, (2002). Reflection: Linking service and learning—linking students and communities. *Journal of Social Issues, 58* (3), 517–534.

Ferrari, J. R., & Worrall, L. (2000). Assessments by community agencies: How "the other side" sees service-learning. *Michigan Journal of Community Service Learning, 7*(1), 35–40.

Fine, M. (1994). Dis-stance and other stances: Negotiations of power inside feminist research. In A. Gitlin (Ed.), *Power and method—Political activism and educational research* (pp. 13–35). New York: Routledge.

Franz, N. (2009). A holistic model of engaged scholarship: Telling the story across higher education's missions. *Journal of Higher Education Outreach and Engagement, 13*(4), 31–49.

Fraser, N. (2001). Social justice in the knowledge society: Redistribution, recognition and participation. Paper presented at the *Wissenschaftszentrum Berlin Fur Socialforschung,* Berlin, Germany. Retrieved from http://www.WISSENGELLSCHAFT.org

Freire, P. (1970). *Pedagogy of the oppressed.* New York: Continuum Publishing.

Green, A. E. (2001). "But you aren't white": Racial perceptions and service-learning. *Michigan Journal of Community Service Learning, 8*(1), 18–26.

Grusky, S. (2000). International service learning: A critical guide from an impassioned advocate. *American Behavioral Scientist, 43*(5), 858–867.

Haig-Brown, C. (2006). *With good intentions : Euro-Canadian and Aboriginal relations in colonial Canada.* Vancouver: UBC Press.

Harris, C. I. (1997). Law professors of color and the academy: Of poets and kings. In A. K Wing (Ed.), *Critical race feminism: A reader* (pp. 101–106). New York: New York University Press.

Henry, F., & Tator, C. (2010). *The colour of democracy: Racism in Canadian society.* Toronto, ON: Nelson Education Ltd.

hooks, b. (1994). *Teaching to transgress—Education as the practice of freedom.* New York: Routledge.

——— (2000). *Where we stand: Class matters.* New York: Routledge.

——— (2003). *Teaching community: A pedagogy of hope.* New York: Routledge.

Illich, I. (1968) "To Hell With Good Intentions" Speech given to *Conference on InterAmerican Student Projects (CIASP) in Cuernavaca, Mexico,* on April 20, 1968.

Jacob, M. D. (2009). *White mother to a dark race: Settler colonialism, maternalism, and the removal of Indigenous children in the American west and Australia, 1880–1940.* Lincoln, NE: University of Nebraska Press.

James, C. E. (2010). *Seeing ourselves: Exploring race, ethnicity and culture.* Toronto, ON: Thompson Educational Publishing.

Kahne, J., Westheimer, J., & Rogers, B. (2000, Fall). Service learning and citizenship in higher education: Directions for research. *Michigan Journal of Community Service Learning,* 42–51.

Keith, N. Z. (2005). Community service learning in the face of globalization: Rethinking theory and practice. *Michigan Journal of Community Service Learning, 11*(2), 5–24.

King, J. E. (1991). Dysconscious racism: Ideology, identity, and the miseducation of teachers. *The Journal of Negro Education, 60*(2), 133–146.

Ladson-Bilings, G., & Tate, W. (1995). Toward a critical race theory of education. *Teachers College Record, 97*(1), 41–62.

Lopes, T., & Thomas, B. (2006). *Dancing on live embers: Challenging racism in organizations.* Toronto: Between the Lines.

Maguire, P. (2001). Uneven ground: Feminisms and action research. In P. Reason, & H. Bradbury (Eds.), *Handbook of Action Research—Participative Inquiry and Practice* (pp. 59–69). Thousand Oaks, CA: SAGE Publication.

Marullo, S., & Edwards, B. (2000). From charity to justice. *American Behavioral Scientist, 43*(5), 895–903.

Masse, A. M., & Hogan, K. J. (Eds.). (2010). *Over ten million served: Gendered service in language and literature workplaces.* Albany, NY: SUNY Press.

Maurrasse, D. J. (2001). *Beyond the campus: How colleges and universities form partnerships with their communities.* New York: Routledge.

Mayuzumi, K., & Shahjahan, R. A. (2008). Whose university is it, anyway? Power and privilege on gendered terrain. In A. Wagner, S. Acker, & K. Mayuzumi (Eds.), *The sacred and resistance within the "prison": The narratives of racially minoritized women faculty* (pp. 187–202). Toronto, ON: Sumach Press.

McCabe, M. (2004). Strengthening pedagogy and praxis in cultural anthropology and service-learning: Insights from postcolonialism. *Michigan Journal of Community Service Learning, 10*(3), 16–29.

McIntyre, A. (1997). *Making meaning of Whiteness: Exploring racial identity with White teachers.* New York: Suny Press.

Minh-ha, T. T. (1989). *Woman, native, other.* Bloomington: University of Indiana Press.

Mirza, Q. (1999). Patricia Williams: Inflecting critical race theory. *Feminist Legal Studies, 7,* 111–132.

Mitchell, C., & Humphries, H. (2007). From notion of charity to social justice in service-learning: The complex experience of communities. *Education as Change, 11*(3), 47–58.

Mitchell, T. D. (2007). Critical service-learning as social justice education: A case study of the Citizen Scholars Program. *Equity and Excellence in Education, 40*(2), 101–112.
Mohanty, C. T. (1997). Under western eyes: Feminist scholarship and colonial discourses. In N. Visvanathan, L. Dugan, L. Nisonoff, & N. Wiegersma (Eds.), *The women, gender and development reader* (pp. 79–86). London: Zed Books.
Monture-Angus, P. (2003). In the way of peace: Confronting "Whiteness" in the university. In R. Luther, E. Whitmore, & B. Moreau (Eds.), *Seen but not heard: Aboriginal women and women of color in the academy* (pp. 29–49). Ottawa, Canada: Canadian Research Institute for the Advancement of Women (CRIAW).
Naples, N. A., & Bojar, K. (Eds.). (2002). *Teaching feminist activism: Strategies from the field*. New York, NY: Routledge.
Nelson, G., & Prilleltensky, I. (2010). *Community psychology: In pursuit of liberation and well-being*. New York: Palgrave.
O'Grady, C. (2000). Integrating service learning and multicultural education: An overview. In C. O'Grady (Ed.), *Integrating service learning and multicultural education in colleges and universities* (pp. 1–19). New Jersey: Lawrence Erlbaum Associates Inc.
Park, S. (2013, December 26). Challenging racism and the problem with White "Allies": A conversation with David Leonard. [weblog post] Retrieved from http://youngist.org/post/71231465066/challenging-racism-and-the-problem-with-white-allies
Philippine Women's Centre of BC (1996). *Housing needs assessment of Filipina domestic workers*. Retrieved from http://pwc.bc.tripod.com/research.html
———— (1997a). *Is this Canada? Domestic workers experience in Vancouver, BC*. Retrieved from http://pwc.bc.tripod.com/research.html
———— (1997b). *Bridging the gap: The legal needs of Filipino youth*. Retrieved from http://pwc.bc.tripod.com/research.html
———— (1997c). *Trapped! Holding onto the knife's edge: Economic violence against Filipino migrant/immigrant women*. Retrieved from http://pwc.bc.tripod.com/research.html.
———— (2000). *Filipino nurses doing domestic work in Canada: A stalled development* (2000). Retrieved from http://pwc.bc.tripod.com/research.html
Pratt, G. in collaboration with the Philippine Women Centre of BC (2009). Circulating sadness; Witnessing Filipino mothers' stories of family separation. *Gender Place and Culture, 16*, 3–22.
Razack, S. (1998). *Looking white people in the eye*. Toronto: University of Toronto Press.
Regan, P. (2010). *Unsettling the settler within: Indian residential schools, truth telling, and reconciliation in Canada*. Vancouver: UBC Press.
Said, E. (1997). *Covering Islam: How the media and the experts determine how we see the rest of the world*. New York: Vintage Books.
Schick, C. (2000). Keeping the ivory tower white: Discourses of racial domination. *Canadian Journal of Law and Society, 15*(2), 71–90.

Shome, R. (2000). Outing Whiteness. *Critical Studies in Mediated Communication*, *15*, 366–371.
Sleeter, C. E. (2000). Strengthening multicultural education with community-based service learning. In C. O'Grady (Ed.), *Integrating service learning and multicultural education in colleges and universities* (pp. 263–276). New Jersey: Lawrence Erlbaum Associates. Inc.
Stoecker, R., & Tryon, E. (2009). Unheard voices. In R. Stoecker & E. A. Tryon (Eds.), *The unheard voices: Community organizations and service learning* (pp. 1–18). Philadelphia: Temple University Press.
Vargas, S. R. L. (2003). Critical race theory in education: Theory, praxis and recommendations. In G. R. Lopez & L. Parker (Eds.), *Interrogating racism in qualitative research methodology* (pp. 1–18). New York: Peter Lang Publishing.
Verjee, B. (November 2010). Service-learning: Charity-based or transformative? *Transformative dialogues: Teaching and learning eJournal*, *4*(2), 1–13. Retrieved from http://kwantlen.ca/TD/TD.4.2/TD.4.2.2_Vergee_Service_Learning.pdf
────── (2012). Critical race feminism: A transformative vision for service-learning engagement. *Journal of Community Engagement and Scholarship*, *5*(1), 57–69. Retrieved from http://jces.ua.edu/critical-race-feminism-a-transformative-vision-for-service-learning-engagement/
Weerts, D. J., & Sandmann, L. R. (2008). Building a two-way street: Challenges and opportunities for community engagement at research universities. *The Review of Higher Education*, *32*(1), 73–106.
Westheimer, J., & Kahne, J. (2004). What kind of citizen? The politics of educating for democracy. *American Educational Research Journal*, *41*(2), 237–269.
Williams, R. M. (1994) Consenting to Whiteness. In A. Callari (Ed.), *Marxism in the postmodern age* (pp. 301–308). New York: Guilford.
Yosso, T. (2005). Whose culture has capital? A critical race theory discussion of community cultural wealth. *Race Ethnicity and Education*, *8*(1), 69–91.
Zaman, H., Diocson, C., & West, R. (2007). *Workplace rights for immigrants in BC: The case of Filipino workers*. Canadian Centre for Policy Alternatives. Retrieved from http://www.policyalternatives.ca/reports/2007/12/reportsstudies1775/?pa=A2286B2A

CHAPTER 4

Role Modeling Community Engagement for College Students: Narratives from Women Faculty and Staff of Color

Jasmine Mena and Annemarie Vaccaro

In this chapter, we attempt to push the boundaries of the traditional service-learning and civic engagement literature by explicating how women of color serve as civic educators by role modeling authentic, collaborative, and justice-based community engagement (CE). We begin the chapter by summarizing the rich, but infrequently cited, scholarship describing the unique ways women and people of color conceptualize community and engage in community work. We provide an overview of the writings by women of color (e.g., Black feminists, Chicana feminists, womanists, Africana womanists, Third World feminists) and CE scholars of color who argue that community engagement is, and has historically been, a critical aspect of the identities, daily activities, and group survival strategies of people of color. Next, we share insights gleaned from a critical ethnographic study of 13 women of color. Study participants were socialized from a young age by family members, educators, and neighbors to value CE that addressed specific community needs, challenged social inequalities, and improved the quality of life in their communities via empowerment (hooks, 2000). Women learned the value of CE through informal interactions with respected community role models and mentors as opposed to formal classroom education (e.g., service-learning courses). They felt a duty to pay forward this informal education by supporting students of color and role modeling the importance of community activism for group survival. Education via role modeling might not be traditional, but such teaching aligns with the writings of womanists and feminists of color who argue that teaching community activism can take many forms (Clark, 1962; Collins, 1991; hooks, 2000). We purport rich learning can occur when college students observe women role models and emulate their CE actions. We conclude the chapter with recommendations for higher education institutions.

Community Engagement through a Critical Lens

Community engaged learning with the aim of increasing moral and civic responsibility is increasingly common in institutions of higher education globally (Colby, Ehrlich, Beaumont, & Stephens, 2003; McCarthy, Damrongmanee, Pushpalatha, Chithra, & Yamamoto, 2005; Vickers, Harris, & McCarthy, 2004). CE and service-learning have been associated with a host of individual gains such as enhanced learning, interpersonal skill building, and a sense of civic responsibility (Astin & Sax, 1998; Bowman, Brandenberger, Lapsley, Hill, & Quaranto, 2010; Eyler & Giles, 1999; Jones & Abes, 2004). Research by Bowman et al. (2010) also begins to shed some light on broader societal impacts by observing that service-learning in college was associated with greater rates of adult volunteering and prosocial orientation 13 years later.

While the writings about CE and service-learning are largely positive, a growing body of literature highlights challenges (Gorski, 2011; Stewart & Webster, 2011; Vaccaro, 2009, 2011; Vickers, Harris, & McCarthy, 2004). Some scholars warn that when people with privileged identities (e.g., White, middle/upper class people) engage in service with underserved communities, there are real dangers in reinforcing stereotypes, engaging in inauthentic or harmful relationships, or doing service work that benefits the volunteer more than the community (Gorski, 2011; Vaccaro, 2009, 2011). Vickers et al. (2004) aptly note that without a focus on reflection, the social justice impact of CE is missed and is rendered a mere "feel good" activity (Artz, 2001). The critical service-learning movement arose in response to some of these challenges. Mitchell (2008) explicates how critical service-learning requires learners to analyze social inequities, challenge social structures, and develop authentic community relationships.

Service-learning and CE literature often assumes that those "engaged in service-learning will undoubtedly have greater societal privilege than those whom they encounter" in community settings (Mitchell, 2008, p. 56). We believe that this argument is steeped in bias and assumes that only those with economic and race privilege engage in service. While privileged college students are participating in service at increasing rates, we contend that women and people of color have historically participated in CE even though their actions have not always been recognized as such by mainstream literature. Evans, Taylor, Dunlap, and Miller (2009) also challenge the paradigm that only those with privilege engage in their communities. They show that community engagement in African-American communities manifests itself in everyday actions and demonstrate its centrality to their identities and daily life:

> Community service may take the form, for example, of ushering at church, rearing extended blood and nonblood kin, looking after neighborhood children before or after school, sitting in shifts at the hospital when friends and neighbors are sick, cooking food to bring to funerals and community events, and organizing the community for participation and activism in the municipal governing processes. (Evans et al., 2009, p. 12)

They go on to explain how people of color break from traditional forms of CE by engaging with their communities in everyday life because they believe "we are" our communities, thus giving to their community is "a natural part of their cultural or familial legacy and survival" (Evans et al., 2009, p. 12). Similarly, Blake (2009) argues that CE or a "sense of caring for all members of the community...was a way of life" for people of color long before the term community engagement was adopted in higher education (p. 242).

In sum, much of the higher education literature emphasizes traditional forms of CE that focus on the individual growth of those "doing" the service—namely privileged college students. According to Mitchell (2008), "The service work most service-learners participate in—e.g., tutoring, soup kitchens, afterschool enrichment programs—are shaped for the benefit of the students" and based on their educational goals (p. 54). In contrast, change-oriented CE necessitates collaboration with communities, is harder to accomplish, and requires delayed gratification because, "Social justice will never be achieved in a single semester" (Mitchell, 2008, p. 54). We believe it is important for students to experience more collectivist and change-oriented ways of engaging with community. As arbiters of this historical tradition, women of color can serve as powerful examples of, and educators about, this type of CE.

Community Engagement among Women of Color

In the United States, women of color appear to share a commitment to CE as social justice work (not charity) due to their history of marginalization and oppression. For women of color, CE has historically addressed basic needs, corrected inequalities, changed social structures, redistributed resources, and ultimately improved quality of life for women and people of color (hooks, 2000; Hudson-Weems, 2003). Blake (2009) argued that "civic engagement has been a linchpin for survival for African Americans" since the time of slavery (p. 245). For example, life-changing initiatives spearheaded by Ida B. Wells-Barnett, the preeminent community organizer, included the establishment of nursing homes, day-care centers, orphanages; as well as, anti-lynching and antirape campaigns (Collins, 1991; Stall & Stoecker, 2008; Taylor, 2005).

In their work examining community strategies to combat gendered violence, Rojas Durazo, Bierria, and Kim (2012) highlight how women of color have long recognized the damaging effects of structural systems of oppression, causing them to seek change at that level. INCITE!, "a national, activist organization of radical feminists of color" who "mobilize to end all forms of violence against women, gender non-conforming, and trans people of color and our communities" represents an example of a collective fighting toward structural changes for the improvement of the lives of women of color (INCITE!, 2013).

Women of color often bring this historical backdrop of CE to their work as faculty and staff at institutions of higher education. Evans (2009) explains how her research on Black women in higher education from 1850–1954 shaped her perspectives on scholarship and community work. Today, four foundational criteria shape Evans' scholarly endeavors as a woman of color: "lived experience, standpoint, challenging the status quo, and social responsibility" (Evans, p. xviii). Like Evans, many women of color argue that CE is integral to their professional roles as staff and faculty; that inextricable links exist between one's service to the community and her professional role (Reyes & Rios, 2005). Unfortunately, tremendous disincentives are associated with community-based teaching, research, and service (Marullo & Edwards, 2000; Reyes & Rios, 2005). For instance, Rios (in her autobiographical reflection in Reyes and Rios) explained the warnings she has received,

> I am hearing that advocacy and community involvement are personal goals that are separate and distant from scholarship as it is conceptualized by academia, especially in research institutions. The pressure is on to pursue the funding that will legitimize my research and mentoring

activities before my involvement. This seems counterintuitive to me in view of the immediate needs of our communities. (p. 384)

Despite such discouragement, women of color engage with their communities because participating in sociopolitical action for community group survival is at the core of their identities.

We contend that women of color do not merely do engagement through formal and informal venues in the academy; women faculty and staff of color teach college students the importance of CE toward sociopolitical action via role modeling. Modeling change-oriented CE takes the form of demonstrating or leading by example. We conducted a critical ethnographic study seeking to better understand the experiences of women faculty and staff of color in a predominantly White institution of higher education. In this project, we observed that role modeling often went beyond mere demonstrating and leading to include implicit and explicit messages of advice, challenge, and empowerment. As such, we argue that leading by example, combined with explicit and implicit messages about the significance of CE, can serve as a form of teaching by role models who foster reflection, inspire growth and encourage activism in young people. This perspective aligns with the intersections of teaching as political activism for community group survival as described by Collins (1991) who argues,

> Teaching reflects a form of Afrocentric feminist political activism essential to the struggle for group survival. By placing family, children, education and community at the center of our political activism, African American women draw on Afrocentric conceptualizations of mothering, family, community, and empowerment... Teaching becomes an arena for political activism wherever it occurs. (p. 150)

Based on the perspectives noted above we can glean that women of color tend to identify with a collectivistic community-oriented perspective. Instead of a "do for" relationship typical of service that upholds the status quo and benefits privileged university learners, women of color establish "do with" relationships with communities; a transformational approach to CE (Marullo & Edwards, 2000). We argue that women of color have the potential to be role models who teach college students the importance of CE as identity work and activism geared at community group survival.

The Study

This chapter emerged from data gleaned from a larger critical ethnographic study examining the experiences of women faculty and staff of color in a predominantly White institution of higher education. Critical ethnographers seek to create positive sociopolitical change through their research (Carspecken & Apple, 1992). They situate the lived experiences of a culture-sharing group in the context of oppressive social structures and social inequality, challenge the status quo, and empower participants (Carspecken, 2013). The overarching aims of this study were to describe the experiences of women faculty and staff of color with rich detail and use the findings to effect change in their institution. Research questions focused on the participants' career trajectories, sense of belonging at their institution, and community involvement. The research included two components typical for ethnographic research: in-depth interviewing and participant observation.

Mena engaged in participant observations of a campus organization for women faculty and staff of color (Organization for Women of Color, OWC) for a period of 12 months. Additionally, 13 key informants participated in retrospective interviews exploring their experiences as women of color in higher education. Qualitative interviewing was deemed an ideal data gathering strategy because of the ability to delve below the surface on issues that may be sensitive in nature (Rubin & Rubin, 2011). Sample open-ended questions included: What is your professional role at this institution? What's your definition of community? and Can you describe the communities of which you are a member? Process consent was used to empower key informants (Usher & Arthur, 1998). Process consent involves a commitment by the researcher to engage in an interactive and collaborative relationship with participants where consent is revisited and renegotiated on an ongoing basis. If at any point the participant wishes to terminate participation in the study she can do so without penalty (Usher & Arthur, 1998). Interviews lasted between 50 and 120 minutes.

The women who participated in individual interviews came from diverse backgrounds. Participant ages ranged from 30 to 63 years of age. Eleven participants identified as Black or African American while two identified as Asian, and one as Latina. All of the women in this study held graduate degrees (seven Masters & six PhD degrees); ten participants were employed in staff positions while three held faculty appointments. The number of years employed at the institution ranged from 1.5 to 22 years. While two participants did not report their sexual orientation, two identified as lesbian and nine as heterosexual or straight. With respect to relationship status, four participants were single, two divorced, and seven were partnered. With the exception of two participants who did not report a religion and one participant who identified as "spiritual," all reported engagement in organized religion. All participants' names and references to others in their lives have been changed to protect confidentiality.

While there are diverse perspectives about analyzing ethnographic data, Coffey (1996) argues there is agreement about the goals of the analysis process. Coffey writes, "analysing and representing are not simply about coding and writing in some distant way. What we are actually concerned with is the reconstruction and reproduction of lives and experiences through critical engagement with our data" (p. 136). As critical scholars, we reviewed interview transcripts with the goal of capturing the unique experiences of women of color who are both a culture sharing (Wolcott, 1999) and historically minoritized group. In line with Wolcott's notion of finding patterned regularities, we reviewed the transcripts and field notes multiple times with the goal of identifying regularities in women's narratives. Wolcott explains that ethnographers find patterned regularities by "positioning and examining patterns as reflected in life cycle events, pervasive themes, annual cycles of activities, observance of rituals, worldview, or through cultural patterning revealed in well-contextualized personal life histories" (p. 256). As we reviewed the interview transcripts and reflected on field observations, we noticed patterned regularities in women's life cycle events, perspectives and activities related to CE, and worldviews as women of color. By delving deeply into these patterned regularities, four themes emerged as salient: definitions of community, engagement as identity and group survival, role modeling as CE, and socialization of younger generations. We used these patterned regularities to form the basis for first-level coding. This basic coding was followed by the identification of subthemes. Once themes and subthemes were identified, both authors reviewed the themes and transcripts to ensure that the reconstruction of women's lives into these patterned regularities was an accurate representation of the culture-sharing group. Finally, as critical ethnographers, we situated these themes and subthemes in the context of oppressive social and educational realities described by the women themselves.

To ensure trustworthiness and credibility (Jones, Torres, & Arminio, 2013) of study findings, a variety of strategies were implemented. Data from the interviews were triangulated with observation notes for the purposes of corroboration. We also made use of analytic triangulation (Patton, 2002) whereby codes were selected for use only upon consensus among the researchers. We utilized member checking and peer reviews to ensure credibility of our emergent themes. Finally, we addressed issues of relational competence (Jones et al., 2013) through reflexivity (Glesne, 1999) in regard to our social identities, positionality, power relationships, and pre-understandings (Jones et al., 2013). We identify as a woman of color who was also participant-observer in the Organization for Women of Color and a White woman who had no connection to the organization. Despite our commonality as critical scholars, our social identities, and corresponding life experiences of minoritization and privilege, surely shaped our analysis. We engaged in deep conversations surrounding our identities, positionality, assumptions, and power relationships throughout the analysis and writing process.

Defining, Teaching, and Modeling Community Engagement: Narratives from Women of Color

Defining Community

In order for us to comprehend conceptions of CE held by women of color, it was first important to understand how women defined and described the term community. Family was a term that seemed to be at the heart of a sense of community for all participants. Kendra explained, "When I think of the word community, I think of family." For many women, community and family included more than biological relatives. Mary shared, "when I think of community I'm really thinking of my family, and then my church, or the small [ethnic] community that I belong to." Amy explained that "growing up in the housing projects, people absolutely looked out for one another. There was a community based situation, for sure." Amy's description is similar to that of Stack (1974) who described how working-class women of color often relied on neighbors and "fictive" kin (nonbiological relatives) to raise families and support each other. Women of color in Stack's study understood they needed "a steady source of cooperative support to survive" (p. 32). Support from nonbiological kin can come from neighbors and religious organizations. Other writers of color have described similar phenomena related to a sense of collectivist CE for people of color (Blake, 2009; Evans et al., 2009).

Study participants also used the term community to refer to other women of color on campus and in the Organization for Women of Color (OWC). Women of color expressed dissatisfaction with many campus community groups. Dissatisfaction coupled with shared experiences with racism and sexism on campus prompted participants to seek specific connections with other women of color at the university. As a result, all of the participants joined the OWC on campus. Like many of her peers, community was intricately tied to Nancy's ethnic identity. As a person who identified as "a woman from the African Diaspora," feeling a sense of community meant finding women with a shared background. She explained, "You have to find community where you fit in and surround yourself with those people." Sonia also described how having a sense of community ideally meant being in the presence of people of color.

Tanya offered a multifaceted description of community that encapsulated many of the emergent themes shared by women in the study regarding their definitions of community (e.g., family, women of color, religious communities, neighbors/"fictive kin"). For Tanya and her peers, the bounds of community shifted depending on location and the shared identities of individuals in those environments. She explained,

> Community on my home front is connecting with my daughter and my sister and my aunt...we can be honest with each other and we can help each other. We know that we can rely on each other...On my job, my community...it's about women...who, when they see me, I feel like they care about what's happening to me and it's not just the peripheral stuff...For my neighborhood, and my people on my street, that's another extended community that I feel tied to...Every morning when I hit my front stairs to leave to go to work, I pray for the whole community and all my neighbors...My church community is a place of growth...I go there mainly for the fellowship as well...Yeah so community for me is all of those pieces.

In sum, for Tanya and the other women of color in this study, community included biological family, nonbiological kin, neighbors, religious organizations, and individuals who shared their marginalized identities as women and people of color. Tanya and other participants were immersed in these communities in a "do with" transformative form of CE described by Marullo and Edwards (2000). This fashion of CE raises the stakes since they do not leave their communities when their time is done as in traditional service-learning (Mitchell, 2008). Instead they remain embedded and active in their community and can observe the changes they helped bring about.

Community Engagement as Identity and Group Survival

The definition of CE described by participants highlighted that CE was an important aspect of their identity. Community engagement was not merely something they *did*, it was a central part of who they *were* as people. Such connections between community, identity, and activism align with feminist and womanist writings explicating similar intersections (Collins, 1991; hooks, 2000; Moraga & Anzaldúa, 2002).

When asked by the interviewer, "Tell me a little bit about your identities," Xiomara replied, "I'm a professor. I'm a student of [discipline]. I'm a mother, daughter... sister, all of these things. You know upstanding member of my community, I hope." Even as she approached retirement from her paid university position, Celeste explained how educating young people of color would remain a central part of her life work and her identity. She shared, "I had lots of support and that's why I believe now in order to help kids, you gotta have support within the community... So that will always be my work even as an older woman."

Since CE was intricately tied to their identities as woman of color and their corresponding desire to promote group survival (Collins, 1991; hooks, 2000; Hudson-Weems, 2003; Reyes & Rios, 2005), most participants intentionally engaged in organizations that served low income youth, women, and people of color. Judy shared how she was:

> involved with domestic violence [and] the women's center. I used to run a support group for women dealing with the issue. I used to do an informative group for women who had not been in that situation yet, but to be able to recognize the signs of an abusive person.

Celeste was passionate about supporting young people and families and believed she had a role to play in creating and sustaining healthy communities of color. In line with her professional role as a family educator, she spent countless hours teaching parenting skills. Celeste explained how her goal was to create healthy families; her own and others. As she approached retirement, she explained how, "I wanna be grandma now." Yet she also continued to facilitate "parenting workshops... to try to teach [young people] that... what you say to your child enforces their development." This quote suggests that Celeste saw her educational efforts with minoritized families as an essential part of community group survival (Collins, 1991; hooks, 2000).

Through formal workshops and informal conversations, Celeste also taught young people to navigate racist educational systems. She shared, "I want to work with young women in my community to teach them how to maneuver through the school system." Her advice to those young people was offered in the spirit of empowering marginalized youth not only to survive, but to also thrive in a racist and classist world. She explained, "I take that information back to the community... to empower people and to help people... You gotta work the system."

Scholars who study CE of African Americans have argued that young people of color are often socialized from an early age to understand the importance of being an active member of their communities (Blake, 2009; Evans et al., 2009). In alignment with that scholarship, most of the women in the study began engaging with their communities from a young age. In high school, Tanya volunteered at a local elementary school where she read to children. This engagement unleashed her passion for working with youth, which prompted her later involvement as an advocate for children and families in the foster care system. Kendra grew up in a war-torn country where she saw many opportunities to serve her community. She explained how there were

> a lot of children who were just orphaned by the war...so there was this opportunity for me to teach first grade...and I found it so fulfilling. So that's how I started working with students, especially the ones that...barely had...food to eat.

Now living in the United States, Kendra tries to remain engaged in her community of origin from afar. One of her dreams was to start a resource center to replace the libraries destroyed during the war. During the conversation, Kendra noted that there are many well-intentioned and privileged individuals and organizations that want to help the country in a charitable way. Yet, she believed that their lack of understanding of the community and their "outsider" and "do for" perspectives led to programs and services that were unnecessary or well-intentioned failures. She shared,

> There are so many humanitarian organizations, they're good hard working honest people who are very kind and looking to help poor countries. So there are some individuals who will write proposals and say, "This is what I want to do."...And then they get the money and...they probably don't do what they want to do. I don't want to be a part of that. It sickens me because, like I said, I experienced the war...So I know the need.

This quote emphasizes the differences between charity work and long-term CE for social justice (Marullo & Edwards, 2000). Kendra believed that those doing charity often did not follow through with their efforts because a deep commitment to community justice was not present. She also distinguished between community outsiders who do not understand the culture or the real community "needs" and community insiders who had an intimate knowledge of the lived realities of community members. Her concerns mirror the growing body of literature about the challenges associated with privileged individuals engaging in service with minoritized communities (Gorski, 2011; Vaccaro, 2009, 2011).

The narratives of women of color in this study show that they engaged in their communities because it was a part of their identities as women of color committed to community progress and group survival (Collins, 1991; hooks, 2000; Hudson-Weems, 2003; Reyes & Rios, 2005). It was not a form of traditional service-learning (Mitchell, 2008) or charity work (Marullo & Edwards, 2000) for "others" done out of guilt or to fulfill a requirement. Instead CE was a "do with" form of authentic CE (Marullo & Edwards, 2000) that was a crucial aspect of their identities and life work as women of color.

Role Modeling and Community Socialization

The practice of CE as identity and group survival strategies employed by participants in this study are in line with women writers of color who have long argued that teaching about community survival is a form of political action that occurs in both formal and informal settings (Clark, 1962; Collins, 1991; hooks, 2000). From a young age, participants in this study were taught group survival skills and the importance of CE by role models and mentors in their homes, neighborhoods, religious organizations, and schools. They also received implicit and explicit messages from role models about empowerment and perseverance in the face of oppression. Through this community teaching (Collins, 1991) via role models, women learned to value themselves, their families, and their communities and were taught the importance of being community activists who inspired and empowered future generations.

Powerful women in Celeste's life helped her gain self-esteem and the grit to push through racism to succeed. She said,

> So it was instilled in me... My mom would say, "You know you are beautiful. You are Black and you have to work very hard and you have to work doubly hard." And my grandmother use to say to us, "When you go on a job... watch your back!"

Gina felt blessed to have role models who gave her the inspiration and self-confidence to believe that she too could be successful. As a child, she was inspired by strong women. "The librarian... I looked up to her and wanted to be like her. She was very helpful to me... And then my aunt was a school teacher and one of her friends was a school librarian. Of course they were both Black... so I had role models which helped." These women, especially the Black librarian, inspired her to think: "If Ms. Jones could do this, I could do this."

Women learned from role models and mentors the importance of CE for group survival. From local community members, Celeste began to see how important it was to teach youth essential skills to succeed academically and thrive in a racist world. She explained, "This man in our neighborhood,

Mr. Johnson...and the other lady...Ms. Willer. They start working with us kids on polishing our skills in terms of public speaking, writing, and stuff like that." Mr. Johnson remained in Celeste's life for decades. Through his mentoring, she learned to write an effective college essay and later to navigate overt and covert forms of bias and political pitfalls at work. During high school, Mr. Johnson took Celeste and five other students of color to Washington DC. In addition to seeing the museums and memorials, he also took the students to the poor section of town. She explained, "He took us to see that so that you would know that you need to give back."

Faculty and staff mentors and role models often helped women persevere in the face of racism and sexism in the academy. These individuals were essential for women's survival as students and later in life as faculty and staff members. As an adult, Judy returned to college to complete her degree. She recalled a time when a mentor convinced her to stay at school after an oppressive encounter with a professor. She shared,

> I remember, I came into her office so upset because a professor wrote insulting comments on my paper...I was so enraged and I remember coming to the office and saying "I want to know how to quit."...She talked to me for a while and I was still saying, "I'm out of here"....She stood in front of the door and said "I'm not letting you leave." I remember laughing and I was thinking...you have a lot of chutzpa. She got me to stay...I always remember her. If I left I would have never come back.

Linda leaned on mentors when she experienced racism at work. She explained how she needs:

> women of color...that I can talk to when I feel that I have been marginalized...Even though it is not going to change [I need] to have someone to go to and say this is what I feel today and have someone say, "I understand." I need to have mentors that I can listen to and follow and see what they have done.

For Mary, having a supervisor of color who emphasized self-confidence and support was invaluable. She explained, "he's just wonderful, in terms of mentoring and kind of helping me gain the set of experiences that I need to be more effective in administration and leadership positions." Mary's supervisor was role modeling community investment he received and teaching her to do the same. Similarly, other women of color in this study were socialized to value CE that addressed community needs, challenged inequities, and improved the quality of life through empowerment (hooks, 2000).

This teaching as feminist political activism (Collins, 1991) often happened in informal settings by women observing and later imitating community engaged behaviors exhibited by family members, teachers, and community role models.

Paying It Forward with Students on Campus

For the women in this study, role models were integral to the realization that self-interested, traditional forms of CE were problematic, and alternatively, that change-oriented and collectivistic forms of CE were essential. As part of their conceptions of CE, women believed it was their responsibility to pay it forward by serving as educators, supporters, and role models to young people on campus. While the traditional service-learning and CE literature does not describe such perspectives and behaviors as CE, we argue that paying it forward was an invaluable form of CE. Women's desire to serve as role models who educated and supported future generations aligns with the body of nontraditional CE and womanist literature that emphasizes the significance of engagement, activism, and teaching for community group survival (Blake, 2009; Collins, 1991; Evans, 2009; hooks, 2000).

Even though each of these women "paid it forward" in different ways, support for young women of color was at the core of their campus efforts. Nancy shared, "I believe that women need to support women. I believe that 100%." Judy explained how important it was to socialize youth to share the values of CE. She said, "One of the things I raised my son to believe was; if you are not part of the solution, you are part of the problem. I raised him to feel empowered and a sense of responsibility to his community, and righting things that were wrong." To this day, Judy takes every opportunity to instill these same messages in the students she works with on campus.

Nancy believed it was her duty to help younger women learn to make their way through racist, sexist, and classist educational and work environments. She explained, "you always learn something from the person that is ahead of you. I think that is what is critical." All of the women in this study seemed to share this sentiment; supporting younger generations of women of color was a deeply held value, a responsibility, and a part of their identities as women. Women of color often described their efforts to engage with younger women as reciprocal, "do with" (Marullo & Edwards, 2000) endeavors. They recognized that while they could offer mentoring and advice, they could also grow and benefit from relationships with younger women. For Tanya, supporting other women was a form of CE that formed the core of her identity and served as a source of positivity in her life. She shared,

To connect with younger women of color, it does something for me. I don't know if it's something way back in genetics, but it does something for me and so I always try to connect... I think I have a feeling of pride in seeing women coming together and being supportive in sharing our struggles and our successes and how we made it through all of that.

Similarly, Amy explained how supporting "our young sisters" is "really important and something that helps me feel connected as well." Linda also described engagement with young women of color as "so gratifying."

Some of the participants talked about specific perspectives or skills that they hoped to role model and teach students of color. Jennifer wanted to teach women of color that any career was possible. Just by doing her job and being herself (i.e., role modeling success), Jennifer hoped she would influence young people to say to themselves, "there is someone that looks like me that works in these offices... maybe [that job] is something I can do." Similarly, Linda recognized that when students of color entered her office they "would just be shocked to see a person of color at this level." She hoped that visibility of women of color (like herself), in respected positions would teach students of color that anything was possible. She also hoped to inspire them to set high goals for themselves.

Other women talked about the importance of teaching young people of color that they had immense value. In her interactions with students of color, Kendra attempted to convey messages of inspiration. She often told students, "Yes you can do it! If you put your mind to it, you can do it." Women hoped that these messages of inspiration would bolster self-esteem and serve as protective factors helping students persevere in hostile environments. Kendra explained how she did this through role modeling and advice giving:

> I was trying to set up an example. Because I didn't want them to think... "I should settle for this because of my situation." You have to be able to go after whatever it is that you want. No matter what it is that come (*sic*) your way, as long as you are alive to overcome it you should continue as long as it doesn't kill you. You should... preserve and get strong from it... I believe I got stronger based on every single obstacle I was able to overcome.

Youth in communities of color and low income communities often trail their privileged peers in access to social capital or networks where they can glean valuable relationships and information (Stevens, 2009). Jennifer was committed to helping students of color learn how to gain such capital.

She said, "I'm in this job to educate students to make connections and that's what I am going to do." Tanya was also committed to helping young women of color develop networks and the skills to navigate racist political environments. She might approach another woman and say, "Hey girlfriend, if you need to talk, come and talk to me and I can tell you how it works here."

Women learned the importance of role modeling as a result of both positive and negative experiences. In graduate school, Tina had a "horrible" advisor followed by one who was "amazing" and who "could identify people's strengths and cultivate them." Today, when she works with students, Tina tries to emulate the skills modeled by that amazing professor. She said, "I know that I've been very well mentored in my career starting from very early on so I feel very compelled, it's a compelling thing for me to do." Xiomara also strives to mentor students who she "feel[s] responsible for." Such a perspective aligns with the insider and "do with" (Marullo & Edwards, 2000) perspectives espoused in critical CE literature.

Judy deeply appreciated the impact that mentors had on her life and career trajectory. In turn, she sought to be a role model, mentor, and supporter for students of color. There were many young people on her campus who needed support and guidance. Yet, she was only one person. To meet vast student needs, she created a peer-mentoring program on her campus. She reflected,

> I was telling my mentors today; "You have no idea how much impact you can have on people and how little you can do that becomes so important to them"... That's what I'm hoping for with the peer mentors.

Amy not only role modeled CE, but she also designed service opportunities for undergraduate students. At one of the universities where she worked, Amy involved undergraduates in a community project related to the Underground Railroad. She shared,

> At [University X] in upstate New York, I discovered that the students back in the 1830s were involved in the Underground Railroad and anti-slavery activity. I got the students involved in that. As a result of finding these faces that were carved in the church basement in Syracuse, we started to do some of the digging and research and found that there was a diary that one of the students from the university left that is now in the archives. It describes the anti-slavery movement... That work is still going on.

While Amy was the only woman who described offering what might be considered a traditional service-learning opportunity to students, *all* of the women taught and role modeled CE in a fashion that aligned with the writings of womanists and feminists of color.

As described in the previous section, all of the women in this study learned from role models how important it was to invest in the future of their communities and to "pay it forward" with students on campus. In turn, their role modeling and community teaching served not only as powerful forms of activism geared at community survival for students of color (Collins, 1991; hooks, 2000; Hudson-Weems, 2003; Reyes & Rios, 2005), but also provided a blueprint for CE from which young people could learn.

Expanding Notions of Community Engagement in the Academy

Throughout this chapter we have suggested that young people can, and do, learn about the power of CE from mentors and role models. Women in our study described CE as identity work and a form of group survival. They also explicated their desire to pay forward their values of, and strategies for, CE. These engagement processes happened organically for women in this study. However, we suggest that with appropriate university support, engaged teaching and modeling could be institutionalized so that more students and communities can be impacted. To accomplish this task, universities must recognize women of color as rich and invaluable resources and invite them to serve as experts in the development of programs and structures that promote an expanded vision of CE (e.g., critical, self-reflexive, authentic, and empowering). At the least, doing so requires privileged faculty and staff to expand their comfort zones by engaging with women of color, thus challenging oppressive structures which often render women of color and their competencies invisible. Institutions can combat the invisibility of women of color and expand visions of CE by intentionally highlighting the engagement work of women of color in university reports, websites, and alumni magazines. Universities can also expand university definitions of CE that push the bounds of traditional CE literature in university manuals, hiring, tenure and promotion processes, and curriculum guidelines.

Universities can develop formal mentoring programs that pair faculty and staff of color with students from similar minoritized backgrounds. We do not intend to essentialize women of color and we understand that two people with similar racial identities may report diametrically opposed experiences and views. Despite the risks associated with assuming a shared experience, women of color in this study highlighted the immense value of connecting with others who were also underrepresented. We encourage a form of mentoring that acknowledges individual and collective experiences and honors the importance of engagement as community group survival. This type of mentoring was central to the success of women in this study and aligns with writings of womanists and feminists of color (Collins, 1991; hooks, 2000; Hudson-Weems, 2003; Reyes & Rios, 2005). Writings about mentoring as feminist praxis can provide a roadmap for university planned mentoring efforts (Moss, Debres, Cravey, Hyndman, Hirshboeck, & Masucci, 1999). Moss et al. explain that "through engaging in mentoring, we share knowledge, experience and practical strategies that promote women, people of colour and others who are less favourably positioned within the academy" (p. 414). The participants in this study benefited from both formal and information mentorship and no discrepancies were observed with respect to the mentorship impact or quality. However, given the grassroots and informal nature of CE described in the engagement literature regarding communities of color (Blake, 2009; Evans, 2009; Rojas Durazo et al., 2012) and feminist and womanist writings from women of color (Clark, 1962; Collins, 1991; hooks, 2000), we acknowledge that formalizing mentorship may result in unintended, and possibly negative, consequences.

In addition to formal mentoring programs, universities can promote and support the development of affinity organizations such as the Organization for Women of Color. Women faculty and staff of color can find such organizations to be safe spaces where they give and glean support, advice, and mentoring. They can also discuss their community engaged identities and sociopolitical action with other women of color who "get it." Because of their desires to pay it forward, women involved in this particular campus group invited female students of color to attend selected meetings. In those sessions, faculty and staff role modeled feminist political activism (Collins, 1991) and CE for students of color. We contend that through formal and informal relationships, mentors can share strategies for survival in the ivory tower and also role model and explicitly encourage mentees to engage with their communities outside academe.

Universities can also highlight the CE of people of color through campus programming and curriculum. Many of the women in this study were regularly invited to serve as panelists and guest lecturers for diversity classes, campus events, and diverse student organizations. In these venues, women shared their CE narratives with women and people of color. In a different five-year study with students of color, Vaccaro and Camba (2012) found that female students of color often described these panel presentations and guest lectures as the most enriching and empowering experiences of their college careers. Hearing the community narratives of women of color inspired these students to persevere despite oppression and engage in their communities. Universities should invest resources into campus lectures, panels, and presentations where women of color are invited to share their CE experiences.

Universities that promote CE and service-learning in the curriculum must assess whether that curriculum reinforces "do for" perspectives that resemble charity (Marullo & Edwards, 2000) or critical CE that emphasizes authentic relationships, recognizes social forces that cause inequality, and challenges oppressive structures (Mitchell, 2008). We also suggest expanding traditional CE curriculum materials to include historic and contemporary writings by women and people of color that offer more inclusive definitions of community and examples of CE that highlight the significance of community group survival and fighting oppression (e.g., Blake, 2009; Clark, 1962; Evans, 2009; Evans et al., 2009; Stewart & Webster, 2011; Taylor, 2005).

We understand that we have made recommendations that will fall, in large part, upon the shoulders of women of color. We contend that they are the experts who can role model socially just forms of CE. Women and people of color already engage with students and service at greater rates than their White counterparts (Masse & Hogan, 2010; Reyes & Rios, 2005; Wyche & Graves, 1992). For women of color in this study, CE was a valued aspect of identity, an imperative form of group survival, and social justice work that challenged inequitable social structures.

We also recognize that such efforts can take incredible amounts of time and emotional energy. Additionally, this form of feminist activism is often discouraged or devalued in the academy, putting women of color in compromising positions during performance reviews and potentially hindering career advancement. As such, we recommend that universities reevaluate formal and informal reward structures so it is clear that all forms of engagement are valued. One way to accomplish this is to invite women of color to model engagement (e.g., paying it forward with students) and reward their engagement as essential aspects of their campus roles. These suggestions, and others noted in this chapter, however, require a willingness on behalf of higher education institutions to recognize the limits of traditional notions of service and engagement. Moreover, schools must expand their paradigms to recognize the power of authentic, collaborative, and justice-based activism for social change. Doing so is critical for the survival and empowerment of minoritized individuals and their communities and provides college students with a rich resource from which they can learn the value of collaborative and justice-based community engagement.

References

Artz, L. (2001). Critical ethnography for communication studies: Dialogue and social justice in service-learning. *The Southern Communication Journals, 66,* 239–250.

Astin, A. W., & Sax, L. J. (1998). How undergraduates are affected by service participation. *Journal of College Student Development, 39,* 251–263.

Blake, D. F. (2009). Final word: African Americans and community engagement: The challenge and opportunity for higher education. In S. Evans, C. Taylor, M. Dunlap, & D. Miller (Eds.), *African Americans and community engagement in higher education* (pp. 241–248). Albany, NY: SUNY Press.

Bowman, N., Brandenberger, J., Lapsley, D., Hill, P., & Quaranto, J. (2010). Community engagement during the college years predict adult well-being? *Applied Psychology: Health and Well-Being, 2,* 14–34.

Carspecken, F. P. (2013). *Critical ethnography in educational research: A theoretical and practical guide.* New York, NY: Routledge.

Carspecken, P. F., & Apple, M. (1992). Critical qualitative research: Theory, methodology, and practice. In M. L. LeCompte, W. L. Millroy, & J. Preissle (Eds.), *The handbook of qualitative research in education* (pp. 507–553). San Diego, CA: Academic Press.

Clark, S. (1962). *Echo in my soul.* New York: Dutton.

Coffey, A. (1999). *The ethnographic self: Fieldwork and the representation of identity.* London: Sage.

Colby, A., Ehrlich, T., Beaumont, E., & Stephens, J. (2003). *Educating citizens: Preparing America's undergraduates for lives of moral and civic responsibility.* San Francisco, CA: Jossey-Bass.

Collins, P. H. (1991). *Black feminist thought: Knowledge, consciousness, and the politics of empowerment.* New York, NY: Routledge.

Evans, S. Y. (2009). Preface: Using history, experience and theory to balance relationships in community engagement. In S. Evans, C. Taylor, M. Dunlap, & D. Miller (Eds.), *African Americans and community engagement in higher education* (pp. xi–xix). Albany, NY: SUNY Press.

Evans, S. Y., Taylor, C. M., Dunlap, M. R., & Miller, D. S. (2009). Community service, volunteerism and engagement. In S. Evans, C. Taylor, M. Dunlap, & D. Miller (Eds.), *African Americans and community engagement in higher education* (pp. 11–15). Albany, NY: SUNY Press

Eyler, J., & Giles, Jr., D. E. (1999). *Where's the learning in service-learning?* San Francisco, CA: Jossey-Bass.

Glesne, C. (1999). *Becoming qualitative researchers: An introduction* (2nd ed.). NY: Wesley Longman.

Gorski, P. (2011). Foreword. In N. Webster & T. Stevens (Eds.), *Exploring cultural dynamics and tensions within service-learning* (pp. xv–xii). Charlotte, NC: Information Age Publishers.

hooks, b. (2000). *Feminist theory: From margin to center* (2nd ed.). Cambridge, MA: South End.

Hudson-Weems, C. (2003). Africana womanism: An overview. In D. P. Aldridge & C. Young (Eds.), *Out of the revolution: The development of Africana studies*. Lanham, MD: Lexington Books.

INCITE! (2013). *Vision*. Retrieved from http://www.incite-national.org/home

Jones, S. R., & Abes, E. S. (2004). Enduring influences of service-learning on college students' identity development. *Journal of College Student Development, 45*(2), 149–166.

Jones, S. R., Torres, V., & Arminio, J. (2013). *Negotiating the complexities of qualitative research in higher education: Fundamental elements and issues* (2nd ed.). New York, NY: Routledge.

Marullo, S., & Edwards, B. (2000). From charity to justice: The potential of university-community collaboration for social change. *American Behavioral Scientist, 43*(5), 895–912.

Masse, A. M., & Hogan, K. J. (Eds.). (2010). *Over ten million served: Gendered service in language and literature workplaces*. Albany, NY: SUNY Press.

McCarthy, F. E., Damrongmanee, Y., Pushpalatha, M., Chithra, J., & Yamamoto, K. (2005). The practices and possibilities of service-learning among colleges and universities in Asia. *Pacific Asian Education, 17*(2), 59–70.

Mitchell, T. D. (2008, Spring). Traditional vs. critical service learning: Engaging the literature to differentiate two models. *Michigan Journal of Service Learning, 14*(2), 50–65.

Moraga, C. L., & Anzaldúa, G. E. (Eds.) (2002). *This bridge called my back: Writings by radical women of color*. Berkeley, CA: Third Woman Press.

Moss, P., Debres, K. J., Cravey, A., Hyndman, J., Hirschboeck, K. K., & Masucci, M. (1999). Toward mentoring as feminist praxis: Strategies for ourselves and others. *Journal of Geography in Higher Education, 23*(3), 413–427.

Patton, M. Q. (2002). *Qualitative research and evaluation methods* (3rd ed.). Thousand Oaks, CA: Sage.

Reyes, X. A., & Ríos, D. I. (2005). Dialoguing the Latina experience in higher education. *Journal of Hispanic Higher Education, 4*, 377–391.

Rojas Durazo, A. C., Bierria, A., & Kim, M. (2012). Community accountability: Emerging movements to transform violence. *Social Justice: A Journal of Crime, Conflict and World Order, 37*, 1–11.

Rubin, H. J., & Rubin, I. S. (2011). *Qualitative interviewing: The art of hearing data*. Los Angeles: Sage.

Saltmarsh, J., & Driscoll, A. (n.d.). *Classification description: Community engagement elective classification*. Stanford, CA: Carnegie Foundation for the Advancement of Teaching. Retrieved from http://classifications.carnegiefoundation.org/descriptions/community_engagement.php

Stack, C. B. (1974). *All our kin: Strategies for survival in a Black community*. New York: Basic.

Stall, S., & Stoecker, R. (2008). Community organizing or organizing community? Gender and the crafts of empowerment. In J. DeFilippis & S. Saergert (Eds.), *The community development reader* (pp. 241–248). New York, NY: Routledge.

Stevens, M. L. (2009). *Creating a class: College admissions and the education of elites.* Cambridge, MA: Harvard University Press.
Stewart, T., & Webster, N. (Eds.). (2011). *Exploring cultural dynamics and tensions within service-learning.* Charlotte, NC: Information Age Publishers.
Taylor, D. (2005). American environmentalism: The role of race, class, and gender in shaping activism, 1820–1995. In L. King & D. McCarthy (Eds.), *Environmental sociology: From analysis to action,* (pp. 87–106). Oxford, UK: Rowman and Littlefield.
Usher, K. J., & Arthur, D. (1998). Process consent: A model for enhancing informed consent in mental health nursing. *Journal of Advanced Nursing, 27*(4), 692–697.
Vaccaro, A. (2009). Racial identity and the ethics of service learning as pedagogy. In S. Evans, C. Taylor, M. Dunlap, & D. Miller (Eds.), *African Americans and community engagement in higher education* (pp. 119–134). Albany, NY: SUNY Press.
— (2011). Challenging privileged paradigms through service-learning: Exposing dominant ideology, unlearning deficit thinking, and debunking the myth of meritocracy. In T. Stewart & N. Webster (Eds.), *Exploring cultural dynamics and tensions within service-learning* (pp. 45–62). Charlotte, NC: Information Age Publishers.
Vaccaro, A. & Camba, M. J. (2012, March). *No one wants to be called a racist.* Research presentation at the NASPA Annual Convention, Phoenix, Arizona.
Vickers, M., Harris, C., & McCarthy, F. (2004). University-community engagement: Exploring service-learning options within the practicum. *Asia-Pacific Journal of Teacher Education, 32,* 129–141.
Wolcott, H. F. (1999). *Ethnography: A way of seeing.* Walnut Creek, CA: AltaMira.
Wyche, K. F., & Graves, S. B. (1992). Minority women in academia: Access and barriers to professional participation. *Psychology of Women Quarterly. Special Issue: Women and Power, 1992, 16,* 429–437.

CHAPTER 5

Social Media for Social Justice: Cyberfeminism in the Digital Village

*Carolyn M. Cunningham and
Heather M. Crandall*

Cyberfeminism, which examines women's relationship to the Internet, considers issues such as how power operates in online spaces, who has access to digital technologies, and how the design of online architecture may reproduce gender inequities. As social media becomes essential for nonprofit organizations to establish an online presence, attract supporters, and help ensure sustainable organizations, nonprofits become critical sites for examining the interplay of gender and technology and offer opportunities for applying cyberfeminist goals.

In this chapter, we reflect on our experience teaching a graduate-level course entitled *Communication, Technology and Social Change*. We designed the course to have both online and face-to-face opportunities for students to examine the social, economic, and political forces influencing the use of communication technologies. Central to students' class experience was a community engagement project through which they consulted for two nonprofit organizations. Students' goal was to share their experiences and expertise in persuasive and rhetorical techniques to increase each nonprofit's reach via social media. Throughout the project, we met with students to critically reflect on ways gender and power manifested in their work.

We offer our experiences of designing and teaching this class as context for making sense of gender inequities as they relate to social media use in nonprofits. We begin with a grounding in literature on cyberfeminism and its application to nonprofit spaces. We then share two vignettes from our experience in order to highlight tensions involved in engaging this work with students. Finally, we discuss the contributions cyberfeminism makes to ongoing conversations of community engagement, reflecting on lessons we have learned.

Cyberfeminism

There are many strands of cyberfeminism (Consalvo, 2003). Broadly, cyberfeminism is an umbrella term for the intersection of gender and the Internet. Cyberfeminists in the 1990s, such as Sadie Plant (1997) and Donna Haraway (1998), saw the Internet as a space that would free women from the social and physical constraints of the material world, offering new opportunities for more egalitarian gender relations. The Internet, they believed, would also offer an avenue for feminist organizing. Cyberfeminists assumed that empowerment for women could be achieved through women's increased use of new media. This utopian vision, however, has been criticized for being overly optimistic, ignoring the imbalance of power that exists when looking at how structures of power are embedded in technological systems (Wacjman, 1991).

Since its inception in the 1990s, cyberfeminist scholarship has taken a more critical turn, examining the limitations of social media for social change. As Kenway and Nixon (1999) write, there are multiple modalities of cyberfeminism, including an analysis of structural issues that impact usage, such as access, cost, availability, and literacy. Similarly, Eudey's (2012) definition of cyberfeminism includes "critical reflection of the ways in which sexism and other oppressions are components of the online experience" (p. 241). Gajjala and Oh (2012) write, "cyberfeminism necessitates an awareness of how power plays not only in different locations online but also institutions that shape the layout and experience of cyberspace" (p. 1). In their edited collection, they ask questions about what it means to be a cyberfeminist when women's participation in online spaces is mainly passive rather than active and consumerist. Their work tackles post-feminist contexts in which feminist activism is no longer necessary because women occupy virtual spaces. Contrary to the optimistic tone of early cyberfeminists, Gajjala and Oh (2012) argue that participation in online spaces does not necessarily lead to empowerment but instead serves self-interest, potentially limiting social change goals.

Technofeminism is a strand of cyberfeminism that enables a more nuanced analysis of relationships between gender and technology (Puente, 2008). Technofeminism sees technology use as both a source and consequence of gender relations (Wacjman, 2004). Gender relations are materialized in technology and both masculinity and femininity acquire meaning through their connection with machines. The social construction of gender provides a framework in which masculinity is linked with technical expertise whereas femininity is not (Oldenziel, 1999). This connection has led to a number of structural issues including persistent under-representation of women in science, technology, engineering, and mathematics (STEM) fields, women's lack of confidence in their technological abilities, and online architectures, such as the collection of personal data, that do not favor women's interests (Crowe, 2003; Fancsali, 2002; Ramsey & McCorduck, 2005). In this chapter we attend to how gender influences technology use in nonprofits.

Nonprofits, Gender, and Social Media

Social media is an important tool for bringing about social change and civic engagement; thus, it is essential for nonprofits to use these tools effectively (Lovejoy & Saxton, 2012; Nah & Saxton, 2013). Research shows that nonprofits can be slow to adopt new communication technologies for a number of reasons, including scarce resources, overreliance on volunteers, limited technology budgets, and lack of knowledge about how these technologies work (Burt & Taylor, 2000; Kenix, 2008; Merkel, Farooq, Xiao, Ganoe, Rosson, & Carroll, 2007).

Hardly utopian as imagined by early cyberfeminists, women's experiences of cyberspace have included multiple forms of oppression. Scholars attest to the persistence of gender disparities in the adoption and use of communication technologies (Bertot, 2003; Cooper & Weaver, 2003; Hargittai & Hinnant, 2008; Harp & Tremayne, 2006), and specifically in the nonprofit sector (Curtis, Edwards, Fraser, Gudelsky, Holmquist, Thornton, & Sweetser, 2009). Women staff the majority of nonprofit organizations in the United States; yet, as Lennon (2013) found, females only held 45 percent of CEO positions in these organizations.

Gender differences can also influence how nonprofits are able to utilize communication technologies. For example, Eyrich, Padman, and Sweetser (2008) found that men adopted a greater number of social media tools than women. Lack of knowledge of how to use communication technologies can hinder feminist goals. Irving and English (2011), in their analysis of 100 websites for feminist organizations in Canada, found that feminist organizations missed opportunities to engage in community-based learning, share knowledge, and give voice to marginalized groups with which they work.

Thus, it is important to critically examine the benefits and limitations of the Internet as a tool for social change. This becomes even more relevant with social media since the tools allow for interactivity that can lead to harassment and silencing of women's voices. In this chapter, we draw broadly on cyberfeminism, and more specifically on technofeminism, to understand the challenges to cyberfeminist practices (Puente, 2008). We ask how social media (re)produces gender relations and what types of ideologies of gender are embedded in their design and usage.

The Course

Theoretical Grounding of the Course

The design of the course, *Communication, Technology, and Social Change*, integrated cyberfeminist pedagogy. Cyberfeminist pedagogy includes goals of feminist pedagogy. Stake and Hoffman (2001) identify four characteristics of feminist pedagogy that engage students in dialogue about gender equality and create a classroom culture to promote these ideals. These include participatory learning, validation of personal experience, encouragement of social understanding and activism, and development of critical thinking and open-mindedness (Stake & Hoffman, 2001). As Richards (2011) writes, cyberfeminist pedagogy "attend[s] to the ways in which digital technologies both subvert and reinscribe gender, race and other corporeal hierarchies in virtual space" (p. 6). Beyond the theoretical implications, cyberfeminist pedagogy integrates feminist pedagogical principles including an "ethics of care, community-based curriculum, collaboration, and embodied praxis" (Richards, 2011, p. 7).

Our intentions for the class were for students to engage and better understand a community organization, and to help that organization better communicate its vision for social change through the use of communication technology. We strove for *participatory learning* by working in community to understand the problem and then collaboratively uncover what it might take to help solve it.

Course Goals

As instructors who work with graduate students in the field of communication, we designed this hybrid course so that students could better understand how race, class, and gender structure access to communication technologies. Class discussions and reflections were designed as spaces for students to consider their own context, experience, and assumptions about social media use and social change. Students, for instance, had to think critically about how forms of electronic communication shape who has access to online technologies and how effectively different groups can communicate.

The course materials provided students with a foundation with which to examine the rhetorical strategies of social movements as well as the use of communication technologies for social change. For example, our required textbook was *Readings on the Rhetoric of Social Protest 2nd Edition* by Morris and Browne (2006). This edited collection offered historical perspectives on the various ways social movements communicated their messages. Readings such as Winner's (1980) *Do Artifacts Have Politics?* Mitchell's (1999) *Equitable Access to the Online World* offered critical perspectives on how social, cultural, and economic forces shape the design and use of communication technologies. McGaw's (1996) *Why Feminine Technologies Matter* shows the intersection of gender and technology. Youmans' and York's (2012) *Social Media and the Activist Toolkit* offered practical tools that students could implement for social change.

One goal for the course was for students to become aware of the many ways activists are working to direct our attention to accomplish social change. Students completed a case study assignment where they examined the rhetorical strategies of a social change organization. Another goal of the course was to have students apply their knowledge through a community engagement project. The community engagement component of the course was a three-day on-campus requirement where the students worked with two local nonprofit organizations. The purpose of this assignment was to collaborate with a local nonprofit organization to improve its communication strategies using a variety of communication technologies.

Before students ever stepped into the community, we introduced them to major concepts related to social movements and the role that communication and technologies play in social change. We examined the study of social change from a communication perspective, asking questions such as: how do social movements form?; what communication strategies do they use to accomplish their goals?; and, what are the barriers to their success? Critical perspectives such as cyberfeminism were used to examine how race, class, and gender are articulated in social movements. Online, students engaged in facilitated discussions on the readings and wrote reading response papers to help synthesize the readings. Students also conducted a case study in which they selected and evaluated a social change organization's use of communication technology. Students chose textbook chapters to create a "learn by teaching" assignment that engaged their peers in discussions. Students enhanced their communication skills in the areas of writing, group and team skills, auditing and research tools, training, and technology decisions and implementation. At this point, students were ready to transform their new knowledge into action at a specific community site.

Community Engagement Component

To select our nonprofits, we worked with our campus' service-learning center. First, we crafted a proposal about what our students could offer a nonprofit in terms of using communication technology for social change. The service-learning center sent our proposal to their network and a number of nonprofits volunteered to have our students come to their sites. We met with each organization to discuss expectations. This process led us to choose two female-run nonprofit community partners, *Our Home Community Ministry*, a service center that provides food, clothing, and shelter for those in need, and *International Refugee Center* (IRC), a resource center for refugees. The IRC was founded in 2006 and its mission is to "improve the lives of local refugee and low income families through building community ties, advocacy, increasing intercultural awareness, and life skills training and education." Once the selections were made, the community engagement portion of the course began.

In what follows, we present two vignettes that illustrate the complexity and importance of how community engagement and feminist pedagogy are used to make cyberfeminist concepts concrete. While these vignettes only show a small piece of students' community engagement experiences, they provide insight into dynamics of gender, technology, and inequality in practice in nonprofits. In addition, we reflect on how these vignettes show the unexamined biases of race, class, and gender.

Vignette One: "We Need a Video"

The women who run *Our Home* are elderly White nuns. In our planning meetings with the nuns, they told us they needed a video to showcase their outreach to church audiences and potential funders but lacked time, tools, and expertise necessary to produce it.

On a crisp summer morning in June, having arrived on campus from all over the United States, five students piled into a university van and rode to *Our Home*. The van passed buildings like the courthouse, the health department, the prison, and then turned into a gravel clearing to park at *Our Home*, as students chatted excitedly. With notebooks, cameras, and video equipment, the students climbed out and were greeted by Sr. Ann who escorted us to the kitchen entrance. The hand-drawn "welcome students" sign beside two plates of assorted cookies made us feel like guests. From here

Sr. Ann led us down a small hall of offices to a waiting area. While students were taking notes and pictures, Sr. Ann explained that in half an hour needy people who qualify would come through this front door. The waiting area was comfortable with soft chairs and tables that held platters of cookies. Posters peppered the walls offering information about services for families in crisis. Partitions cordoned off the waiting room and created cubicles for one-on-one meetings with the volunteers.

From here, Sr. Ann showed us a large back room where boxes of produce sat on tables beside metal shelves stacked high with canned and dry goods. Volunteers stood ready to instruct visitors about amounts of food, hygiene, and baby supplies to take. The loading dock outside this large room signaled the end of the tour.

Students huddled together to plan their strategy. As the doors opened, our students went to work. Students roamed around taking pictures and interviewing those who consented. Our "high tech" student Henry Jones asked if he could meet the person in charge of *Our Home's* website. Through his thick southern accent we could tell he was conversant in the latest applications to handle complex social media relations. Ever polite, Sr. Ann showed Henry to a small office to talk with Stacy who greeted Henry with a tentative smile. Noting Stacy's shyness, one of us casually monitored their interaction.

Stacy sat down at the computer in her tiny office as Henry looked over her shoulder at the website she had launched for *Our Home*. Henry fired off the many ideas he had about how to help. Stacy showed signs of defensiveness as she explained the website she had built, how, and why. She was at once proud of her progress and resistant to his help. Henry was at a loss. He desperately wanted to help Stacy, but hit a wall with her defensiveness. Stacy had neither requested this help nor had the leaders of the organization.

When *Our Home* closed its doors, students thanked everyone and loaded into the van. Henry wasn't done. He wanted to explore more ways to help the nuns with their cause. After some discussion with both Henry and Sr. Ann, it was agreed that he could stay. As Henry and the nuns sat down at the kitchen table, the rest of the team returned to campus, excited for the work ahead. That afternoon, Henry returned to campus with a smile on his face and a watermelon in his hands.

Class that day was spent eating watermelon and revisiting the course material in light of this participatory learning experience. The students discussed how organized and well-run *Our Home* was, the social issues that give rise to nonprofits like *Our Home*, and the surprising number of children and young families served. After listening to students share their experience, our goal as teachers was to bring them to a deeper understanding of course material. First, we directed their reflection to issues of power, specifically discussing the readings on gender, technology, and the digital divide. Students could see how the readings aligned with their experiences noting that women ran the nonprofit and lacked the resources to achieve their goals that require technology. Also, Stacy, in the way she interacted with Henry, exemplified the finding that women's confidence impedes their abilities to use technology.

Vignette Two: "They Are Seeking Refuge"
In our planning meetings with Karen, the founder and executive director of IRC, she spoke about her clients as members of her own family. Karen is African American with long braided hair wrapped in a printed scarf. She dresses in African clothing acquired on mission trips to Kenya. IRC fills the gap that other refugee organizations leave, and as Karen explains, "we invited them here but we didn't tell anyone they were coming." Her maternal approach to her work shines through when she tells us, "they are refugees, so they are seeking refuge."

The mission of IRC is broad and it is clear they lack the resources to carry out many of their goals. For example, IRC is volunteer-run and even Karen works part-time at another job to support herself. It was agreed that our students would help IRC build a new website that was easier to navigate and conveyed a consistent message. Students would also create an informational video about the organization. Based on our conversations with Karen, we were excited about how our students could provide help. From the beginning of the course, students were engaged in discussions online about how they would approach the project. Yet, throughout the three-day residency, tension arose between our students and Karen. Differences of opinion emerged regarding project roles. This tension came to a head on the second day during an impromptu lunch that Karen organized.

Students planned to interview local refugees for the video. However, that morning Karen announced that she arranged for a family from Kenya to cook everyone lunch. The students had to switch gears to accommodate this plan and expressed some dissent about how useful the lunch would be. Karen's motivation was to expose students to a cultural experience with refugee families. Students, on the other hand, were focused on finishing the project. They decided to attend the lunch and use it as a central focus of the video.

The family lived in an apartment complex on the south side of town. When we arrived, children were playing in the courtyard. The lunch was in Maria's apartment, which we immediately identified from the smells of spices and cooked meat. Maria arrived in the Northwest United States a year ago, coming from Kenya with her mother and three daughters, age 8, 10, and 12. The women cooked an impressive lunch with fried yams, chicken wings, and pickled vegetables. As we stood around the table eyeing the food, Maria talked about how difficult it was to find the ingredients for her recipes. Her daughters hid behind her as she spoke, nervous of the strangers in their house but curious about their camera equipment.

Sharing food seemed to be a common practice among Karen's clients; yet, the experience of going to the lunch required our students to confront issues of privilege. Two of our students followed gluten-free diets and chose not to eat. Because of language barriers, they could not ensure the food followed their dietary restrictions. Marie and Karen were obviously offended by these students, setting up a tension that existed during the time we were there.

Over lunch, students took pictures of the food and interviewed Maria who spoke about Kenya and her transition to the Northwest. A few of the students work professionally in the field of broadcasting and public relations and had grand ideas about what they were hoping to accomplish in the three days of fieldwork. They brought cameras, tripods, and microphones with them, ready to produce a high-quality video. However, what they did not anticipate was how difficult it would be to work with Karen. Through their interactions, it was clear that Karen wanted to control the image of the organization and would not let the students have access to her clients without her present. In the process, the focus of the video became about Karen as the founder, rather than the stories of the refugees.

Discussion

We now describe the key tensions that emerged in each of these vignettes, drawing upon cyberfeminism and technofeminism as our theoretical lenses. These tensions help us to reflect on what we can accomplish as educators when faced with the intersections of race, class, gender, power, and technological inequality in community engagement projects.

Politics of Race and Community Engagement

In vignette two, one of the key tensions was racial differences between students and the organization. During the time we set aside for classroom reflection about making the video, students expressed their frustrations with the process. They had an idea of what elements they wanted in the video, including interviews with refugees. However, Karen wanted to be present during all of the interviews. This created an uncomfortable dynamic because the students believed that the refugees were not speaking candidly about their experiences because Karen was present. Additionally, Karen believed that it was important for students to spend time getting to know the refugees instead of creating a video. Karen planned the lunch at Maria's house before changing the plan or letting us know her new vision.

Also, in the classroom we guided students through a discussion of gender and power as it emerged in their community engagement as well as how race operated. Students were unwilling to think of the tension in terms of race, some of them stating that they lived in diverse communities themselves. Karen is African American, and the refugees are primarily from African countries; our students, in contrast, come from positions of privilege and are primarily White; and we are White instructors. As Daniels (2009) writes, cyberfeminism is slow to address issues of race and class and we experienced this firsthand through our community engagement. Cyberfeminist writing tends to celebrate the disembodiment that the Internet and virtual space allows. Yet, this disembodiment can mask other inequalities, such as those that emerge because of racial differences (Daniels, 2009). This same dynamic was present in a face-to-face context. Our students were focused on using the technology, including making a video and designing a website to "tell the story" of IRC. Yet, in the process, they were unwilling or unsure of how to examine issues of privilege and race. Karen felt it necessary to shape the story because she sees the refugees as a vulnerable population who have been victims in our local community. Karen controlled students' access to and the settings in which interactions occurred. As a result, the student-produced video features Karen prominently, rather than the families. Throughout the process, students commented that Karen was getting in the way of completing the project. As teachers, we saw that the process of negotiating these complexities offered important learning opportunities for students. However, students saw the end technological product as most important.

Given that critiques of cyberfeminist discourse bring up issues of racial difference, this vignette shows the tensions when practicing cyberfeminism in community engagement projects. Uncritical use of technology can reify the very practices cyberfeminists try to change. Although our readings provided a critical perspective to students, students gravitated toward their own technological expertise to accomplish the goals of the course. Classroom discussions did not illuminate the politics of race and technological inequality as much as we would have liked. Granted, the students had a limited amount of time to complete their projects and were graded on the work. In our future classes, it would be important to have discussions about internal biases and unexamined assumptions about privilege before they step into the community.

We perceived that the power imbalance with the students became uncomfortable for Karen. On the last day of the residency, she spoke with us about how students talked with the refugees and how uncomfortable she was with their lack of knowledge about where the refugees were from. This is something we did not anticipate but raises questions about the importance of cyberfeminist lenses for addressing racial inequality in community engagement projects, suggesting strategies such as participatory video production. Our students came in with a plan based on their consultations with Karen. However, it may have been useful to have the refugees be a part of learning how to use the technology to develop their own stories.

Social Media Does Not Solve Nonprofits' Problems

Through community engagement, students learned that technology does not always solve problems, even ones for which people requested help. Technologies and our use of them are embedded in larger systems of power. In vignette two, our students approached the video one way, but Karen questioned this angle and what would be produced. Additionally, our students suggested that she integrate social media as part of the organization's communication plan, but she was uncomfortable because she may no longer be able to control information about the organization. To do so would require that she change her view that the refugees were vulnerable and needed her protection.

Using a cyberfeminist lens, this vignette offers some interesting perspectives about the intersections of gender, technology, and power. Karen, the organization's founder, wanted to control the message of her organization and had a difficult time allowing our students to act as consultants. In our planning meetings, we explained the process and she agreed, but it became difficult in practice. Resonating with scholarship on women in nonprofits (Curtis et al., 2009), Karen lacked the technical resources and skills to launch the type of website she wanted. She was skeptical about the use of a new platform, WordPress, that would revamp her original site. Through the process of students' community engagement, she grew wary and did not see the benefits of social media for her clients, since many of them lacked access to the Internet and mobile technologies. The students, though, were uneasy shifting the plan that they developed. They believed that they had the "right" answer and went forward. In the end, the students created a Wordpress site, a new Facebook page, and a YouTube channel with a promotional video. Unfortunately, the organization is not using the newly designed site, and the new Facebook page remains inactive. IRC continues to use the original website; however, they did embed the YouTube videos the students produced on their home page.

Through the lens of technofeminism, it would be too simplistic to argue that Karen's perspective was uninformed. Karen's struggle with using new technologies suggested by the students was embedded in her prior technological choices. Her website was on a platform using the proprietary software DreamWeaver. The students wanted her to move to free software that they perceived as more usable, but she wanted to use that in which she had invested to accomplish her goals.

Throughout the community engagement piece, a struggle persisted over the meaning of what was considered technical and how technology could be used to communicate a message. As Wacjman (2008) writes, a technofeminist perspective redefines the problem of exclusion of groups of people from technological domains and activities; it "reveals how the concrete practices of design and innovation lead to the absence of specific users" (p. 17). Social media invites (virtual) dialogue, comments, and interactions with the general public. For Karen, who wanted to control the message of her organization, this was threatening. As an organization that works with refugee populations who are vulnerable to discrimination and who come from cultural and political contexts, IRC worked to protect their clients' privacy and anonymity. Posting pictures of vulnerable people without their consent may lead to negative consequences for this population. Additionally, nonprofits need to protect themselves from negative publicity that may occur in social media spaces. In these ways, a technofeminist lens offers insight into the challenges nonprofits face online. Further, this lens illuminates how the architecture of different online platforms determines the types of communication that take place.

Gender and Technical Expertise in Practice

Vignette one offers insight into the dynamics of gender and technical expertise. In our classroom discussions, we asked students to think about the importance of technology for *Our Home's* goals. Since cyberfeminism celebrates the Internet for opening up access, we needed students to critically think about this in practice. We talked about power and technology and who gets to be "technical," and the limits of certain media for giving voice. After this discussion, students came to the idea that their video should be produced and posted online to give voice to the work of these women, to the social issues at work, and the people who consented to be interviewed.

However, while the readings and community engagement allowed students the opportunity to help the organization tell its story, some gender dynamics that were evident in the making of the video are worth mentioning. Technofeminism, which unveils the mutual shaping of gender and technology, was useful for understanding the gender dynamics between Stacy and Henry. It explains Stacy and Henry's difficult interaction over technical expertise as a gendered struggle of confidence and knowledge. Henry exemplifies the confidence with which men tend to approach technology. Henry used technology instrumentally, as something he could master. Stacy had the insight of the needs of the organization but not the efficacy to match Henry's technological confidence. She also had not asked for the help Henry was offering. Henry was tech savvy but implementing his tools effectively was neither simple nor obvious. Through their experience at the site, the class learned that you have to understand the organization, its struggles and goals *and* the way gender relations interact with technology in order to help the organization with their social change goals in effective ways.

Implications and Conclusions

There is undeniable value in carefully designed and well-executed community engagement projects, and our experience designing and teaching *Communication, Technology and Social Change* shows that communication technologies have potential benefits for community engagement. Benefits include helping solve real-world problems and being able to witness and discuss the reality of gender differences on and offline. Our students read about and discussed social change and the gender and technology dynamics of nonprofits, but stepping into *Our Home* and IRC reinforced the course material in a way that would not have been captured otherwise. These "real-world" experiences make course material come alive and they make vital the useful the practical nature of education, but it isn't easy. We experienced some challenges that will inform future versions of our course. For example, once students engaged in the community, they reverted to their default ways of thinking about technology. We thought that through class discussion and classwork on a topic like technology and gender equality, our students would perceive these connections in the community engagement portion of the course. Instead, they operated with the assumption that technology would help solve the organizations' problems. We had to revisit our goals for the students, their roles, and talk about their positionalities and limitations often. In evaluating community engagement as a vehicle to empower students' social understanding and activism, we see the practice of working with community organizations complicated by students' own assumptions about their roles in the process.

Cyberfeminism offers a critical perspective on how gender influences technology design and use. Yet, still more can be learned about how we as educators might apply these insights to community engagement projects. Technology became the starting point for us to unpack the dynamics of race, class, and gender as it relates to social change; yet, we also struggled with what was and was not possible to accomplish with technologies. Our students created finished products of which they were proud, but in the case of IRC, the products did not adequately address the organization's needs and were not implemented. In the process, students' focus on product (completing their technology projects) left them unable or unwilling to discuss some of the dynamics that emerged. We see the need to restructure the assignment so that the end product does not have as much weight as classroom discussion and reflection. In the process, we see the need for further reflection on the practice of cyberfeminism.

In all, experiencing these tensions through working in community with our students allowed us to see the reality that critical feminists are unavoidably aware of. A tremendous amount of social change is still needed if we are to be socially just with one another in a normative democratic society or enlarge that social justice to an increasingly global context and take seriously an ethical commitment to our communication practices. Judging by what we had to do in teaching our students about their experience, we have a lot of work ahead. Our course goals were theoretically sound, but our students needed more making connections in the face of real and complicated experiences. Upon reflection, we would do more work prior to community engagement on what being open-minded is like and to help students investigate their own biases.

Many opportunities exist to integrate cyberfeminism in community engagement efforts, expanding the reach, tools, and scope of feminist activism. Cyberfeminism challenges assumptions of the Internet's potential for democratic communication and shows that we need to attend to the many barriers in achieving these goals. Harassment, cyber bullying, and cyber stalking continue to disproportionately impact women more so than men (Citron, 2009).

We wholeheartedly agree that to be effective, it is important for educators and students to work directly with nonprofits in order to understand the nature of what is truly involved in achieving social change goals. We cannot work together to achieve goals when we lack an ability to detect the dynamics of gender and technology constructions, when we lack ways to talk about race and privilege at work, and when we carry unexamined expectations about what problems technology can and cannot solve.

References

Bertot, J. C. (2003). The multiple dimensions of the digital divide: More than the technology "haves" and "have nots." *Government Information Quarterly, 20*(2), 185–191.

Burt, E., & Taylor, J. A. (2000). Information and communication technologies: Reshaping voluntary organizations? *Nonprofit Management and Leadership, 11*(2), 131–143. doi:10.1002/nml.11201

Citron, D. K. (2009). Law's expressive value in combating cyber gender harassment. *Michigan Law Review, 108,* 373–415.

Consalvo, M. (2003). Cyberfeminism. In S. Jones (Ed.), *Encyclopedia of new media* (pp. 108–110). Thousand Oaks, CA: SAGE Publications.

Cooper, J., & Weaver, K. D. (2003). *Gender and computers: Understanding the digital divide.* Mahwah, NJ: Lawrence Erlbaum.

Crowe, M. (2003). Jump for the Sun II: Can a monthly program change girls' and women's attitudes about STEM? *Journal of Women and Minorities in Engineering, 9,* 323–332.

Curtis, L., Edwards, C., Fraser, K. L., Gudelsky, S., Holmquist, J., Thornton, K., & Sweetser, K. D. (2009). Adoption of social media for public relations by nonprofit organizations. *Public Relations Review, 36*(1), 90–92.

Daniels, J. (2009). Rethinking cyberfeminism(s): Race, gender, and embodiment. *Women's Studies Quarterly, 37*(1–2), 101–124.

Eudey, B. (2012). Civic engagement, cyberfeminism, and online learning: Activism and service learning in women's and gender studies courses. *Feminist Teacher, 22*(3), 233–250.

Eyrich, N., Padman, M. L., & Sweetser, K. D. (2008). PR practitioners' use of social media tools and communication technology. *Public Relations Review, 34*(4), 412–414. doi: http://dx.doi.org/10.1016/j.pubrev.2008.09.010

Fancsali, C. (2002). *What we know about girls, STEM, and afterschool programs: A summary.* Washington, DC: Educational Equity Concepts, Inc.

Gajjala, R., & Oh, Y. J. (2012). Cyberfeminism 2.0: Where have all the cyberfeminists gone? In R. Gajjala & Y. J. Oh (Eds.), *Cyberfeminism 2.0* (pp. 1–9). New York: PeterLang.

Haraway, D. J. (1998). A cyborg manifesto: Science, technology and socialist-feminism in the late twentieth century. In P. D. Hopkins (Ed.), *Sex/machine: Readings in culture, gender, and technology* (pp. 434–467). Bloomington, IN: Indiana University Press.

Hargittai, E., & Hinnant, A. (2008). Digital inequality: Differences in young adults' use of the internet. *Communication Research, 35*(5), 602–621.

Harp, D., & Treymane, M. (2006). The gendered blogosphere: Examining inequality using network and feminist theory. *Journalism & Mass Communication Quarterly, 83*(2), 247–264.

Irving, C. J., & English, L. M. (2011). Community in cyberspace: Gender, social movement learning, and the internet. *Adult Education Quarterly, 61*(3), 262–278.

Kenix, L. J. (2008). Nonprofit organizations' perceptions and uses of the internet. *Television & New Media, 9*(5), 407–428. doi:10.1177/1527476408315501

Kenway, J., & Nixon, H. (1999). Cyberfeminisms, cyberliteracies, and educational cyberspheres. *Educational Theory, 49*(4), 457–474.

Lennon, T. (2013). *Benchmarking women's leadership in the United States, 2013*. Denver, CO: University of Denver-Colorado Women's College.

Lovejoy, K., & Saxton, G. (2012). Information, community, and action: How nonprofit organizations use social media. *Journal of Computer-Mediated Communication, 17*(3), 337–353.

McGaw, J. A. (1996). Why feminine technologies matter. In N. Lerman, R. Oldenziel, & A. P. Mohun (Eds.), *Gender and technology: A reader* (pp. 13–36). Baltimore, MD: Johns Hopkins University Press.

Merkel, C. B., Farooq, U., Xiao, L., Ganoe, C., Rosson, M. B., & Carroll, J. M. (2007). Managing technology use and learning in nonprofit community organizations: Methodological challenges and opportunities. In E. Kandogan & P. M. Jones (Eds.), *Proceedings of the 2007 Symposium on Computer Human Interaction for Management of Information Technology.* Paper presented at CHMIT 07, Cambridge, MA, March 30–31 (pp. 1–10). Cambridge, MA: ACM.

Mitchell, W. J. (1999). Equitable access to the online world. In D. Schon, B. Danyal, & W. J. Mitchell (Eds.), *High technology and low income communities: Prospects for the positive use of advanced information technology* (135–161). Cambridge, MA: MIT Press.

Morris, C. E., & Browne, S. H. (Eds.). (2006). *Readings on the rhetoric of social protest* (2nd ed.). State College, PA: Strata Publishing.

Nah, S., & Saxton, G. (2013). Modeling the adoption and use of social media by nonprofit organizations. *New Media & Society, 15*(2), 294–313.

Oldenziel, R. (1999). *Making technology masculine: Men, women and modern machines in America, 1870–1945*. Amsterdam: Amsterdam University Press.

Plant, S. (1997). *Zeros + ones—digital women + the new technoculture*. New York: Doubleday.

Puente, S. N. (2008). From cyberfeminism to technofeminism: From an essentialist perspective to social cyberfeminism in certain feminist practices in Spain. *Women's Studies International Forum, 31*, 434–440.

Ramsey, N., & McCorduck, P. (2005). *Where are the women in information technology?* Boulder, CO: National Center for Women and Information Technology.

Richards, R. S. (2011). "I could have told you *that* wouldn't work": Cyberfeminist pedagogy in action. *Feminist Teacher, 22*(1), 5–22.

Stake, J. E., & Hoffmann, F. L. (2001). Changes in student social attitudes, activism, and personal confidence in higher education: The role of Women's Studies. *American Educational Research Journal, 38*(2), 411–436.

Wacjman, J. (1991). *Feminism confronts technology*. University Park, PA: Pennsylvania State University Press.

———. (2004). *Technofeminism*. Malden, MA: Polity Press.

———. (2008). TechnoCapitalism meets TechnoFeminism: Women and technology in a wireless world. *Labour & Industry, 16*(3), 7–20.

Winner, L. (1980). Do artifacts have politics? *Daedalus, 109*(1), 121–136. Retrieved from http://www.jstor.org/stable/20024652

Youmans, W. L., & York, J. C. (2012). Social media and the activist toolkit: User agreements, corporate interests, and the information infrastructure of modern social movements. *Journal of Communication, 62,* 315–329. doi:10.1111/j.1460-2466.2012.01636.x

CHAPTER 6

Transgressing *Intellectual* Boundaries Begins with Transgressing *Physical* Ones: Feminist Community Engagement as Activist-Apprentice Pedagogy

Dana Bisignani

In every class I have taught, I have endeavored to create space for students to engage critically with the language around them as it shapes our art, media, politics, and public policy. Early on, I placed a great deal of importance in my course planning on exposing my students to the complex and ever-evolving social, political, and ideological structures that lead to systemic injustice. Like many well-meaning activists, I was driven by the belief that individuals merely needed to understand the roots of injustice in their world, believing that once they came to *know* they would automatically *act* on this knowledge. Yet when commenting on assigned readings, my students would often express disappointment: "I really liked what the author said... but she didn't tell us how to *change* it." Though we analyzed power, privilege, and oppression in classes, for my students, a clear bridge to action was still missing.

As educators and intellectuals, it is easy to assume that students' lack of political participation, or even our fellow citizens' inaction, is the result of apathy, particularly if we are feeling disheartened or disillusioned ourselves. But this presumption fails to acknowledge the ways individuals are systematically disempowered by the very structures they are being asked to question. Listening to my students, I came to understand that by ushering them into critical awareness without giving them any tools or methods to create change—that is, without involving them in *praxis*—I was not empowering them to act. In fact, I was sending them off newly burdened. Rather than helping to liberate my students, I risked making them cynical but passive intellects. Any educator who is committed to raising students' critical consciousness and who wishes to educate future ethical and *active* citizens must commit to practicing a pedagogy that transcends mere awareness; that is, our pedagogy must help students to build a bridge between knowledge and action and must offer a practical ethics that students can apply in the actual communities in which they live. What's more, a bridge that aims to cross *intellectual* borders must also bridge the *physical* one that separates the classroom within the academy from the surrounding community. So long as the environments of our educational institutions continue to embody the hierarchical and authoritarian structures that barricade certain forms of knowledge, our classrooms will continue to be limited spaces where our efforts at liberatory practices are frustrated.

In this chapter, I first discuss some of the challenges that both students and instructors face in attempting to engage with critical pedagogy and service-learning within the confines of the academy. Then, by situating service-learning within an historical context of other radical educational experiments, I argue for the transformative potential of constructing countersites beyond university walls. Political philosophies regarding intentional exodus can help instructors to better theorize how their service-learning projects engage their students with available infrastructures and tools of resistance at these countersites. Finally, building on current feminist service-learning praxis as well as anarchist theories of education, I propose an activist-apprentice model of service-learning and describe the project I undertook with my introductory women's studies students. While traditional service-learning projects often have students volunteer with members from underprivileged groups in the community, activist-apprentice pedagogy pairs students with experienced organizers. This relationship not only fosters students' critical awareness of the structural roots of injustice (theory), giving them set of skills that they then apply in their own endeavors to create change (praxis), but also provides students with a site outside the academy in which to practice these skills under the guidance of a mentor.

Free Market Feminism

Increasingly, college-aged women and men enter our classrooms with maligned images of feminism and of political activists. Such images work to divorce strong and successful women from feminism and also to divorce feminist activism from its radical goals of restructuring society. Many of our students fail to see "their fixation on pursuing individual occupational success and consumer satisfaction" as antithetical to feminism (Rinehart, 2002, p. 27), or even a participatory democracy, and such fixations are rarely challenged by educational institutions. Rinehart argues that this belief on the part of students "reflects a refusal to believe that they have any power to change the rules of the game" and an acceptance that "they can only hope to be successful players" (p. 27). However, this is also evidence of the deliberate miseducation our students have received from news media and popular culture that presents what Manzano (2000) dubs "free market feminism." This brand of co-opted empowerment, marketed to Third Wave feminists,

> focuses on personal freedoms instead of women's rights, personal maneuvering instead of structural oppression, and personal choices instead of collective action. Under the lens of free-market feminism, "independence" doesn't mean liberation and self actualization. The free-market feminist spin on "independence" emphasizes detachment and equanimity. (p. 10)

Echoing this detachment, Robin Morgan (2001) observes that "the genius of patriarchy" lies in its practice of "compartmentalization, the capacity for institutionalizing disconnection. Intellect severed from emotion. Thought separated from action" (p. 51). The academy embodies this compartmentalization and detachment, from the separation of its colleges to its tower-like remove from the surrounding community; and as bodies trained within it, we are often fragmented ourselves, many of us internalizing the lie that we may either *know* (inside) or *act* (outside) but not both, a lie that our students inherit unless we work to model a more integrated way of learning and being in the world. For our pedagogy to be liberatory, it must work to reconnect that which has been compartmentalized. For feminists, this includes challenging the separation of theory and practice.

The prevalence of these "free market" values—values that dramatically limit the possibilities students might imagine for their lives and for their communities—necessitates that our liberatory pedagogies emphasize collective organizing that moves students into new spaces where they might see in practice a set of values rooted not in individualism and consumerism but in collective responsibility and problem-solving. In order to avoid mere "detached study of activism, activists, or social change" (Noterman & Pusey, 2012, p. 177), we must arrange the context of our students' learning so that they might realize what Novek (1999) describes as "a world that coheres through human connection rather than through systems of rules" (p. 233). This experience is integral to students' understanding how to live by an ethic of care and mutual aid rather than "acting out of competitive self-interest" (p. 233).

Institutional Challenges to Liberatory Practice

Rather than converting students to a particular ideology, both feminist and anarchist educators work to subvert the authoritarian practices of education that reinforce passive learning.

In particular, feminist pedagogues have advocated for transformation of the traditional power dynamic of the classroom that positions the instructor as the sole expert and unquestioned authority in the room (Bauer, 2009; Maher & Tetreault, 1994; Powers-Stubbs, 1992). Indeed, this top-down dissemination of knowledge is reflected in and reinforced by the built environments of most college classrooms: the instructor stands at the front and lectures while her students sit facing her, uncritically accepting the information she deposits—what Paulo Freire (1970) dubbed the banking model of education. Rinehart (2002) argues that "the tension between subversion and conversion is basically about how 'authority' is constructed and the effects of its different constructions" on how students relate to both what and how they are learning (p. 25). A primary goal of feminist pedagogy then is to question and reconstruct this teacher-student hierarchy, and to decenter the instructor's authority so that students actively engage in critical problem-solving and participate in *constructing* their knowledge rather than simply *receiving* it.

However, when confined to the classroom, students' participation in knowledge-making (a central tenet of feminist pedagogy) remains limited by unconscious rules learned over years of conditioning within environments created to reinforce hierarchy and individualism. Cushman (1999) observes that "teachers often apply liberating teaching *only in the classroom*, and they are hard pressed to create solidarity and dialogue within the institutionalized social structure of American schools" (emphasis mine, p. 333). As space *within* the academy, the classroom is fraught territory:

> as students and academics, we are grappling with [the academy] as a messy and contested space of, often contradictory, values and ethics. On the one

hand the role of the university is (increasingly) about social reproduction: creating docile, debt-ridden workers for capital. On the other hand, the university is a potential space of community and commons. (Noterman & Pusey, 2012, p. 180)

This struggle is even greater when epistemology renders institutional norms invisible or normal, certainly to our students if not also at times to instructors.

Service-Learning in the Academy

Instructors who engage their students in service-learning have consistently had to negotiate such contradictory ethics. Despite the growing popularity of service-learning in college courses around the country, many professors prefer to frame their projects as *civic engagement* while actively steering clear of anything resembling *political activism*. While students may avoid activism because they associate it with images of angry protesters, professors more often seek to distance their practices from it for fear of accusations that they are practicing politics in the classroom. In the academy, while it is acceptable that we learn *about* social justice (as part of history, for example), administrators grow anxious when instructors appear to be *doing* social justice, particularly if they appear to be requiring their students do it. Perhaps nowhere is this tension more evident than in the academy's simultaneous promotion and undermining of ethnic and women's studies programs (Hu-DeHart, 2000, p. 21).

This institutional anxiety about activism is rooted in the belief that it is possible (indeed that it is preferable) to divorce the classroom from politics.[1] bell hooks (1989) argues that we

> have been seduced by the false assumption that the goal of academic freedom is best served by postures of political neutrality, by teaching methods that belie the reality that our very choice of subject matter, manner and style of presentation embodies ideological and political signifiers. (pp. 64–65)

For many students and instructors, the boundary that divides the campus from the surrounding community is also the boundary that maintains a division between the assumed political neutrality of the "protected" (read: enclosed) educational environment and the "politically contaminated" community outside. As if the university—who can afford to be there, whose voices are reflected in the curriculum, who receives tenure and funding—was not already a political space designed to maintain particular power structures. Henry A. Giroux and Susan Searls Giroux (2004) remind us that "pedagogy is political because it is always tangled up with power, ideologies, and the acquisition of knowledge and skills necessary for critical participation in public life" (p. 8). So as educators, we must first acknowledge that, even if we frame what students are doing as civic engagement, politics are still at work that we must critically examine.

Many early civic engagement and service-learning projects failed to interrogate the politics at work between the university and community, and feminist scholars seriously questioned this uncritical practice. These projects often reproduced power and privilege between those at the university (i.e., the repository of "official" knowledge) and those in the community, considered "impoverished" (whether intellectually, economically, artistically, etc.) in their surroundings. Webb, Cole, and Skeen (2007) observe that "older service-learning projects posited students as 'knower' and the members of the community as the 'other' who needed the 'knower's' expertise" (p. 238). Early examples of service-learning projects often positioned students as volunteer tutors working with underprivileged children in community centers. Without asking students to critically analyze the power relations at work in such an endeavor, such projects merely reinforce students' belief in their role as "knowers," and the relationship remains unidirectional (p. 240). Cushman (1999) argues that "if the university representatives understand themselves as coming to the rescue of community residents, students will enact this missionary ideology in their [volunteer activities]" (p. 332).

Projects that place students in direct contact with marginalized populations outside the academy often risk reinforcing students' understanding of their work simply as charity or philanthropy where they help the less fortunate; however, this framework fails to develop students' critical understanding of *why* some of us are "less fortunate." Bickford and Reynolds (2002) offer this helpful distinction:

> roughly speaking, service addresses people, and activism addresses structures. One of service-learning's biggest limitations, admittedly, is that it induces students to ask only, "How can we help these people?" instead of the harder question, "Why are conditions this way?" (p. 231)

Service-learning informed by feminist praxis, however, does move students in this direction.

"Current examples of service-learning share feminism's goal of building reciprocal relationships between the university and the community in a way that complicates the relationship between 'knower' and 'other'" (Webb at al., 2007, p. 239). In particular, feminists within the academy have argued both for the potential of service-learning to encourage students activism and for the importance of recognizing the politics involved in such pedagogical practices. In addition, service-learning projects that focus on activism situate contemporary grassroots organizing in a larger historical context, as something ongoing, enabling students to see themselves as continuing the work of the social and political movements they study in class. For these reasons, it makes a profound difference for students, as well as for members of the community, when students understand what they're doing as *activism* and not simply as the more "neutral-sounding" community service or civic engagement: changing the language of the project dramatically reframes the relationships they build with the community and deepens the questions that students will take with them into the field (Bickford & Reynolds, 2002).

A University-Without-Walls

Like many anarchist educators experimenting with Free Skools in the 1950s and 1960s,[2] Adrienne Rich understood that spaces of learning *outside* the university held great transformative potential. The existence of such countersites "allows for some autonomy from...the restrictions of mainstream education" and provides "the imaginal, if not the material, means for undermining state and capital relations and authorities both ideological and structural" (Shantz, 2012, p. 125). For anarchists, such spaces are "important sites for skills development, for learning and practicing those skills which are underdeveloped in authoritarian social relations" (p. 125). Such spaces serve as sites of personal transition and are *prefigurative*; that is, temporary spaces that embody "the new world in the shell of the old" (p. 143), wherein individuals might model *what could be*, practicing their vision of the future in the here and now.

Indeed, Rich (1979) doubted whether institutions of higher learning would ever be capable of supporting truly revolutionary thinking and practice, even as the feminist movement moved inside its walls in the form of the first Women's Studies programs. For this reason, maintaining an autonomous space outside the university remained crucial for Rich as a radical lesbian feminist, poet, and scholar. In "Toward a Woman-Centered University," Rich (1979) argues for a women's "university-without-walls," a network of women creating and sharing knowledge that extends beyond the confines of the university. However, she also recognized the university as a "potential space of community and commons" to which women and minorities needed access. The educational transformation Rich envisioned in 1979 addressed not only the university, but the community outside its gates as well:

In a sense the solution I am proposing is anarchistic: that the university should address itself to the microcosms of national problems and issues that exist locally, and that it should do so with the greatest possible sense that it will not simply be giving, but be receiving, because academe has a great deal to learn from women and from other unprivileged people. (p. 152)

Like radical feminism, anarchist education is rooted in an analysis of power and oppression (in the case of anarchism, between the individual and the State) and a desire to radically restructure social and political organizations (Suissa, 2006). Feminists have sought to collapse many dualisms, including the one that separates theory/practice as well as university/community (Williams & McKenna, 2002, p. 141). In Rich's proposal for a university-without-walls, we find an early model of feminist service-learning characterized by a reciprocal exchange of knowledge that challenges the university/community divide.

Like Rich, Giroux (1988) recognized that borders delineate not just lines on a map but also "particular identities, individual capacities, and social forms" (p. 166). As scholars and as students, we may need to cross such borders, real or imagined, to abandon our assigned roles. If "subversive teaching aims to communicate an 'oppositional imagination': an ability to think past received habits of thought and action" (Rinehart, 2002, p. 24), then developing an "oppositional imagination" has everything to do with a willingness to enter oppositional *spaces*. Entering such spaces then becomes a practice of abandoning particular identities and/or social forms in search of new possibilities. That is, if we truly want to realize the potential for education to become a practice of freedom, then we must actively transgress not just the *intellectual* boundaries established by the academy, but the *physical* ones as well in order to envision new ways of knowledge-making and skill-sharing.

Such an exodus from the academy leads to "an element of defamiliarization," something that King (2004) argues is necessary for critical reflection to occur (p. 125). Defamiliarization requires that what students recognize and take for granted becomes strange and/or unavailable to them. Absent the cues of their familiar environment, both students and instructors will necessarily struggle to discover new roles and methods. As King attests, "Where defamiliarization occurs...new information, situations, and perspectives are not simply assimilated into students' existing belief systems but serve to disrupt those systems in such a way that they themselves become the subject of critical examination" (p. 136). In this way, students are challenged to become more self-reflexive about their own behaviors and assumptions, even as they are learning from and forming relationships with their collaborators in the field.

Rinehart (2002) tells us that "practicing subversion means constructing the classroom as a public space" (p. 24). This means, for starters, not only addressing the *content* of our classrooms to public problems, as Rich recommended, but also literally opening the classroom to the ideas, skills, and other models of authority that are traditionally located outside the walls of the university. Doing so would necessarily blur the boundaries between university and surrounding community, and between which forms of knowledge and experience are allowed in and which kept out. In working with members of the community, the instructor becomes *one* authority among many from whom students learn. Additionally, students are able to put their classroom learning in dialogue with their learning out in the field, so "[s]ervice learning asks students...to test the merit of what they learn in a university classroom against their experiences as a volunteer at local sites" (Cushman, 1999, p. 330). This ongoing field-test is an effective model of decentering the instructor's *institutional* authority that still allows for his/her *personal* authority as an experienced practitioner in collaborative relationship with other practitioners working in interconnected contexts.

Activist-Apprentice Pedagogy

Like anarchistic Free Skool projects that encourage skill-sharing and collective organizing (Shantz, 2012), an activist-apprentice model of service-learning is based on intergenerational teaching of collective organizing skills as well as local organizing history, including successes and failures, and calls into question the relationship between knowledge and institutional authority. In this model, students enter the community as learners rather than as teachers, a shift that facilitates the defamiliarization that creates space for critical self-reflection. In addition, occupying the position of learner means that the goals and services of a collaboration between students and their community partner are not fully established beforehand (Schutz & Gere, 1998, p. 145)—much like anarchist educators' refusal to dictate the aims of education prior to knowing particular students and their needs in specific contexts (Suissa, 2006, p. 100).

Rather than volunteering directly with the populations that their organizations target (e.g., the homeless or women and children leaving abusive partners), small groups of students are paired with a community organizer from a local nonprofit who can engage them in learning about the structure and goals of the organization, the particular challenges it faces while working for social justice, as well as its successes and failures over the years. This *apprenticeship* with an experienced activist prioritizes students' learning practical grassroots organizing tools and provides an affirmation of the real possibility of change—in effect, local organizers train a new generation of practitioners in a set of skills that they are then able to practice on their own. Unlike the traditional teacher-student relationship where the student passively absorbs knowledge, an apprentice agrees to work alongside a more experienced practitioner for a period of time with the understanding that he or she will then enter the trade.

An apprenticeship that focuses on sharing practical skills that students can then apply to their own organizing endeavors is one example of what Shantz (2010) describes as "constructive anarchy," or "projects that provide examples of politics grounded in everyday resistance" (p. 1). Students might use the organizing tools they acquire to act for any cause; in this way, students do not learn a particular political agenda from their organizer so much as a set of skills to respond to and participate in a whole field of politics. "In nonfoundational knowing and teaching, the project is not 'getting it' but 'doing it,'" which is "not about an individual grasping an object [i.e., an idea or theory], but about individuals (teachers and students) building relationships with one another and negotiating agreements about what makes sense" (Rinehart, 2002, p. 25). Activist-apprentice pedagogy that prioritizes sharing these skills with students ensures an active citizenship, not one active political party. Ultimately, projects that prioritize students' acquiring tools to enact social justice and to work critically to change oppressive structures ultimately build a student, and eventually citizen, body that has the skills to mobilize others and to start and sustain dissent in their multiple communities. Such projects also work on a larger scale to decriminalize acts of dissent among citizens.

Course Project

The service-learning project I designed for my introductory Women's Studies course coincided with a Women's History Month event, spearheaded by the new director of our Women's, Gender, and Sexuality Studies (WGSS) program. *The March at Purdue: Celebrating 100 Years of Public Action* (1913–2013) was a collaborative effort among multiple departments, offices, and graduate and undergraduate students at the university aimed at creating greater visibility for the WGSS program and injecting the campus with a spirit of activism and change. As an activist, I saw in this event the potential for coalition-building across borders, between the university and the local community, and as an instructor, I recognized the value of an opportunity to introduce students to more experienced organizers with knowledge of local politics. Toward these ends, I redesigned my syllabus to incorporate a feminist service-learning component and met with representatives of several local nonprofit organizations to determine how they felt they might benefit from working with my students. Several organizations expressed interest in the undertaking, including the Lafayette Area Peace Coalition (LAPC), Lafayette Urban Ministries (LUM), Pride Lafayette, the Lafayette Crisis Center, and the League of Women Voters.

Many community organizations that partnered with my class had strict guidelines for volunteers that would have made it nearly impossible for students to work directly with the people that they served, even if the students had wanted to do so. For example, the Crisis Center, who often fielded calls regarding incidences of domestic violence or sexual assault, required that their volunteers undergo 20 hours of training before staffing the phones, a task that could not reasonably be completed by students within the time frame of the course project. While such guidelines initially seemed like obstacles as I was planning the project, they forced me to reconsider alternative ways to involve students with local organizations: rather than having students volunteer to work in the homeless shelter or tutor in the after-school urban ministries program, they would partner directly with the community organizers who formed or ran these nonprofits.

At the start of the semester, students selected a nonprofit group with which to partner for approximately eight weeks and created working groups based on their interests.[3] Students began their fieldwork by researching their organization's history and social justice work and interviewing at least one of its members. Each group presented their research to the class, educating others about their organizations' missions, priorities, and actions. These presentations opened fruitful discussions about how the individuals at each organization understood their work as part of a larger effort and how their missions, or philosophy, shaped their understanding of social justice and informed their actions within the community. By sharing their research with each other, students were exposed not just to the work of their collaborating organization, but to a variety of grassroots efforts happening within the community that connected with course content covered in readings and lectures. During this process, students also worked alongside members of their organizations to accomplish practical organizing tasks, determined during meetings with their community partner (CP). Tasks ranged from writing an article for the organization's newsletter to representing their CP at a city council meeting, to drafting letters to area schools, churches, and organizations to promote their CP's services to different audiences.

During this time, we were also reading and discussing excerpts from Baumgardner's and Richards's (2005) book *Grassroots: A Field Guide for Feminist Activism*.[4] In their text, aimed specifically at college students, the authors describe their first forays into campus activism, as well as successful activist projects undertaken by students at a number of universities. Their book became an important resource for the class for several reasons. First, the writers' accounts of their own successes and failures, and the examples of student organizing they provided within the book's pages, helped to challenge and broaden students' understanding of who activists are and what activism looks like in our daily lives. In her introduction to the book, Winona LaDuke (2005) also questions our associations with the label of "activist." "My own life as an identified activist," she writes, "has made me wonder at the term itself. What separates simple 'responsibility' in life...from the fine line that one crosses to become an 'activist'?" (p. xii); "our most personal lives," she insists, "are actually embroidered in the reality of public policy, foreign policy, military aid, and economics" (p. xv). While most of our students have grown up steeped in the American ideal of individualism and the belief in a meritocracy, LaDuke emphasizes collectivity and communal welfare. In a later chapter, Richards describes the moment she came to realize that her participation in voter registration drives as a young White woman coming from privilege was not motivated by a desire to " 'help' the poor, disenfranchised black people in the South, but because *I* wasn't served if I didn't live in a participatory democracy" (Baumgardner & Richards, 2005, p. 56, italics in original).

While LaDuke, and Baumgardner and Richards challenged students to think about how activist efforts get started and who starts them, we spent another class discussing the often troubled relationship between philanthropy and social activism.[5] In a consumer culture, we are often presented with the option of donating money to causes, or purchasing a product, as a means of combating injustice. Of course, nonprofits are often able to conduct their work thanks to donations; however, throwing money at a problem creates a distance between those with the resources to donate funds and those most directly affected by or working on the problem. This distance is a form of social privilege in itself and can effectively deny us an opportunity to confront and solve such problems within our own communities. In short, by enabling another to act on our behalf, we disable our own engagement with those directly affected by such problems. Activism requires our direct and compassionate involvement with the people, communities, and problems at hand, and a complex understanding of our interconnectedness. This is the difference I hoped my students would feel by becoming involved within their local organizers.

For the last part of the project, students collaborated with their community partners to form a delegation for the Women's History Month march, attending large planning meetings and helping to publicize the event in the community. Students and their community partners then collaborated to prepare their delegations, designing signs, banners, T-shirts, and sashes for the participants to wear on the day of the event. In order to fund their projects, two students from the class volunteered to draft a proposal and apply for a Service-Learning Grant through Purdue's Office of Engagement. With some assistance creating an itemized budget and collecting all the participating community partners' signatures, the class was awarded a total of $1,000 from the university, which was used to purchase supplies for their community partners as well as poster boards and refreshments for their end-of-semester symposium, where they showcased their service-learning projects to fellow students, faculty, and administrators alongside the community partners they had apprenticed with.

The goals of the project were: 1) to put students in contact with individuals and organizations involved with local grassroots activism; 2) to demonstrate how practical feminist ethics might be applied within their own lives as well as within multiple communities; 3) to help students develop practical organizing skills that they might employ beyond their time in class; 4) to build relationships between community partners and the university community and its students; and 5) to potentially provide area organizations with new volunteers and/or "ambassadors for their causes," a phrase penned by one of the students who wrote the grant proposal.

Reflection

As nearly any instructor who has undertaken service-learning with a class will admit, the process often resembles organized chaos, especially compared with a more traditionally organized classroom where the instructor is solely in charge of lessons and learning. Despite moments when the class, with all its overlapping activities, mentors and ideas, felt like a too-fast car taking a curve, the final reflective papers I received from my students convinced me of the value of an activist-apprentice service-learning pedagogy.

In several papers, students noted that their earlier stereotypes of activists as angry protesters shouting at people on the street had been transformed. Many of them now openly claimed "activist" as part of their identities. One student took the organizing skills he learned from reading *Grassroots* (Baumgardner & Richards, 2005), and from working with the Feminist Action Coalition for Today (FACT), back to his work as a member of the National Residence Hall Honorary, and in turn tapped into his work in the residence halls to garner more student support for FACT's rape crisis center petition. This cross-organization coalition-building was just one example of the ways that students applied the skills they learned while apprenticing to other projects and other communities in their lives. For many students, the service-learning project solidified their theoretical learning in class and presented opportunities to practice the applied feminist ethics we had discussed in class. A young woman also apprenticing with FACT observed, "The service-learning project I feel was the reason I could actually relate the things I learned in class to real life. Just learning feminism is nothing like actually working with people who identify as feminist."

One young woman from class who had grown up in the local community critically compared her service-learning experience from the class with her years of mandatory volunteer work in Catholic local schools:

> Coming from a Catholic school, we were required each semester to do a certain amount of service hours for our community, school, family, and parish. These hours became very repetitive [such] that it came to the point [where] they did not mean much anymore. I expected the same from service-learning. To my surprise, my service-learning experience was an eye-opening, life changing experience.

This same student continued to volunteer with the organization beyond the semester's end, having formed lasting relationships with the Pride Lafayette members with whom she apprenticed.

A number of students cited the intergenerational collaboration as an unexpectedly positive experience. The core members of both the League of Women Voters and the LAPC were in their fifties and sixties. While both groups were excited to collaborate with my students, at least a few members of the LAPC bought into the stereotype that young people were apathetic (unlike their generation, they said), while some of the students were surprised by how politically active these older members of the community continued to be. Both the experienced organizers of the LAPC and the students who worked with them surprised one another. One young woman who worked with the League of Women Voters wrote that, not only had she discovered the power of her own voice, but, she said, "I feel that it is now my duty to follow [this older] generation with educating the public about the importance of voting." This student cited the willingness of the older women on the League to include her as an equal in their planning outreach to young people about voter registration as a transformative experience for her. This seemed, at least in part, a realization that, despite her young age, she had useful information and insight to offer even more experienced activists who wanted to collaborate with more young people. In a critical reflection on his generation, one African-American student compared the activity of the older members of the LAPC with "the inactiveness most people attribute to youth;" what he gleaned from this reflection was that "it's not that youth is lethargic, but unconfident and unknowing." Over the course of the semester, this student became increasingly active in several protests in response to racist incidents that occurred on campus. By the spring, he was one of the activists leading chants on the steps of the campus's main administration building while I stood as a member of the crowd, repeating his words in unison.

Not only were the students able to list the practical skills that they learned working alongside community activists in their papers, but many professed a desire to continue their activist work in some capacity, either by staying on with the organizations with whom they had partnered, by joining student organizations on campus, or in the case of my graduating senior, by laying out a plan for how he would apply a feminist lens to all of his working relationships and future event-planning in his career in College Student Personnel. In effect, students were no longer apprentices, they had successfully entered the trade.

While the students in my class reported that they learned a great deal from their apprenticeships with the activists in their organizations, they also faced several challenges along the way. Some of these were mundane and expected, for example, difficulty with time management and coordinating group members' schedules outside of class. Students were informed of the service-learning component on the first day of class and were strongly encouraged to consider whether this section of the course, which required significant work outside of scheduled class meetings, was right for them considering their schedules. Predictably, some students complained abut the extra work outside of class, despite the course days marked off for their volunteer hours. One group procrastinated their community partner interview for so long that they failed their group presentation due to a lack of content; however, they later reported that this had been a significant learning experience for them. They took more responsibility after this and their commitment to their CP, and their work, improved greatly.

One oft-repeated complaint at the start of the project involved transportation and the perceived difficulty of leaving campus and entering the community. A few students balked at the suggestion that they take public transportation, which is free for students. This concern seemed rooted in anxiety about class difference as much as unfamiliarity with the bus schedules (some students associated the bus with poverty, or with urban communities and therefore the expectation that the buses were "unsafe"). However, such assumptions provided for class discussion about the role of borders and border-crossing. At least one student group reported that the community partner who had agreed to work with them was consistently difficult to contact, and this proved frustrating for both the students and for me.

Only one student commented on the course evaluation that s/he felt it was wrong for an instructor to require students to "participate in a protest," referring to the *March at Purdue,* as the student felt that this put him/her in a position of supporting political causes with which he/she did not agree. It should be noted that while students were able to choose the organization with which they wished to partner for their project, the culminating march around campus comprised not only of the community partners working with my class, but also several independent student groups that focused on issues such as promoting women's reproductive rights and marriage equality. While the march was not organized to be a political protest, some student groups did use it as a venue to engage the student body with their particular issues.

Perhaps the greatest challenge I faced as an instructor involved implementing a service-learning project in an introductory course where students were still learning core concepts as they were working in the field. In addition, because the course was an elective, students ranged from first-year undergraduates to graduating seniors, and so brought a range of skills and confidence levels with them. I underestimated how much class time I would need to discuss the details of their assignments and project responsibilities,[6] as well as addressing questions and concerns that arose from challenges they faced in the field. Indeed, one of the challenges I faced was remaining flexible—that is, gaining a level of comfort with not positing the aims of every class meeting before checking in with my students to see where they were and what their frequently shifting contexts required from me as their guide.

Conclusion

In closing, I offer reflections on something that is seldom mentioned in the literature on service-learning, even in those resources that address specifically *feminist* service-learning. If such projects clearly benefit both students and members of the community working for social justice, they also benefit instructors. This is particularly true for instructors committed to practicing liberatory pedagogies, who identify as radical feminist and/or anarchist, or who ever find themselves disheartened or disillusioned from the daily struggle of working in an institution that professes freedom and equal education but that seems increasingly to be losing a battle with budget cuts and corporate influence.

In her chapter for *Teaching Feminist Activism,* Naples (2002) observes that the act of collaborating with her students and with members of the community "continually reinspired my own sense of political possibilities for a new generation" (p. 75). As feminist-instructors invested in liberatory practices, it is also imperative that we continue to recognize and to change the structures and practices of the university that work to estrange feminist instructors from the activist practices of their own scholarship and teaching, so that we do not become alienated from the radical goals that inspired so many of us in the first place. Activist-apprentice pedagogy then, by realizing Rich's "university-without-walls," might be one method by which feminists and other radicals committed to liberatory practices find a home within the academy without betraying themselves. For if our students need social justice courses in any discipline to embody both the "No!" to injustice as well as the affirmation of the possibility of real change, as instructors, we need them to do so as well.

Notes

1. Henry A. Giroux and Susan Searls Giroux (2004) trace this "retreat from politics" (p. 4) to academic and political backlash in the post-civil rights era that brought about changes to literary canons and other curricula as well as affirmative action (p. 10).
2. Shantz (2012) notes that such experiments were "an effort to develop alternative forms of education and self-development in a context that was considered increasingly alienating, rationalized, and industrial" (p. 127), much like critical service-learning pedagogies in the present.
3. One group of students would decide to work with a campus organization, the Feminist Action Coalition for Today (FACT), after their community partner, the local YWCA, unexpectedly withdrew from the project just as it was starting. This was an obstacle that neither the students nor I foresaw, and it necessitated all of us working together to find a solution. By working with FACT, the students were able to remain focused on the issue that had interested them in the YWCA to begin with, which was violence against women.
4. Students were assigned the Introduction and Prologue, plus Chap. 3 "Rebels with Causes," Chap. 6, "Creating Activism," Chap. 7 "The Revolutionary Next Door," and Appendix A: "A Glossary of the Most Common Forms of Activism." For their final papers, students were asked to reflect on how their experiences working in the field with their community partners compared to the activist endeavors and tools presented in the text; in particular, I asked them which tools they learned in the field would translate effectively to student activism on campus.
5. This dialogue was particularly important since many students at Purdue were heavily involved in Greek organizations that stressed philanthropy, and because

this was an especial point of pride for many of the students who volunteered for and organized such activities. My notes from the class discussion of philanthropy and activism can be found online on my course blog, *The Gender Press*, at the following URL: http://genderpressing.wordpress.com/2013/02/04/philanthropyvssocialactivism-2/.

6. Students seemed to need extra reassurance during particular phases of the project when they were faced with particularly unfamiliar territory, both intellectual and geographical. While some might dismiss spending extra class time walking students through particular tasks, we might just as easily consider this necessary scaffolding for learners acquiring new skills.

References

Bauer, D. M. (2009). Authority. In R. Crabtree, D. Sapp, & A. Licona (Eds.), *Feminist pedagogy: Looking back to move forward* (pp. 23–26). Baltimore: Johns Hopkins University Press.

Baumgardner, J., & Richards, A. (2005). *Grassroots: A field guide for feminist activism*. New York: Farrar, Straus, & Giroux.

Bickford, D., & Reynolds, N. (2002). Activism and service-learning: Reframing volunteerism as acts of dissent. *Pedagogy, 2*(2), 229–252.

Cushman, E. (1999). The public intellectual, service learning, and activist research. *College English, 61*(3), 328–336.

Freire, P. (1970). *Pedagogy of the oppressed*. New York: Continuum.

Giroux, H. (1988). Border pedagogy in the age of postmodernism. *Journal of Education, 170*(3), 162–181.

Giroux, H. A, & Giroux, S. S. (2004). *Take back higher education: Race, youth, and the crisis of democracy in the post-civil rights era*. New York: Palgrave Macmillan.

hooks, b. (1989). *Talking back: Thinking feminist, thinking black*. Boston: South End Press.

Hu-DeHart, E. (2000). The diversity project: Institutionalizing multiculturalism or managing difference? *Academe, 86*(5), 38–42.

King, J. (2004). Service-learning as a site for critical pedagogy: A case of collaboration, caring, and defamiliarization across borders. *Journal of Experiential Education, 26*(3), 121–137.

LaDuke, W. (2005). Introduction. In J. Baumgartner & A. Richards (Eds.), *Grassroots: A field guide to feminist activism* (pp. xi–xv). New York: Farrar, Straus, and Giroux.

Maher, F., & Tetreault, M. K. T. (1994). *The feminist classroom*. New York: Basic Books.

Manzano, A. (2000). Charlie's angels: Free-market feminism. *Off Our Backs, 30*(11), 10.

Morgan, R. (2001). *Demon-lover: The roots of terrorism*. New York: Washington Square Press.

Naples, N. (2002). Collaborative learning, subversive teaching, and activism. In N. Naples & K. Bojar (Eds.), *Teaching feminist activism: Strategies from the field* (pp. 71–94). New York: Routledge.

Noterman, E., & Pusey, A. (2012). Inside, outside, and on the edge of the academy: Experiments in radical pedagogies. In R. Haworth (Ed.), *Anarchist pedagogies: Collective actions, theories, and critical reflections on education* (pp. 175–199). Oakland: PM Press.

Novek, E. (1999). Service-learning is a feminist issue: Transforming communication pedagogy. *Women's Studies in Communication, 22*(2), 230–240.

Powers-Stubbs, K. (1992). Watching ourselves: Feminist teachers and authority. *College Composition and Communication 43*(3), 311–315.

Rich, A. (1979). *On lies, secrets, and silence: Selected prose 1966–1978*. New York: W.W. Norton.

Rinehart, J. (2002). Collaborative learning, subversive teaching, and activism. In N. Naples & K. Bojar (Eds.), *Teaching feminist activism: Strategies from the field* (pp. 22–35). New York: Routledge.

Schutz, A., & Gere, A. R. (1998). Service learning and English studies: Rethinking "public" service. *College English, 60*(2), 129–129.

Shantz, J. (2010). *Constructive anarchy: Building infrastructures of resistance.* Farnham, UK: Ashgate.

———. (2012). Spaces of learning: The anarchist Free Skool. In R. Haworth (Ed.), *Anarchist pedagogies: Collective actions, theories, and critical reflections on education* (pp. 124–144). Oakland: PM Press.

Suissa, J. (2006). *Anarchism and education: A philosophical perspective.* New York: Routledge.

Webb, P., Cole, K., & Skeen, T. (2007). Feminist social projects: Building bridges between communities and universities. *College English, 69*(3), 238–259.

Williams, T., & McKenna, E. (2002). Negotiating subject positions in a service-learning context: Toward a feminist critique of experiential learning. In A. Macdonald & S. Sánchez-Casal (Eds.), *Twenty-first-century feminist classrooms: Pedagogies of identity and difference* (pp. 135–154). New York: Palgrave Macmillan.

PART II
Feminist Applications

CHAPTER 7

Feminist Student Philanthropy: Possibilities and Poignancies of a Service-Learning and Student Philanthropy Initiative

Christin L. Seher

Introduction

The implementation of service-learning, as one type of experiential education, is increasing in collegiate classrooms across the United States. As an active-learning pedagogy, service-learning strives to connect academic information with professional praxis in new and creative ways. Broadly grounded in Boyer's (1996) "scholarship of engagement," the literature is ripe with examples of the benefits of service-learning. Whether enhancing academic learning outcomes (Conway, Amel, & Gerwein, 2009; Eyler & Giles, 1999; Astin, Vogelgesang, Ikeda, & Yee, 2000), developing cultural competence (Chen, McAdams-Jones, Tay, & Packer, 2012; Einfeld & Collins, 2008; Kezar, 2002), facilitating campus-community partnerships (Jacoby, 2003), promoting student identity development (Eyler & Giles, 1999; Iverson & James, 2013), fostering a more engaged, active citizenry (Einfeld & Collins, 2008; Eyler & Giles, 1999; HERI, 2000), or working toward social responsibility and justice (Allan & Iverson, 2004; Bickford & Reynolds, 2002; Cipolle, 2010; James & Iverson, 2009; Kinefuchi, 2010), there is little doubt among scholars, educators, administrators, and, increasingly, politicians and policy makers, that service-learning has value in an academic classroom (Hartley, Harkavy, & Benson, 2005).

Feminist educators, however, have remained reluctant to fully embrace service-learning as a pedagogical strategy, critiquing the charitable, often patronizing, orientation of most service-learning efforts (Bickford & Reynolds, 2002; Eyler & Giles, 1999; Naples & Bojar, 2002). Specifically, feminist scholars contend that service-learning opportunities typically do not go far enough in promoting social/political action—and thereby risk unintentionally reinforcing power structures and discourses that support the continued marginalization of specific social groups, like women, people of color, or members of the gay, lesbian, bisexual, or transgender community. For similar reasons, feminists critique community service, and other volunteer-based, charity-oriented or philanthropic student learning experiences, noting that often traditional conceptions of "service" avoid the political activism needed to bring about social change (Walker, 2000). A feminist lens holds great possibility as a philosophical framework for designing educational experiences that push students beyond the boundaries of traditional service-learning.

In this chapter, I employ a feminist lens as I reflect upon the implementation of a student philanthropy project in my senior-level community nutrition course. This project was not designed with explicitly feminist aims in mind, for reasons I explain later; however, having since reflected upon the experience, I see great possibility in re-visioning this project as a feminist— community engagement strategy and use this chapter as a space to initiate that process. I offer my story and reflection, as a novice faculty member and emerging feminist scholar, in the hopes that it sparks a discussion— most acutely on the potential for feminist student philanthropy, and—the possibility for feminist community engagement—to enhance the field of nutrition and dietetics. More broadly, to provoke thought on the ways in which feminist identity emerges, on the process of becoming a feminist educator, and on the fluidity and tensions experienced in this journey. Before discussing lessons learned, I first contextualize the project and introduce the concept of student philanthropy.

Possibilities of Student Philanthropy: Pay It Forward

Pay It Forward (PIF) is a service-learning and student philanthropy initiative that connects college students to nonprofit agencies in their local community, linking academic coursework to community need in an experiential learning strategy that pays—literally. Students enrolled in PIF courses complete academic projects in close consultation with nonprofit community agency representatives to develop products (e.g., a Request for Proposals, client education materials, community needs assessment, grant proposals, marketing strategies, social media sites, etc.) that have an immediate, tangible impact for the organization. In this regard, PIF is an initiative that reflects core elements of service-learning—meeting academic competencies through real-world experience and application, while simultaneously serving the needs of the surrounding community. What distinguishes PIF from other types of service-learning is that financial support allows each academic course participating in PIF to award money to one nonprofit agency with whom they collaborate. To this end, PIF adopts a philanthropic orientation, teaching students about the importance of giving within one's community. PIF is unique in that it takes the service and academic components of service-learning, and blends it with the charitable aspect of philanthropy. This hybrid approach is representative of a new form of experiential learning—known as "student philanthropy" (Olberding, 2009, 2012)—trending on college campuses in response to a growing concern over the lack of civic engagement, volunteerism, and philanthropy in today's college students (The Sillerman Center for the Advancement of Philanthropy, 2014).

PIF was first established in 2009 by three state affiliate chapters (Ohio, Kentucky, and Michigan) of Campus Compact, a nationwide coalition of colleges and universities committed to furthering the public purpose of higher education and teaching students about citizenship (Campus Compact, 2014). The idea for PIF grew from the successes of a smaller pilot program, *Campus Connects*, which was funded by a private donor-philanthropist and implemented on campuses in Ohio and Kentucky during 2007–2008 (Ohio Campus Compact, 2014). PIF began on my home campus, The University of Akron (UA), in 2010 sponsored in part by Ohio Campus Compact. Since the initial grant, funding continues through the United Way of Summit County allowing approximately 5–7 courses per semester at UA to participate in PIF. According to the developers who brought PIF to UA, the primary goals of implementing this initiative on campus were to provide a way to further engage university constituents within the local community, to foster understanding and community connectedness in UA students, and to facilitate a spirit of philanthropy and volunteerism on campus. In total, more than 50 individual classes with over 1,000 students from a variety of disciplines at UA (i.e., law, accounting, English composition, nutrition, chemistry, health education, exercise physiology, and psychology, to name a few) have participated in PIF since its inception. No single course or academic discipline is best suited for PIF; rather, it is the integration of PIF with specific academic learning outcomes and the variety of nonprofit partners that makes each PIF course experience truly unique.

PIF has changed throughout its history at UA. Initially, students in courses (funded by the original grant) participated in a group decision-making process to award money ($5000) to nonprofit agencies who responded to a Request for Proposals (RFP) generated by their class. Students studied social issues affecting their nonprofit partners, and through a collaborative process, determined as a class how to prioritize and distribute their allocated funds. The current PIF initiative at UA is designed more like a "traditional" service-learning project; students must volunteer for at least 15 hours of work with a designated nonprofit agency, and complete an academic project assigned by their course instructor based on discipline-specific learning outcomes. At the end of the experience, one nonprofit agency is selected to receive the monetary award (typically ranging between $1000 and $2500) by a panel of community leaders and philanthropists who judge both the merit of the students' work in meeting community needs, and the ability of students to *advocate* on behalf of their nonprofit organization, its cause, and its need during a culminating presentation at the end of the semester. The money, therefore, does not necessarily go to the students producing the best academic work; rather, it is given to the organization represented by the group of students that fosters an authentic, passionate, and collaborative relationship with their agency, who conveys understanding of their agency's role and mission in the community, and who have developed a sustainable product to meet an agency-determined priority.

PIF is positioned by UA to university constituents, partner agencies, and the surrounding community as "volunteer-oriented" service-learning and philanthropy. In this regard, and by many accounts, the PIF initiative has been quite successful. Data obtained from end-of-term student reflections and survey instruments note positive outcomes of enrolling in PIF courses—both at UA and across institutions in Ohio, Michigan, and Kentucky—the three states actively involved in PIF through their respective state affiliate chapters of Campus Compact. Outcomes data indicate that after participating in a PIF course, students are more likely to report they will engage with their community in the future through donating their time or money, and demonstrate a greater understanding of the important role nonprofit agencies play in the community (The Sillerman Center for the Advancement of Philanthropy, 2014).

Many recognize, however, that PIF, and similar service-learning or student philanthropy initiatives, can (and, perhaps, should) prompt students to go further than volunteerism or charity—to move *beyond* philanthropy. The Senior Vice President of Community Impact for The United Way of Summit County explains PIF to UA students in an introductory letter by stating:

You will learn yet again [through the PIF experience] that *the world is not fair*, that people struggle every day with meeting basic needs: housing, food, health care. The nonprofit will share statistics with you and the numbers will be shocking. *This may be uncomfortable for you.* Difficult economic realities are sometimes hard to think about and often slip from our minds as we focus on our own day to day activities. Your role is to learn, to *question*, and to understand (emphasis added).

PIF then represents the *possibility* of more. Through my experience in teaching a PIF course, I have come to realize that student philanthropy, when intentionally designed, might serve as an excellent platform to introduce students to the philosophical aims of feminism and feminist community engagement principles (see Iverson & James, Chapter 2). I propose the term, *feminist student philanthropy*, to describe student philanthropy initiatives that intentionally incorporate opportunities for consciousness-raising and strive to facilitate activist strategies for equality and justice. I argue this approach has the potential to promote social responsibility in students and spark a passion for change. Specific to PIF—which is active on more than 30 campuses across Ohio, Michigan, and Kentucky—incorporating feminist principles into student philanthropy initiatives can intentionally challenge students to move beyond learning paradigms that typically do not question, disrupt, or seek to eliminate hierarchical and categorical social relationships.

Possibilities of Feminism: A Conceptual Framework

My belief in the possibilities of PIF as a space for feminist service-learning and student philanthropy is influenced most directly by feminist scholarship that aims to problematize, contest, and disrupt dichotomous notions of gender, race, class, sexuality, ability and other social factors and to illuminate the power dynamics inherent in the creation of meaning. I assert that like service-learning, student philanthropy can be viewed as both pedagogy and philosophy. The scholarship on feminist philanthropy is limited (McCarthy, 1996; Ostrander, 2004, 2005) and a focus on critical or feminist *student* philanthropy is absent; thus, I extend the thinking of critical and feminist scholars (Freire, 1970/2000; Giroux, 1983; hooks, 1994) to this experiential learning platform. In particular, I believe that service-learning and student philanthropy are teaching strategies that align with the foundations of feminism in that they challenge the learning hierarchy of traditional pedagogies, encouraging students to collaboratively generate (and contest) knowledge (Novak, 1999).

I believe the possibilities of feminist student philanthropy can only be fully realized when educators utilize antifoundational conceptions (Butin, 2010)—seeking to disrupt taken for granted assumptions and challenging students to consider "notions of themselves and others as gendered, racial, and status-bound individuals" (Butin, 2003, p. 1683) in the process. By asking students to purposefully consider the communities in which they work, the work that they do, and the intentions of that work (Iverson & James, Chapter 2), educators can use feminist student philanthropy as a platform to introduce conversations on gender, race, and status, while reinforcing the need for activism and social responsibility as future citizens and professionals.

Adopting this position challenges me to think about the possibility of student philanthropy initiatives like PIF for striving toward transformative ends. I agree with and extend the critiques of those who have written critically on philanthropy, challenging the notion that philanthropy and/or charitable endeavors are not political (Reckhow & Snyder, 2014); rather, these acts, through the monetary support they give to organizations, often "favor social continuity over change, and operate in a very cautious manner" (Ostrander, 2005, p. 43). My aim, therefore, by (re)positioning PIF as the *possibility* of feminist student philanthropy is to draw explicit attention to the artificial and conflated distinction between the "politics" of activism and the safety of "service"—the latter being presented as nonpartisan, private, apolitical, and virtuous (Walker, 2000). Rather, I argue feminist educators can (and should) reclaim student philanthropy for what it already is—an inherently political teaching strategy that presents the opportunity to teach activism—in that the underlying social issues often at the center of philanthropic initiatives (e.g., hunger, access to health care, health disparities, violence against women) are some of the most pressing social concerns of our time affecting women. I further recognize that the "ideology of service" (Walker, 2000, p. 30) is powerful and contributes to the disillusioned notion that social problems can be rectified through individual action—an idea feminist student philanthropy can contest by reframing service as a necessary prepolitical step to more forthright acts of activism and dissent and by requiring students to advocate for *collective* social change through their philanthropic experience (Walker, 2000).

I acknowledge that conceptions underlying "service" are historically situated, and gender-bound, with direct (charitable) service and volunteerism (often the only arenas available to women) continuing to be devalued in a patriarchal US culture where access to policy making, fundraising, and advocacy is not equitable (Damon-Moore, 2000). Adopting an activist conception of student philanthropy, therefore, extends the notions of "service" found in service-learning, and underlying student philanthropy, invoke the (Second Wave) feminist movement, and intentional acts of dissent (Bickford & Reynolds, 2002; Damon-Moore, 2000).

Finally, I also acknowledge that service-learning and, by extension, student philanthropy, often disparately serves those in power—typically those actually *doing* the service—in this case, members of the academy who have relative privilege based upon their educational background and social class (Butin, 2003, 2005). Furthermore, by participating in (charitable) service or philanthropic activities, the risk remains that gendered, raced, and classed notions can be reinforced and (re)inscribed in the process (Trigg & Balliet, 2000; Walker, 2000). In the design and delivery of feminist student philanthropy initiatives, therefore, educators should strive toward reciprocity with community partners (Jacoby, 2003), to acknowledge mutual respect and authenticity among all participants, and to foster reflexivity in the form of critical consciousness-raising in all involved—including the educators responsible for the design of learning experiences (Allan & Iverson, 2004; Cipolle, 2010; Kinefuchi, 2010; Sifers, 2012). It is in this spirit of critical reflexivity I now offer my reflections on lessons learned through my PIF experience as an instructor in an effort to cultivate a discussion of the need to reconceptualize and reclaim the possibilities of student philanthropy.

My Story: Exploring the Possibilities of PIF

I learned about PIF immediately prior to starting my first semester as junior faculty at The University of Akron, where I began my position mid-year, hired to replace a retiring colleague who was part of the original grant that brought PIF to our campus. It was in taking over one of her courses that I found myself working with PIF. As I began to plan the logistics of the project, I quickly became excited as I realized the potential of PIF to go further than an experiential learning exercise. Having been exposed to the philosophical and pedagogical possibilities of feminism (and, more broadly, critical theory) as a doctoral student, and having come to identify as a criticalist, I saw PIF as providing a platform to push at the boundaries of traditional classroom learning by asking students to think critically and systemically and to question the social determinants of nutrition-related problems they would come to experience through their time in the community. Given the timeframe for implementation to get the project off and running for spring term (less than a month), and as a result of working within the bounds of an existing project design and with the cautious exploration that comes in being a new faculty member, I found myself approaching my first time teaching a PIF course as an exploratory endeavor. Therefore, I did not design the PIF experience explicitly with feminist aims in mind; rather, from the outset, I simply pushed myself to consider the ways I could extend my adoption of PIF beyond a "traditional" service-learning classroom exercise toward one with more transformative ends.

PIF Project Design

PIF was included in my *Community Nutrition II* (CN2) senior-level dietetics course enrolling 39 students in the spring 2014 semester. Prior to the start of term, I worked with the Institute of Teaching and Learning on campus to identify nonprofit organizations whose mission and services were nutrition-related. While the final organizations were ultimately selected for their ability to meet course-specific learning objectives, I gave significant attention to collaborating with agencies that would provide a platform to push students' thinking about specific social issues (e.g., hunger, violence against women, access to health care, nutritious foods, and nutrition education, etc.), or allow exposure to marginalized social groups (e.g. low-income, minority, displaced, HIV+). Nine agencies collaborated with my class including a battered women's shelter; a local food pantry and assistance center; a local organic farm working on farm-to-school programming; an agency providing housing and transitional assistance to pregnant, displaced teenage women; a local Boys & Girls Club affiliate; a local Head Start program; an agency bringing meals to the elderly, homebound population; an advocacy agency for HIV positive individuals, primarily in the LGBT community; and an agency providing life skills training and residential facilities for developmentally challenged adults.

As the academic component of the PIF project, students generated a grant proposal to help address a nutrition concern for their agency/population. The assignment guidelines were specific to format and general content (e.g., all papers had to include background data, goals/objectives and a timeline for implementation, a budget), but each group was able to work with their agency to craft a proposal that best filled an agency need. Groups typically advocated for the inclusion of nutrition education or wellness programming, requested equipment (like a commercial dehydrator, oven, or cooking supplies), or built infrastructure (e.g., one group proposed to establish a nonemergency food pantry on site at their agency). One group even wrote their proposal requesting to help purchase a commercial van for the emergency food assistance center to help streamline their donation collection process. In this aspect of the project, the groups and their agency contacts had full creative capacity to propose a solution to their specific nutrition problem.

As the semester progressed, a series of opportunities to bring a reflexive element to the PIF project was included in class. I allotted time for intergroup dialogue in class on the project, in conjunction with course content. I asked students to complete a standardized survey used by UA for all students participating in PIF courses; among other things, this instrument collects basic demographic information, and asks a series of nine Likert scale questions, assessing things like *As a result of my service-learning experience, I have an increased awareness of cultural differences and attitudes toward helping others* and *As a result of my service-learning experience, I have an improved sense of civic and social responsibility*. Finally, I designed a series of reflective writing prompts for students to complete at the end of the project encouraging them to consider (a) what the PIF experience has taught them about themselves and their future work as health professionals; (b) what they learned about the population and organization with whom they were collaborating; and (c) about their responsibility to take action in light of what they now know. Specifically, I asked students *what will you do differently tomorrow* (Steinem, 1983) *based upon what you now know about yourself, the population, the organization, or the broader issue you investigated?* in the hopes that they would be pushed to reflect upon their level of social responsibility, commitment to creating change, and plans for continued community engagement beyond the scope of this class.

The project, by most accounts was incredibly successful. Although students initially viewed the project as a lot of work and somewhat intimidating, in the end they responded very favorably to the experience. The students' presentations were widely attended, and accolades came to both me and my students as a result of our work by colleagues and administration. But after the pageantry and the semester concluded, I reflected more deeply on my first student philanthropy experience, and wondered what a feminist analysis might offer. I knew I had transformative aims for the project going in, designing the experience to hopefully push my students to examine issues of power and equity related to nutrition, and wondered what, if anything, PIF was able to facilitate for my students. Furthermore, as a novice educator grappling with the distinctions between critical and feminist pedagogy, I was left wondering what might be possible if PIF was re-visioned as explicitly *feminist* student philanthropy.

To spark this process, I analyzed student responses to the reflective writing prompts I assigned with the following research question in mind: *what understandings of themselves, of their community, of service and social responsibility, do students take away from their experience with PIF?* I was particularly interested to see if students' responses to these questions were change-oriented, approached from a systemic perspective, and couched within the context of a personal or professional responsibility. A thematic analysis provided insight into students' thinking. Responses were read and coded for all 39 students to represent possible meanings (Rubin & Rubin, 2005); codes were collapsed into themes in an effort to subsume the "particulars into the general" (Miles & Huberman, 1994, p. 245). In the section that follows, I describe the themes, illustrating with excerpts from students' writing, which inform my process of re-visioning PIF into an example of feminist student philanthropy.

The Possibilities of (Feminist) Student Philanthropy

Analysis of responses to the assigned writing prompts indicated that PIF did, indeed, provide students with the opportunity to consider their social responsibility as future nutrition professionals. Students experienced gains in awareness of self and others, of community need, of the role of service, and demonstrated greater recognition for the need to be philanthropically involved as they move into their professional roles. However, differences emerged in the depth of responses from students with some articulating a change-oriented mindset and describing concrete acts of advocacy and activism they envision moving forward.

Toward Awareness

Students' reflective writing suggests that through the PIF experience, they were able to reflect—upon self, upon the needs of others, upon the role of their nonprofit organization in meeting community needs, and upon the value of service. Most common were responses that demonstrate a shift in personal awareness after working on the PIF project, as exemplified by this student, who found herself thinking about her life experiences while reflecting upon a visit to the teen pregnancy shelter:

> I do not have experience in crisis shelters or homelessness. I have no personal experience with these issues and it was shocking to see girls younger than me dealing with these issues. After the first visit, I reflected on my life and I wondered where I would go if my family kicked me out like some of the girls at the [organization] experienced. I mean, I have no clue what I would do. It was a humbling experience. (Paige)

While many students showed a shift in self-awareness as a result of the PIF experience, some engaged on a deeper level through these reflective exercises, noting how stereotypical beliefs were challenged, their views of others expanded, or their ability to empathize with diverse populations strengthened:

> I used to think that everyone who contracted HIV in the U.S. did so because of his or her own risky behaviors whether it's drug use or unprotected sex. I felt like I didn't have much sympathy for this population. I learned, however, that this is not always the case and how much the cycle of HIV, food insecurity, and malnutrition helps to reveal the desperation to stay alive that many inner-city populations experience. (Ashley)

> This experience taught me that working with populations outside of your comfort zone can be a very rewarding experience... I sometimes tend to blame the drug abuse population of making poor choices leading to their situation due to personal experiences; however, in the future I will keep a much more open mind... I realize that over time, I have allowed a personal situation to cloud my vision of this particular population, when in reality each person has a different situation. (Rebecca)

Many students also noted how PIF provides the opportunity to experience first-hand, the difference nonprofit agencies make in the community. "This project helped me explore my inner philanthropist. The opportunities to explore this have been limited thus far in my life," one student wrote. "Before doing this assignment, I did volunteer work every once in a while, and gave $1 when I shopped at Giant Eagle to Harvest for Hunger, but never really thought too much into it. I didn't realize to the full extent how heavily these nonprofits rely on volunteers and philanthropy, until sitting through all the presentations," a second notes. Yet another student thinks about her newfound level of awareness regarding social issues as a result of working on the PIF project:

> After living in Akron, Ohio for the past 4 years while attending UA, it never hit me that so many residents around this area are in poverty and the statistics we found on Summit County are absolutely astounding. It's weird to think that in the past 4 years, I never really new about my surroundings. (Laura)

It was evident through the student responses that the PIF experience facilitated a shift toward awareness—of self, of others, of community need, and of the value of service.

Social and Professional Responsibility

Students directly connected their work through PIF to their future practice as nutrition professionals, describing their obligation to lend their "expertise" in the local community. For most students, the PIF project directly shed light on the need to be socially responsible, engaged citizens; many expressed the desire to volunteer or donate money to similar nonprofit organizations in the future, illustrated by the response of one student, who wrote

> very rarely in the past, I have donated to a canned food drive here and there, but I never understood what the food meant to the people it helped. In the future, not only will I donate regularly to food pantries, but I will make it one of my personal goals as a dietitian to step in wherever I can to impact food security. (Deann)

Less often, but not infrequently, students communicated the desire to advocate on behalf of these organizations; this was often tied to professional obligations, and students found themselves contemplating continued engagement with these agencies since they relate to their field of study. For example, one student writes, "I will advocate more for childhood and pregnancy nutrition because this project made me realize how much of a need there is and how much nutrition makes an impact" (Kerri).

A number of students spoke very concretely of their plans for continued advocacy as a result of this experience. The quotes below illuminate students' thinking in this regard, illustrating the power of participating in experiences like PIF and demonstrating the potential for intentionally designed student philanthropy experiences to introduce students to the concepts of advocacy, activism, collective responsibility, and the need for systemic change:

> After participating in this project, and finishing this class, I see the importance in advocacy for our profession... I feel like now I can question the way policy is administered, and fight to propose policy solutions regarding our communities and country. (Ashley)
>
> I would also want to become actively involved in organizations whose purpose it is to enact change to eradicate food insecurity. (Catherine)
>
> Throughout my career, I plan to make small stands against nutrition-related issues that are in my community. (Julia)
>
> I have been recently telling my friends and family about the little changes they can make to help out others in need. (Erica)
>
> Finding reliable nutrition information today is nearly impossible so I need to step up and be the "poster child" for reliable information. (Paige)

This experience taught me we have a collective responsibility to provide care and support to teenagers that find themselves in crisis situations without the support of family. (Danielle)

As I was analyzing student responses, I was excited to see them starting to reflect upon the ways in which PIF prompted them to consider what role activism and advocacy would play in their future career as nutrition professionals.

(Re)examining PIF through a Feminist Lens

I consider my first time teaching a PIF course as successful—specifically in regards to its ability to raise students' awareness, foster a sense of social responsibility, and highlight the importance of philanthropic work; my outcomes mirror existing research in this regard (The Sillerman Center for the Advancement of Philanthropy, 2014). Yet, I am left grappling with the ways in which this student philanthropy experience might challenge students' thinking and action more deeply if purposefully designed and implemented with feminist aims.

Despite the academic and personal gains in awareness that students displayed through their writing, few were able to engage critically with the reflection questions I posed—even when guided to take a systems-oriented perspective on change. Rather, students more frequently wrote on a personal level about aspects of themselves that were brought to light by participating in PIF, with many framing this discussion in terms of their own privilege compared to the population with whom they were working. A number of students noted how the project prompted them to be "grateful" or feel "lucky" for their life experiences and status—in essence, for the privileged spaces they occupy as members of dominant social groups (e.g., White, heterosexual, middle-class, well-educated). While self-reflection of this nature can be an important first step in facilitating a more critical awareness of self, students need to be pushed to delve deeper in exploring these thoughts, to engage in a more nuanced interrogation of the reasons privilege exists and be asked to challenge the assumptions upon which privilege is built. I now realize that furthering the feminist possibilities of PIF will necessitate the incorporation of a more intentional process that asks students to concurrently explore elements of their social identity along with their PIF experience.

I also realized that while students wrote poignantly about insights gained from the PIF experience, their writing illustrates a continued hierarchical categorization between themselves and the "others" their agency serves. Instead of being reflective of the reciprocity that feminist community engagement tries to build, my students' writing problematically indicated a reinforcement of power dynamics through participating in PIF, noting things such as: "As for now, this experience will definitely teach me to appreciate everything," and "It made me incredibly thankful for what I have in life and realize that I have taken for granted what many children wish they could have." It remains troubling for me that these thoughts could not be further unpacked due to the timing of the reflective writing prompts (they were given at the end of the semester). These excerpts illustrate to me, however, that without ongoing reflexivity, PIF and other student philanthropy initiatives can indeed have the unintended consequences of reinforcing gender and class hierarchies (Trigg & Balliet, 2000).

Given the inherent possibility I see between the aims of PIF and the activist orientation of feminist community engagement, I continue to question how PIF and similar student philanthropy initiatives can go further in encouraging students to form a long-term commitment to activism—to move beyond the boundaries of a specific course project or in working with a specific nonprofit agency on any given social issue. In this regard, student responses were promising, moving beyond what Baumgardner and Richards (2005, p. 13) term "the generic three"—donating money, volunteering time, and contacting politicians—surface-level acts indicative of "knee-jerk, minimally effective answers...that encourage passivity in would be activists" (Baumgardner & Richards, 2005, p. 13). Rather, students (while also talking of volunteerism and donation frequently) indicated a level of prepolitical awareness in their writing that pushed them to begin considering ways in which they could start to *act* to address areas of inequity. They wrote of volunteering their expertise to impact legislation, programming, fundraising; becoming involved in policy generation and coalition building; in starting their own businesses to address community problems; and in participating in education and outreach initiatives in the community. They did so, however, in mostly professional contexts—seeing advocacy as an extension of their responsibilities as future nutrition professionals, and not their responsibility as socially engaged citizens.

Implications for Feminist Student Philanthropy

Through this PIF project, I attempted to foster students' abilities to "critically assess social, political, and economic structures to see beyond surface causes" and to develop students who "[seek] out and addresses areas of injustice" (Westheimer & Kahne, 2004, p. 240). In this, I was partially successful, with some students leaving their PIF experience more ready to engage in action. Other students, despite a heightened sense of awareness of their personal responsibility as citizens, saw this as readily enacted through volunteerism and charity—important acts, but which I argue are not enough. This experience has led me to believe it is necessary to begin a conversation regarding the way we (instructors in general) design student philanthropy experiences, and leaves me reflecting upon what feminist educators can do to more purposefully push at the boundaries of student philanthropy to better align with feminist strategies and contest taken-for-granted assumptions on complex social issues. I maintain that student philanthropy initiatives like PIF can serve as an important prepolitical step enabling students to begin to *think* about the ways they interact in the world, about their views on social issues, and about their sphere of influence. Prepolitical steps like these may be necessary *introductions* to activism, and better aligned with the scope of a single project or class. As Santoro (2010) pushes us to consider,

> School-generated social justice action has the potential to limit students' perception of the scope of social justice work temporally, as occurring within a school year or semester, and spatially, as just another *school* activity that is monitored and assessed by teachers... Of even greater concern is that, despite the best intentions, social justice education has the danger of subverting student *thinking* in efforts to stimulate student *activism* (p. 241, italics in original).

In this regard, Santoro's words (2010) encourage feminist educators to avoid "circles of certainty" (p. 241) in the design of pedagogical exercises, and of feminist student philanthropy experiences more specifically. Rather, we should not underestimate the importance that simply *thinking*—of "dwelling in an ongoing engagement" (p. 242) with pressing social issues—can have for our students. In this regard, I believe a feminist approach to student philanthropy can provide the perfect platform for teaching "in the in-between" (Santoro, p. 244).

Designing service-learning and student philanthropy experiences with transformative aims will not be enough to realize the full possibility of feminist community engagement—feminist educators must do more. We must recognize that positioning matters; the way a project is described (e.g., as a "service" project, or as a social action opportunity) allows for dialogue to occur that pushes students' thinking about social identity, promoting the development of critical consciousness (Allan & Iverson, 2004) necessary to move beyond awareness to action. Community collaborators should be intentionally chosen for their ability to expose students to disenfranchised populations, and for their ability to introduce students to activism—rather than solely for their direct link to academic content.

It is also important to recognize that critical reflection on identity and privilege does not come easily for students, especially on issues of social justice, and must be facilitated very directly. Feminist student philanthropy needs to incorporate structured, *required* opportunities to help move students to "*both* awareness *and* action" (Bickford & Reynolds, 2002, p. 240, emphasis in original) and I now recognize that activism must be intentionally drawn out. This can be done by requiring action-oriented projects through which students must connect the broader sociopolitical and cultural aspects of their experience to a demonstrated act of activism, dissent, or advocacy (Iverson, 2012). It is my hope that with these curricular design changes in mind, I can better utilize PIF as an opportunity to push at the boundaries of my thinking, as well as my students', and help extend the possibilities and potential social impact of feminist student philanthropy.

Conclusion

This project was a learning experience for me, as a novice feminist educator, to fully appreciate the depth of integration needed of *both* feminist theory *and* practice in order to create a space in which students can begin to disrupt, question, and take action toward equality and justice. My story illustrates the messiness in moving from a place of knowing and internalizing feminist theory as a student to the application and creation of feminist praxis as an educator. It underscores the importance of reflexivity in this transition, and has prompted me to consider how to continue pushing at the boundaries of my teaching. As I continue to grapple with the distinction, if any, between my identity as a criticalist and a feminist, I leave this experience questioning the value of suppressing—or if it is even possible to dissociate from—my epistemological orientation, even when feeling the heightened sense of risk that comes with the constraints of junior faculty status. I now realize the need to more fully unpack the hesitation that prompted my first encounter with student philanthropy to be designed as cautiously as it was—because even within taking a tentative approach, promise as a feminist community engagement strategy emerged. I am anxious to re-vision pay it forward with the intentionally it deserves and further the possibilities of feminist student philanthropy.

References

Allan, E., & Iverson, S. V. (2004). Cultivating critical consciousness: Service-learning in higher education. *Inquiry: Critical Thinking Across Disciplines, 23*(1–2), 51–61.

Baumgardener, J., & Richards, A. (2005). *Grassroots: A field guide for feminist activism*. New York: Farrar, Straus and Giroux.

Bickford, D. M., & Reynolds, N. (2002). Activism and service-learning: Reframing volunteerism as acts of dissent. *Pedagogy: Critical Approaches to Teaching Literature, Language, Composition, and Culture, 2*(2), 229–252.

Boyer, E. (1996). The scholarship of engagement. *Journal of Public Service and Outreach, 1*(1), 11–20.

Butin, D. W. (2003). Of what use is it? Multiple conceptualizations of service learning within education. *Teachers College Record, 105,* 1674–1692.

――― (2005). Service-learning as a postmodern pedagogy. In D. W. Butin (Ed.), *Service learning in higher education* (pp. 89–104). New York, NY: Palgrave Macmillan.

――― (2010). *Service-learning in theory and practice: The future of community engagement in higher education*. New York, NY: Palgrave Macmillan.

Campus Compact. (2014). Who we are. Retrieved May 19, 2014 from http://www.compact.org/about/history-mission-vision/

Chen, H. C., McAdams-Jones, D., Tay, D. L., & Packer, J. M. (2012). The impact of service-learning on students' cultural competence. *Teaching and Learning in Nursing, 7,* 67–73.

Cipolle, S. B. (2010). *Service-learning and social justice: Engaging students in social change*. New York, NY: Rowman & Littlefield.

Conway, J. M., Amel, E. M., & Gerwein, D. P. (2009). Teaching and learning in the social context: A meta-analysis of service learning's effects on academic, personal, social and citizenship outcomes. *Teaching of Psychology, 36,* 233–245. doi:10.1080/00986280903172969

Damon-Moore, H. (2000). The history of women and service in the United States: A rich and complex heritage. In B. J. Balliet & K. Heffernan (Eds.), *The practice of change: Concepts and models for service-learning in women's studies* (pp. 46–55). AAHE's Series on Service-Learning in the Disciplines.

Einfeld, A., & Collins, D. (2008). The relationship between service learning, social justice, multicultural competence and civic engagement. *Journal of College Student Development, 49,* 95–109. doi:10.1353/csd.2008.0017.

Eyler, J., & Giles, D. E., Jr. (1999). *Where's the learning in service-learning?* San Francisco, CA: Jossey-Bass.

Freire, P. (2000/1970). *Pedagogy of the oppressed*. New York, NY: Continuum.

Giroux, H. A. (1983). *Theory and resistance in education: A pedagogy for the opposition*. Westport, CT: Bergin & Garvey.

Hartley, M., Harkavy, I., & Benson, L. (2005). Putting down roots in the groves of academe: The challenges of institutionalizing service-learning. In D. W. Butin (Ed.), *Service learning in higher education* (pp. 205–222). New York, NY: Palgrave Macmillan.

Astin, A. W., Vogelgesang, L. J., Ikeda, E. K., & Yee, J. A. (2000). *How service learning affects students: Executive summary*. Los Angeles, CA: University of California, Higher Education Research Institute.

hooks, b. (1994). *Teaching to transgress.* New York, NY: Routledge.
Iverson, S. V. (2012). Multicultural competence for doing social justice: Expanding our awareness, knowledge, and skills. *Journal of Critical Thought and Praxis, 1,* 62–87.
Iverson, S. V., & James, J. H. (2013). Self-authoring a civic identity: A qualitative study of change-oriented service-learning. *Journal of Student Affairs Research and Practice, 50*(1), 88–105.
Jacoby, B. and Associates. (2003). *Building partnerships for service-learning.* San Francisco, CA: Jossey-Bass.
James, J. H., & Iverson, S. V. (2009). Striving for critical citizenship in a teacher education program: Problems and possibilities. *Michigan Journal of Community Service Learning, 16*(1), 33–46.
Kezar, A. (2002). Assessing community service learning: Are we identifying the right outcomes? *About Campus, 7,* 14–20.
Kinefuchi, E. (2010). Critical consciousness and critical service-learning at the intersection of the personal and the structural. *Journal of Applied Learning in Higher Education, 2,* 77–93.
McCarthy, K. D. (1996). Women and philanthropy. *Voluntas: International Journal of Voluntary and Nonprofit Organizations, 7*(4), 331–335.
Miles, M., & Huberman, A. M. (1994). *Qualitative data analysis: An expanded sourcebook of new methods* (2nd ed.). Newbury Park, CA: Sage.
Naples, N. A., & Bojar, K. (Eds.). (2002). *Teaching feminist activism: Strategies from the field.* New York: Routledge.
Novak, E. M. (1999). Service learning is a feminist issue. *Women's Studies in Communication, 22,* 230–240.
Ohio Campus Compact. (2014). Pay-It-Forward: History. Retrieved May 19, 2014 from http://www.ohiocampuscompact.org/programs/pay-it-forward/history/
Olberding, J. C. (2009). "Indirect giving" to non-profit organizations: An emerging model of student philanthropy. *Journal of Public Affairs Education, 15*(4), 463–492.
——— (2012). Does student philanthropy work? A study of long-term effects of the "Learning by Giving" approach. *Innovative Higher Education, 37,* 71–87.
Ostrander, S. A. (2004). Moderating contradictions of feminist philanthropy: Women's community organizations and the Boston Women's Fund, 1995 to 2000. *Gender & Society, 18*(1), 29–46.
——— (2005). Legacy and promise for social justice funding: Charitable foundations and social justice movements, past and present. In D. R. Faber & D. McCarthy (Eds.), *Foundations for social change: Critical perspectives on philanthropy and popular movements* (pp. 33–58). Lanham: Rowman & Littlefield.
Reckhow, S., & Snyder, J. W. (2014). The expanding role of philanthropy in education politics. *Educational Researcher, 43*(4), 186–195.
Rubin, H. J., & Rubin, I. S. (2005). *Qualitative interviewing: The art of hearing data* (2nd ed.). Thousand Oaks: SAGE Publications.

Santoro, D. (2010). Teaching to save the world: Avoiding circles of certainty in social justice education. *Philosophy of Education Archive*, 241–249.

Sifers, S. K. (2012). Reflecting on teaching through reflective service-learning: A pedagogical journey. *Reflective Practice, International and Multidisciplinary Perspectives, 13*, 651–661.

The Sillerman Center for the Advancement of Philanthropy. (2014). Engaging a new generation of philanthropists: Findings from the Pay It Forward student philanthropy initiative. The Heller School for Social Policy and Management, Brandeis University. Available at: http://sillermancenter.brandeis.edu/PDFs/Engaging%20a%20New%20Generation%20Full.pdf.

Steinem, G. (1983). *Outrageous acts and everyday rebellions*. New York: Holt, Rinehart and Winston.

Trigg, M., & Balliet, B. J. (2000). Learning across boundaries: Women's studies, praxis, and community service. In B. J. Balliet & K. Heffernan (Eds.), *The practice of change: Concepts and models for service-learning in women's studies* (pp. 87–102). AAHE's Series on Service-Learning in the Disciplines.

Walker, T. (2000). A feminist challenge to community service: A call to politicize service-learning. In B. J. Balliet & K. Heffernan (Eds.), *The practice of change: Concepts and models for service-learning in women's studies* (pp. 25–38). AAHE's Series on Service-Learning in the Disciplines.

Westheimer, J., & Kahne, J. (2004). What kind of citizen? The politics of education for democracy. *American Educational Research Journal, 41*, 237–269. doi: 10.3102/00028312041002237

CHAPTER 8

The Personal Is the Political: Community Engagement with Men as Feminist Border Crossing

Lamea "Elle" Shaaban-Magaña and Melanie L. Miller

Introduction

The slogan "the personal is the political" popularized throughout the 1960s and 1970s in the United States served as one of the quintessential expressions characterizing important aspects of the Second Wave of the women's liberation movement and aligning more women with the cause. Rooted within feminist ideologies, the phrase was an early challenge to reject binary delineations of the public/private divides, which served to uphold gender oppression, calling instead for recognition of macro-structures as they interact with the life experiences of women and girls.

This chapter orbits this maxim to explore how our university women's center's community engagement with men and boys was, and continues to be, a space for traversing conceptual geographies and simple dualisms. Using feminist research and pedagogies, we negotiate ongoing "border crossings" (Anzaldúa, 1987). We, and our male allies, are challenged with navigating the entanglements of the mutable, often competing boundaries between personal/political, past/present, staff/educator/student roles, service/activism, institution/community, insider/outsider, and the complexity of interactions of self-making/being made. Through our application of this feminist lens we explore a new terrain of politicized community engagement based in a foundation of activism and social justice designed to disrupt traditional constructions of manhood and boyhood. We seek to deepen our understanding of the "messiness" (Lather, 2007) of community engagement that endeavors to live in the in-between in order to contribute to a more equitable society.

Border Crossing/Methodological Considerations

Within this chapter we place ourselves, as well as the students and our community partner, a local elementary school, as multiple centers of inquiry. Using one university women's center's school-based mentoring program with men and boys, we deconstruct our practices and outcomes to foreground our feminist framework. We understand our investigation as an accountability mechanism to make transparent both content and process, baring the construction of our work as part of a nexus of ever-evolving, critical and emancipatory "feminist projects" with politicized agendas to challenge sexist ideologies and practices (Code, 1991; Harding, 1987).

From a legacy of feminist qualitative research traditions, we acknowledge the interconnectedness of researcher positions to this inquiry, and challenge the feasibility or desirability of neutral and objective research. Feminist poststructural methodology encourages the practice of ongoing interrogation as a generative tool. Patti Lather (2007) offers, "It is about seeing ambivalence and difference not as obstacles, but as the very richness of meaning-making and the hope of whatever justice we might work toward" (p. 115). We use "productive disruption" as a tool to offer "truths" of our text and explore the possibilities of community engagement as a conduit for feminist activism (Lather, 2007). We draw from qualitative research methods placing direct observation, document analysis, discursive analysis and survey method in conversation.

Drawing from our experiences as university women's center staff members intricately involved in the administration and development of this program, we utilized a variety of data collection tools. One source of data was derived from our conversations with school personnel, our male coordinators, and student participants. Another source of data was based on field notes and weekly post-session reflection papers documented by program coordinators. Discursive analysis (Lather, 1991, 2007) was applied to the language and content of curriculum modules and program materials such as promotional brochures and websites. Additional data were gathered through student participant surveying at different stages of their experience. We examined our data using a feminist poststructural lens that holds the intertwining of language, discourse, power relations, resistance, lived experience, and gender as key features. Within this theoretical tradition, multiple and fluid subjectivities (or self-in relation) are foregrounded over the notion of fixed "identity."

We combine these methodological approaches with the metaphor of "border crossing" as an interpretive device rooted in critical race feminist scholarship (Anzaldúa, 1987; hooks, 1984; Mohanty, 2003; Narayan & Harding; 1998). Scholar Gloria Anzaldúa (1987) introduced this conceptual "Borderlands" theory, now often circulated within feminist scholarship. She (Anzaldúa, 1987) wrote, "A borderland is a vague and undetermined place created by the emotional residue of an unnatural boundary. It is in a constant state of tension" (p. 357). Anzaldúa (1987, 1990) moves beyond a description of a geographic border, and explodes any understanding of the border as fixed and clearly delineated. Instead she theorizes an ideological border as a state of "in-between," partially outside and partially inside, overlapping, a space of recovery and discovery, negotiation, transition, and ambiguity.

Background: The Women's Center Past/Present

Feminist philosophers Nelson and Nelson (1994) offer, "We start, all of us, always, in the middle of ongoing histories of inquiry" (p. 500). Our scholarly examination relies on our years of work, crossing more than 18 years as women's center directors at a large, public research university in the Southeast United States. We explore border crossing in our negotiations in and with our men's activism initiatives. These have varied in scope and focus, from our early antiviolence groups with males, to the present configuration as the Young Men's Leadership Program (YMLP), a multilayered school-based community mentoring program.

In situating our community engagement, we are clear our movement did not travel from a space of the ahistorical, or a single history. Instead we acknowledge the complexity of the past with the present. As women were mobilized by the consciousness-raising of the liberal feminist movement, women's centers began to emerge during the 1970s at institutions of higher education across the United States. These centers organized to respond to the complex political issues brought to the forefront of the feminist movement of this period. Women's centers provided a space for female students, faculty, and staff to gather to socialize, support, and educate themselves and others (Bengiveno, 2000; Davie, 2002).

While the number of female students now typically outnumbers those of male students attending colleges and universities, shifts in campus landscapes have not seen the elimination of the pervasive sexist concerns that served as a catalyst for the emergence of early women's centers. Most service-oriented centers, which account for the majority of North American women's centers, continue to address many of these original concerns by offering direct client services, and programming efforts to address the needs of women (Boyd, Cavicchia, Lonnquist, Morrow, Robbins, Seaholes, & Wies, 2009). Our center followed a similar path, under Melanie's directorship from 1995 to 2007, then under Elle, as Melanie's successor and the current director. While nonfeminist models of organizational leadership often delineate the "beginning" or "end" of particular services or programs, we recognize this as one of many false tidy perimeters. We acknowledge our roots in a political and social movement as a landscape of historical melding. We transgress borders of linear historicity toward an ongoing becoming and being in and through our community engagement projects.

In 2008, 15 years into the establishment of our center, we, along with our colleagues across the United States, were addressing many of the same initial concerns. Despite employing a multitude of efforts to eliminate the material, social, psychological, and culturally disfiguring effects of patriarchy, they persisted. Robin Kelly (2002) posed, "movements in struggle produce new knowledge and new questions" (p. 152). We were challenged to examine our services and programs, to explore the "ruins" (Lather, 1991) of our feminist ideologies and practices.

Tension and Strand: Feminist Work with Men

In an effort to dig through to our feminist roots, we closely examined our practices of who and how we approached our work, with the ultimate goal of building a more equitable society. We transgressed borders we may have erected ourselves, looking inward as a means of looking outward. What were the remnants of our ideological and methodological delineations that we were unwilling to see, or give up, that limited our movement? As has been critically raised within feminist community engagement work, who was and is the "we" of our work (Ticineto & Fine, 2007)? How did and do we frame and imagine the locus of our work, or define our constituents? Were our feminisms malleable enough to accommodate a "feminist promiscuity" (Childers, Rhee, & Daza, 2013) that exceeds boundaries previously imposed? Were we able to move our center from programs to and for women and girls to include community engagement with men and boys?

Childers et al. (2013) suggest we can engage a feminist wandering to question "what counts" as feminist research and "how its displacement is an investment in its becoming" (p. 518). What would it mean for our women's center to cross this particular border? The founding mission of the center was "to improve campus awareness and responsiveness to women's issues."

Was this work with men consistent with the intended mission and/or our feminist values? Who had the authority to decide?

Inspired by "pro-feminist" men's activism (Katz, 2006; Kaufmann, 1994; Kimmel, 1992; Kivel, 1999; Stoltenberg, 1989), in 1994, our center's early programs included outreach to engage men as part of our commitment to gender justice. Were we "cheating" on or betraying (Childers et al., 2013) our feminisms by focusing on male subjects? Was this an example of progress or a reifying of institutional programs characterized by patriarchal agenda setting? We troubled questions of insider/outsider locations as we "invited" our male students, to come "into" the women's movement as allies. Whose place was it to do the asking? Were the men not already deeply embedded within these same circulating systems? How would an expansion to men's activism in our movement impact circulating power relations? With a feminist ear to the Foucaultian (1984) warning that, "Not everything is bad, but everything is dangerous" (p. 343) and given limited human, financial, and other resources (Clevenger, 1988; Kasper, 2004), was this something we could "afford" to extend? Could we afford not to? Our decisions could only be guided from knowledges that were and are, partial.

History of Our Campus Men's Programs

Programs, such as our initial men's program the "Gentlemen's Agreement" peer education group, were designed to engage male students on campus in increasing awareness of interpersonal violence against women. The program mobilized characteristics of feminist activism and organizing (Faver, 1994; Joseph, Lob, McLaughlin, Mizrah, Peterson, Rosenthal, & Sugarman, 1991) such as emphasis on consciousness-raising and social action. However, the project was anchored in personal responsibility models rather than social responsibility models. Heavy emphasis was placed on individual male behavior without sufficient attention to the pervasive, systemic rape culture. They also centered on problematic notions of "civility" and "men's honor" framing males as extending themselves *on behalf of* females, rather than *alongside* women and girls. This program, and our similar programs that followed, operationalized the underpinnings of systems that we wanted to dismantle.

We were looking for new models and methods to accommodate our "new" knowledges. Susan Geiger (1990) posed, "A feminist researcher's methodology must be receptive to strains, and strains in the overall process, even where 'strain' has a double meaning as simultaneously tension and strand" (p. 407). While we were energized by an optimism of expanding our movement to a broader base of activists, we were simultaneously cautious, even unsure, about the implications of this move.

Working the Ruins: The Young Men's Leadership Program

Our center's early programs with men provided a platform for entry into a broader feminist reach. Fueled by a 'feminist imaginary' (Ticineto & Fine, 2007, p. 258), in our current model, initiated in 2008, we worked through and within this transitional, yet hopeful, space and made the decision to cross a border beyond our strictly campus-based programs "into" the community with the establishment of the YMLP. Modeled loosely after our campus Young Women's Leaders Program, founded at The University of Virginia, we developed our own YMLP curriculum from a range of materials, including scholarly literature and activities to explicitly address gender construction. YMLP paired (and still pairs) young boys and men to explore issues of self-identity and interpersonal relationships. The program focuses on nontraditional male leadership models by encouraging the participants to build on core values of authenticity, respect, and celebrating strength of character, as opposed to physical strength. After an application and interview process to identify and select a diverse group of participants, we form a group of ten to twelve male undergraduate students to serve as mentors to fifth-grade boys from a local elementary school. Mentors are asked to make a one-year commitment.

In the fall, the mentor "Big Brothers" attend ten weekly, two-hour training sessions with structured exercises. These begin to challenge hegemonic masculinity, encourage participants' self-reflection, and promote introspection on the damaging aspects of the socialization of men and boys leading to a sexist culture. During this semester, we facilitate relationship-building among the group members, helping them develop strategies and practice exercises to build rapport with their mentees. The curriculum explores the construction of masculinities and gender roles, and the implications on the lived experiences of boys and men. Selected training topics in the semester include: listening and communication (including sociocultural expectations for masculine restricted emotionality); risk, violence, and socially endorsed tests of courage; identity, difference, and intersectionality; male power and privilege; masculinity, the continuum of harm, and interpersonal violence; ally development and social justice activism.

After completion of the fall semester and a kick-off weekend retreat, bringing together returning and newly trained participants, each student mentor is paired with a fifth-grade boy for the spring. The fifth-graders are recommended for participation by a teacher or school counselor. After school, mentoring sessions are held weekly for an hour-and-half at the elementary school. Each meeting is divided into several components: (1) an introduction to the day's topic, (2) time for each "Big"/"Little Brother" pair to have snacks and discuss the topic one-on-one, and (3) group discussion and activity time.

While interactive exercises are used to form the foundations of the curriculum, we are also reminded of the importance of fun and food to the program. We understand this is not just a bonus, but an integral part of YMLP's richness. In our formalized evaluation of the program, many of the fifth-graders responded that snack time and spending time with their "Big" was the best part of their involvement. We do not read the emphasis on the food as a deficiency of the program, but acknowledge this as due in part to the contextual material realities of this student population.

Mindful of feminist pedagogical practices, the program is participatory, discussion based, and focused on developing participants' critical lens with which to read gender. Topics covered in this semester complement those of the undergraduate mentors, including issues such as: communication and feelings; reframing strength and what it means to be a "man"; identity, self-expression, and self-esteem; exploring difference; goals for the future; and violence prevention. The undergraduate and fifth-grade topic titles reflect the parallel issues and content throughout the curriculum between the two training groups, but contain developmentally appropriate language. For example, the session entitled "Stepping Up as an Ally" in the undergraduate materials was introduced as "My Strength Is Not for Hurting" with the fifth-graders.

The program curriculum intentionally pushes the bounds on previous knowledge gained toward increasingly reflective exercises. For example, the mentors and mentees watch and discuss films used to contest normative frames of masculinity. Jackson Katz' (1999) *Tough Guise: Violence, Media, and the Crisis in Masculinity*, is used to examine how media outlets endorse a guise, or performance, of a violent masculinity as an arbitrary concept of manhood that can and should be challenged. Following the film, participants reflect on their own gender socialization and complicity or engagement along a continuum of harm of sexist behavior, and the personal and societal costs of this.

Similarly, the film viewing and discussion of *Boys Will Be Men* (Weidlinger, 2001) creates an opportunity for participants to explore the complexities of development and growing up male in the United States. The film features clinical psychologist William Pollack commenting:

> Around the ages of 3 and 4 to 5 and 6, boys are prematurely pushed into what I call the "boy code." Put most simply, that's a code that tells boys that they should stand on their own two feet, cut Mama's apron strings

and be an independent person way before it's possible to really achieve that. (Weidlinger, 2001)

Following the film, the coordinator asks the group a series of questions, such as "What specific examples of the 'boy code' can you identify in your own experience?" or "What are some other ways in which parents and teachers teach boys about human emotions? Why is this important?"

Building on this knowledge, in the subsequent sessions, the young and older students explore sensitive and personal issues. Using Paul Kivel's (1999) "Act Like a Man Box" activity, the men and boys respond to questions of characteristics and behaviors commonly associated with being a man, where their ideas of manhood come from, and consequences of violating those norms. As a group they explore their experiences encountering the "man box." They examine limitations placed on boys and men to perform a traditionally celebrated masculinity that emphasizes physical strength, constrained emotional expression, competition over collaboration, and narrow understandings of "successful manhood" marked by sexual prowess and financial success. The close of the spring semester is honored by a group community service project selected by all participants, and a celebratory banquet, where friends and family members are invited.

Crossing Borders: Benefits and Impacts

The YMLP has allowed for a unique territory to explore the benefits of crossing borders. A value we see to our center is the opportunity to use the YMLP as a recruitment tool for men. As predicted, the men's interest increased as they saw an opportunity to "make a difference" in the lives of young boys. The motivations of the applicants are usually evenly split between men who report an understanding of their own privilege and "want to give back," and those who recall difficulties they have overcome in their own childhoods. For most of the men, the initial decision to participate is not articulated through discontent with normative masculinity and a desire to embrace a feminist orientation and worldview. The men are almost exclusively focused on the development of the fifth-grade boys. However, our goals are equally hinged on the education and development of both the men and boys. We hope to examine leadership and mentoring through a broader inquiry on the construction and enactment of gender and masculinities, and the impact of this on individuals and macro-systems.

In spite of these challenges, the remaking of self is common across the men's experiences and part of our reading of the success of YMLP. In closing reflections of their involvement with our center, the mentors speak to the personal significance of the program as changing the lens with which they now view themselves. For example, one male college student suggested, "I am a feminist and I didn't even know I could be one!" Another university student noted insightfully, "I had a lot to work on within myself. I needed to better myself to be able to reach out to the kids." Similarly, a student observed, "I learned just how much my own experiences as a child had affected my adulthood and how it impacted the man I am today." These remarks remind us that the process of forming a gendered self simultaneously pushes against constructions of dominant masculinity and "cultural tyranny" (Anzaldúa, 1987) while opening up to moments and spaces of reflection, resistance, and self-making.

We also interpret the strong connections the members develop for each other as a community across differences, as some of the most powerful elements of this project. As one university participant shared, "There is a very valuable experience learned through having a positive relationship with a mentee and that experience goes both ways. You are able to learn from one another and grow as either child or adult." Similarly, a mentee noted, "I enjoyed learning new things and spending time together." It is in this building of capacity that we acknowledge how the process of deconstructing and then reframing masculinities within and through community are intricately intertwined.

The transformation of YMLP on individual participants' lives and the ripple effect into their communities is evident, when postgraduation, college men provide testimony to the impact the program continues to have on them. One reflected, "I am a better husband and father because of my involvement in this group." Another wrote:

> I am an eighth grade teacher now. One day I shared with my students about my participation in YMLP when I was in college. Afterward, a female student in my class shared with me her history of abuse by a family member. I am so grateful for my training from YMLP, as I knew what to say to her and where to refer her for help.

These, and other conversations, reflect examples of how the men have applied their experiences in this program to gendered issues and their own relationships, long after their participation has ended.

The critical self-reflection facilitated through the program creates a space of alterity for the boys and men to reimagine themselves through the lens of possibility. One focus of the curriculum is on nontraditional forms of leadership. In the post-program evaluations the fifth-grade participants are asked "What makes a strong man?" and "What does it mean to be a leader?"

The boys often articulate the expression of emotion, concern for others, and showing respect as key qualities of a leader. For example, one child offered, "I found out that being a strong man means you should be respectful of others and that it is okay to let your feelings out." Similarly, another reported, "I can help my peers to do better. Caring makes me a strong leader."

Another measure of the curriculum impact is reflected in the boys embracing of nonviolent expressions of masculinity, as can be seen in one participant's response of "being a man means to respect women." Another offered that being a man "means being non-violent and aware of everybody's needs." Yet another said, "it is important to be kind and help others."

From the perspective of the community partner, the program has had tangible benefits. It has provided an after-school enrichment experience for a group of male students, within the context of the school, for over five years now. School personnel, often wary of the transient nature of many campus outreach efforts, value the collaborative communication developed between our women's center staff and the school administration. The fact that the program has continued for more than five years, speaks to the commitment of campus and community partners and the sustainability of the program. School staff members express how beneficial the structure of the program is in providing positive male role models through the mentor/mentee relationships and the value of particular curriculum topics.

For example, one curriculum session includes a panel discussion by prominent community men. One principal noted that this session has a powerful impact on the boys who typically identify their only career options as limited to choices like "professional athlete." She noted that presenting them with the narratives of men such as local attorneys, educators, and police chiefs, who are also representative of the communities in which the boys live, opens their worldview to other possibilities and connects them to the advantages of education.

Another benefit for the school has been the ability to leverage the program to obtain additional funding. Due to the presence and strength of the YMLP, the school was able to use that partnership to obtain additional grant funds to support other enrichment programs. Recently, the school counselor asked if we could be contacted as one of their key partners by the school board's central office to share information about the "success of the program" and the building of our collaborative relationship.

Border Crossing: Lessons and Questions

Within these border travels, we have come to understand that our work is not easily defined or contained, but crosses through and within multiple domains. We operate in a constant state of negotiation and reinvention; however, we have used reflections to guide us through this movement. Our lessons learned include issues of staffing, program promotion, participation, curricular adjustments, building trust, and becoming/being in community.

Staffing

One of the earliest lessons learned centered on staffing of YMLP. This was, and continues to be, a point of unsettled terrain composed of the blending of material of "what could be" with "what is." We did not want to operate with frames of reductionist caricatures of male students, but did want to leave room for possibility. We worried that having a female coordinator could serve as an additional barrier resulting in silence, defensiveness, or guilt of the mentors over their own male privilege. We were concerned about the men censoring themselves to accommodate us or devaluing our ideas because we may be perceived by the participants as educators who did not understand their gendered experiences and realities. We wondered if they would perceive that as female feminists we may have unrealistic, optimistic goals. This sentiment was expressed by one new student facilitator recently as "pie-in-the-sky socialism" in response to learning of our feminist agenda of working toward broad gender equity.

While we have many qualified female staff facilitators, we made the choice to have a male graduate student in the role of facilitator/coordinator. We learned, through our experiences, the complexities of creating a learning environment to allow the group to dig deeply into the curriculum. Having a male peer facilitator to engage them, not in a distanced relationship with the material, but with an intimate look at their own subjectivities, privileges, and relationships, we believed would serve as a bridge to this difficult process.

Program Promotion

We are mindful of the complexity of language and its capacity to shape and reflect. We embrace strategic, yet admittedly problematic practices within the development and implementation of the program. We employ a tactic of "code-switching" (Delpit, 1995)—speaking the language of the dominant group—in our negotiations with the school. For example, we purposefully use the valuable currency of "mentoring" and "leadership" programs to gain access. In our promotion of the program, we intentionally emphasize vague references to "community," "service," and "leadership." This overused lingo glorified in the rhetoric of the institution has come to simultaneously encompass everything and nothing.

Similarly, at campus events, such as recruitment fairs, we use a separate information table to market the program to increase our appeal to potential male volunteers. We omit the word "feminist" in our descriptions of YMLP. This distancing ourselves from our feminisms is an ongoing contention in our work, with the desire to elevate our feminist identity within a climate of backlash, while acknowledging that most students, regardless of their gender identification, do not identify with feminism.

Participation

Another lesson is awareness of challenges to boys' participation, and how our efforts at inclusion might unwittingly reinforce dominant narratives we wish to disrupt. We do not want to contribute to the heavily circulated discourses of the "at-risk" or "underserved" children. Dominant discourses circulating within communities and institutions of education situate boys of color as monolithically oppressed or disadvantaged or dangerous. This is fueled by a "moral panic" of school violence (Barron & Lacombe, 2008; Killingbeck, 2001) and supported by pervasive ideology of "zero tolerance," characterized by a policy climate of strong institutional regulation (Armistead, 2008; Essex, 2004). Boys are alternately measured against competing neoliberal discourses which celebrate meritocracy and individual power, self-determination, and success, through embodiment of a particular masculinity that emphasizes an academically successful, active, and assertive athletic boy who can have it all.

To avoid reproducing these discourses, we market the program as geared to "children in the middle whose potential is not fully developed." This strategy also minimizes the probability that the only referrals to the program are already identified student "leaders" who have resources, and social and cultural capital to excel.

Yet, we also struggle with the choices of "middle" and "potential not fully developed" as eligibility descriptors. What implications do these have on border work of the self, at the margins? What does it signify to be "in the middle?" And in the middle of what and by whose estimation? What does it mean to simultaneously be "in the middle," and still in the margins, experiencing both hyper-visibility and invisibility? What does it mean to be a "mentor" or "mentee," given that there are no neutral words, and these are highly circulated within our educational systems? We complicate our understanding as we explore how the "community" of the school serves a particular container for bounding ourselves, the men and boys, and our interactions with each other.

To what extent does a grand narrative of improved opportunities and achievement—allegedly available to all students—dismiss recognition of barriers of access? How does this tacitly contribute to a stratified status quo of binaries of successful/unsuccessful masculinity, healthy/unhealthy boys, without acknowledging that overwhelmingly normative "successful" student discourses are read through White middle-class able-bodied students? In considering the interchange and border negotiations of self-making and being made of the fifth-grade boys, what are the implications for placing our community engagement work in relation to gender and these school practices? How are boys understood as educational subjects in need of mentoring? What implications does this have on boys' understandings of their own subjectivities and possibilities?

Finally, the boys' ability to persist in the program emerged as a concern. With a limited number of weeks to meet with the boys, an ongoing challenge was inconsistent program attendance of the fifth-grade boys due to school disciplinary actions, such as suspensions, based on alleged "violations." Educational institutions have often turned to the principles of behavior modification based on negative reinforcement and away from the advancement of prosocial behavior development to address behaviors now characterized as criminal and deviant (James & Freeze, 2006). This painful irony of boys being denied positive educational experiences thrives at the margins of a topography in which "opportunity" collides and co-constructs "regulation."

Curricular Adjustments

Within the negotiation of YMLP, we have pushed, and are continually, pushing at boundaries of roles within our center, as we understand that all of us and our curriculum are subjects-in-process, always in the making. We, as the program administrators and developers of the curriculum, usually view ourselves in the role of educators. Within the program; however, we have often become the student, taught by our facilitators, undergraduate and fifth-grade participants, and our school partners.

We have learned to let go of many of our original ideas. Our curriculum may be characterized as a dynamic document, with the coordinators providing input for ongoing adjustments. From our facilitators, we learned to trust them to honor the intent and goals of the work, even if the strategies are modified. They have sometimes politely, sometimes not so politely, provided feedback about the dissonance between the curriculum of our imaginations and the program in operation, the sometimes disconnect between theory and practice, and the powerful opportunities in the interstices when there is room for flexibility.

For example, we incorporated into the curriculum what we thought would be a way to encourage respectful communication during group discussion by incorporating the use of a "talking stick." The stick would be passed around, allowing the person holding the stick to present their ideas. While we thought this would be an excellent pedagogical tool, it proved unsuccessful. The stick became an object mocked by students, an imaginary sword, or other instrument for swinging. We had not considered the unhappiness of the school principal and counselor, at what appeared to them, as us bringing a weapon into the school. We realized that we had succumbed to our own stereotypes of how men and boys communicate and had not accounted for the very dynamic of respect that we sought to cultivate. As the group spent time together, they found in their own becomings, an emerging accountability to each other to regulate their larger group communication. The facilitator reinforced these effective group dynamics by mimicking classroom management techniques utilized by the school.

Building Trust

One of the most challenging yet crucial aspects of the program is creating an environment and interactions with each other that disarms the male posturing commonly used to distance themselves from difficult, emotional topics. We ask that the men and boys engage wholly with the content. In his field notes, one of the coordinators reflected, "It has been a rough few weeks because we had to discuss intense topics, many of which challenged our opinions and beliefs." As center directors we have to resist wanting to step in and immediately resolve silences or tensions, or "fix" the curriculum to avoid the men's resistance to new ideas. A coordinator noted, "Some of the guys were quiet. I noticed they didn't want to bring any attention to themselves, giving off the 'whatever' vibe like they didn't care. I know that's not true as they are present and committed to the program." We struggle with the realization that the students absorbing the content in their own way and timeframe is a necessary part of the process, and is more productive than lecturing. Their encounters with self-making and being made are highlighted as the men and boys grapple with their individual and collective apprehensions over negotiating these expectations as they are challenged to explore alternative conceptions of masculinities.

Becoming/Being in "Community"

Ideally, we seek to operationalize principles of feminist organizing to emphasize the strengths of participants' contributions and the empowerment of individuals and community, while acknowledging these at the margins of structural oppression (Mizrahi, 2007). Our desire is to promote a transformational process for change based on collaboration, inclusiveness, and shared problem-solving. We deploy strategies to move from a simplistic, nostalgic understanding of community service, to engage spaces of activism related to a deeper historical and culturally embedded feminist activist project. We work toward possibilities that are in-line with our feminist understandings of a reciprocal community engagement, taking into account that complicated questions of uncertainties and insecurities are part of our "strain" (Geiger, 1990).

As we enter "into" the broader community, we question what it means for us to conceptualize ourselves as originally somehow apart? Are we moving from an imaginary location and position, to a bounded "other" space? What implications does the conceptualization and articulation of us as separate entities imply for our feminist work? How do we balance this with the reality that our predominantly White and middle- to upper-class students do not reflect the larger demographic of our broader population and school? Our demographics reflect a large economically disadvantaged Black community and growing Latino population.

How can we acknowledge the complex histories of the university with the broader "community"? We are aware of a long legacy of racist university practices, as well as an embracing of philanthropic frameworks of community engagement that often enacted "White savior" notions of community work. What does it take and signify for us to reconceptualize ourselves as part of this community? Whose decision is this to make? How can we develop the program to acknowledge varying levels of privilege, while not invoking us/them or benefactor/recipient binaries?

While aware of these difficulties, we do not let them paralyze our movement forward. An important premise of our community engagement work in schools focuses on contributing to positive social change addressing issues of sexism, racism, classism, and other forms of oppression, using a strengths-based perspective. This framework emphasizes the ability of young people, their families, and communities to recognize internal strengths and identify resources, with a holistic focus on the complexities of real-life experiences. Offering a counter-narrative to traditional deficit models, this perspective acknowledges there are challenges and problems to be addressed; however, it provides a different lens to examine these. Resonant with feminist organizing practices, a strengths-based model views both process and product as constitutive elements of a capacity-building paradigm (Cowger, 1994; Grant & Cadell, 2009).

Conclusions

We appreciate that we are not just simply moving away *from* positivist research traditions, histories of "charity basket" (Donahue, 2000) style community engagement, but moving *toward and within* communities of equity and nonviolence, strengths-based engagement models, and alternative forms of gendered being. From 2008 through the present we have sustained a program that has contributed to the expanded consciousness raising of more than 100 men and boys. It has enriched our collaborative relationships with community partners and expanded our impact in doing gender-focused social justice work.

As our feminist activism has moved to position itself beyond the pedagogical comfort of an academic environment, into the less familiar structure of communities we have made several adaptations to our program model as a result of our ongoing negotiations regarding both process and product. These can serve as a catalyst for women's centers or community organizations wanting to engage men as allies. For example, the topical, interactive curriculum that has evolved provides an effective tool for stimulating transformative self-examination and critical analysis of traditional definitions of masculinity in the development of both college men and younger boys. The training modules, developed and revised over the course of several years, for our male university student mentors, provide a safe space for participating in thoughtful discussions that allow them to make meaning of their own identity development before they enter into communities to mentor others. Such a tool would lend itself for adaptation by those wishing to implement a similar mentoring model.

Feminist activists and community collaborators involved in programs that address equity in gender roles can gain insight from the lessons learned by program staff through the evolution of this university/community partnership. Gender-based programs exploring expansion into community engagement can benefit from attention to the boundary issues reflected in this analysis. Community partners can utilize this program model to examine opportunities to assist university staff and students in identifying community strengths and exploring the creation of spaces to promote honest reflection and mutual, transformative learning for sustainable partnerships.

Through examination of this mentoring model of community engagement work with men and boys, we are left with some questions that warrant further attention. We wonder, how can this model of working with men as allies be applied to other feminist engagement work? Can the framework of "border crossing" be helpful in explaining the challenges of other types of community engagement? How can, and is it necessary, for feminists to reconcile the negotiation of certain border crossings with traditional feminist ideology and values? Our experiences can provide a platform for the broadening of both practical and pedagogical knowledge while extending the conversation.

In response to the question, "What might be gained by bringing a feminist lens to the work of community engagement?" we affirm that while we may not be able to deliver a wide-scale revolution in and through our men's mentoring program, we cross borders to invoke a feminist praxis for community engagement with possibilities of infinite becomings. We aspire to transgress boundaries with the commitment of Anzaldúa's (1987) border "mestiza" of whom the author notes, "She communicates that rupture, documents the struggle. She reinterprets history and, using new symbols, she shapes new myth" (p. 104). We point to the transformative impact in the lives of ourselves, our students, our center, and our community. Our work serves to expose power relationships and helps to empower our males to implicate themselves as part of the solution to enact personal and systemic change.

We hold personally meaningful the opportunity to be part of a continuing legacy of feminist resistance to build critical counter-narratives of individual and community transformation. YMLP has given us ground to maintain a sense of optimism and meaning making despite being committed to the sometimes overwhelming work of dismantling pervasive social inequities. This work has provided a space to apply our scholarship in a way that is not in the abstract or purely theoretical, but is entrenched in real lived experience. We continue to be inspired by the connections we have made to remarkable boys and men as they, and we, have grown in our knowledge of ourselves and others.

References

Anzaldúa, G. E. (1987). *Borderlands/la frontera: The new mestiza*. San Francisco: Aunt Lute Books.

Armistad, R. B. (2008). Zero tolerance: The school woodshed. *Education Week*, 27(41), 24–26.

Ball, S. (1994). *Education reform: A critical and post-structural approach*. Buckingham: Open University Press.

Barron, C., & Lacombe, D. (2008). Moral panic and the nasty girl. *The Canadian Review of Sociology*, 42(1), 51–69.

Bengiveno, T. A. (2000). Feminist consciousness and the potential for change in campus based student staffed women's centers. *Journal of International Women's Studies, 1*(1), 1–11.
Boyd, C., Cavicchia, J., Lonnquist, P., Morrrow, R., Robbins, C., Seaholes, C., & Wies, J. (2009). The role of women student programs and services: CAS standards contextual statement. In L. A. Dean (Ed.), *CAS professional standards for higher education* (7th ed.) (pp. 390–392). Washington, DC: Council for the Advancement of Standards in Higher Education.
Childers, S., Rhee, J., & Daza, S. L. (2013). Promiscuous (use of) feminist methodologies: The dirty theory and messy practice of educational research beyond gender. *International Journal of Qualitative Studies in Education, 26*(5), 507–523.
Clevenger, B. M. (1988). Women centers on campus: A profile. *Initiatives, 51*(2/3), 3–9.
Code, L. (1991). *What can she know? Feminist theory and the construction of knowledge.* Ithaca, NY: Cornell University Press.
Cowger, C. D. (1994). Assessing client strengths: Clinical assessment for client empowerment. *Social Work, (39)*3, 262–268.
Davie, S. L. (Ed.). (2002). *University and college women's centers: A journey toward equity.* Westport, CT: Greenwood Press.
Delpit, L. (1995). *Other people's children: Cultural conflict in the classroom.* New York: The New Press.
Donahue, D. M. (2000). Charity basket or revolution: Beliefs, experiences, and context in preservice teachers' service learning. *Curriculum Inquiry, 30*(4), 429–450.
Essex, N. L. (2004). Student dress codes using zero tolerance? *Education Digest, 84,* 54–57.
Faver, C. A. (1994). Feminist ideology and strategies for social change: An analysis of social movements. *Journal of Applied Social Sciences, 18,* 123–134.
Foucault, M. (1984). On the genealogy of ethics: An overview of work in progress. In R. Rabinow (Ed.), *The Foucault reader* (pp. 340–372). New York, NY: Pantheon Books.
Geiger, S. (1990). What's so feminist about women's oral history? *Journal of Women's History, (2)*1, 169–182.
Grant, J. G., & Cadell, S. (2009). Power, pathological worldviews, and the strengths perspective in social work. *Families in Society, 90*(4), 425–430.
Harding, S. (1987). Introduction: Is there a feminist method? In S. Harding (Ed.), *Feminism and methodology* (pp. 1–14). Bloomington, IN: Indiana Press.
hooks, b. (1984). *Feminist theory: From margin to center.* Boston: South End Press.
James, S., & Freeze, R. (2006). One step forward, two steps back: Immanent critique of the practice of zero tolerance in inclusive schools. *International Journal of Inclusive Education, 10*(6), 581–594.
Joseph, B., Lob, S., McLaughlin, P., Mizrah,T., Peterson, J., Rosenthal, B., & Sugarman, F. (1991). *A framework for feminist organizing: Values, goods, methods, strategies, and role.* New York, NY: Education Center for Community Organizing.

Kasper, B. (2004). Campus-based women's centers: Administration, structure, and resources. *NASPA Journal, 41*(3), 487–499.
Katz, J. (Director), (1999). *Tough guise: Violence, media, and the crisis in masculinity.* [Documentary]. Media Education Foundation.
Katz, J. (2006). *The macho paradox: Why some men hurt women and how all men can help.* Naperville, IL: Sourcebooks.
Kaufman, M. (1994). *Cracking the armour: Power, pain, and the lives of men.* New York: Penguin Press.
Kelly, R. D. (2002). *Freedom dreams; The Black radical imagination.* Boston: Beacon Press.
Killingbeck, D. (2001). The role of television news in the construction of school violence as a "moral panic." *Journal of Criminal Justice and Popular Culture, 8*(3), 186–202.
Kimmel, M. (1992). *Against the tide: Pro-feminist men in the U.S., 1776–1990.* Boston, MA: Beacon Press.
Kivel, P. (1999). *Boys will be men.* British Columbia, Canada: New Society Publishers.
Lather, P. (2007). *Getting lost: Feminist efforts toward a double(d) science.* Albany: State University of New York Press.
────── (1991). *Getting smart: Feminist research and pedagogy with/in the postmodern.* New York, NY: Routledge.
Mizrahi, T. (2007). Women's ways of organizing: Strengths and struggles of women activists over time. *Affilia, 22*(1), 39–55.
Mohanty, C. (2003). *Feminism without borders: Decolonizing theory, practicing solidarity.* New York: Duke University Press.
Narayan, U., & Harding, S. (1998). Introduction. Border crossings: Multicultural and postcolonial feminist challenges to philosophy (part I). *Hypatia, 13*(1), 1–6. doi: 10.1111/j.1527-2001.1998.tb01222
Nelson, J., & Nelson, L. H. (1994). No rush to judgment. *The Monist, 77*(4), 486–508.
Stoltenberg, J. (1989). *Refusing to be a man: Essays on sex and justice.* Portland, OR: Breitenbush.
Ticineto. C. P., & Fine, M. (2007). Activism and pedagogies: Feminist reflections. *Women's Studies Quarterly, 35*(3/4), 255–275.
Weidlinger, T. (Director), (2001). *Boys will be men.* [Documentary]. Bullfrog Films.

CHAPTER 9

Moving from Theory to Practice: The Rocxxy Summer Internship in Feminist Activism and Leadership

Angela Clark-Taylor, Quinlan Mitchell, and KaeLyn Rich

Introduction

The University of Rochester's Susan B. Anthony Institute for Gender and Women's Studies (SBAI) houses a women's studies major, minor, and three concentrations: women, gender, and sexuality studies. As an institute, we provide services beyond the scope of an academic department, offering unique opportunities and support to students and faculty interested in feminist scholarship across disciplines. At SBAI we encourage students to participate in internships and other volunteer activities with the aim of promoting experiential learning, directly correlating their extracurricular activities with academic coursework. Until recently, however, we did not provide students an opportunity to directly participate in feminist activism.

Over the past five years, students, staff, and faculty have discussed this missing (and integral) piece of feminist curriculum. SBAI's approach was to utilize staff to connect students with meaningful volunteer and internship opportunities. As our alumni grew, however, we began to hear more and more stories of students who, despite the opportunities offered through the institute, became confounded or disillusioned with nonprofit and institutionalized activist work after college. We also heard from current students that they and their peers were eager for opportunities to participate in feminist activism, but didn't know where to start. In response to this student and alumni feedback, SBAI was inspired to construct a program that would introduce current students to activist work and create a space where they could reflect on their experiences. What developed was the *Rocxxy*—inspired by Rochester (Roc), the University's mascot Rocky, and inclusive of all sexes and genders (xxy)—*Summer Internship in Feminist Activism and Leadership.*

In this chapter we offer a description of the curriculum, as well as the strengths and challenges in implementing the Rocxxy program. We will briefly discuss women's studies inherent mission as a site of feminist activism as well as look at the value of using feminist pedagogy in engaging all students in activist work. It is important to note that the authors of this chapter include the instructor, a student, and a site supervisor of the Rocxxy program. Each author brings a radically difference lens to the analysis of mutually shared experience. Sharing our experiences from this formative evaluation of the Rocxxy pilot program will add to the growing dialogue on feminist student engagement and best practices for implementing similar programs.

Women's Studies as a Site for Social Change

In the 1960s, women's studies courses began to appear in colleges and universities across the country (Ginsberg, 2008). In 1970, the first official women's studies program began at San Diego State University (Ginsberg, 2008). Situated within the context of the academy, "women's studies had a very clear purpose to transform the university so that knowledge about women was no longer invisible, marginalized, or made 'other'" (p. 10). Boxer states that "from the beginning, the goal of women's studies was not merely to study women's position in the world but to change it" (as cited in Ginsberg, 2008, p. 10). Although a majority of women's studies scholars agree on this as a general purpose of feminism, they do not agree on how to implement this in the women's studies curriculum.

Bubriski and Semaan (2009) assert that teaching and discussing feminist literature written by and about women does constitute activism, pointing out that integrating women's and gender studies into college and university curricula is a radical act and an important step toward broader social change. Yet, they argue that women's studies programs must see promoting feminist scholarship as a beginning point, not an end, adding, "Course readings and classroom discussions are critical for understanding feminist discourse and analysis, but we must also teach students to merge feminist theory with social action in order to transform systemic gender, class, and race inequalities" (Bubriski & Semaan, 2009, p. 91). We must go a step further than consciousness-raising to encourage students to implement what they are learning about social inequality and social change in their communities.

Rocxxy: Summer Internship in Feminist Activism and Leadership

When we piloted the Rocxxy program in summer 2013, the integration of theory and practice was our main goal. The program was 12 weeks in length and open to all undergraduate students at the University of Rochester. Rocxxy combined a professional internship experience with visits from guest speakers, field trips to historic sites, and reflection on feminist activism and leadership. This combination of academic, experiential, and professional experience was meant to inspire students to become stronger, more resilient agents of social change upon graduation as well as equip them with the necessary skills for realizing feminist ideals in their post-college lives.

A cohort of four students (three female and one male) participated in the pilot program. Many of the applicants had taken women's studies courses, but none of the four selected was a women's studies major or minor. The cohort was comprised of three sophomores and one senior. Three of the students self-identified as people of color. Two of the students were originally from the greater Rochester area, one was living on campus due to another summer program, and the last student was residing in off-campus housing. At the end of the Rocxxy program, one student declared a women's studies minor.

Rocxxy members worked for 20 hours per week for the 12-week summer semester—May 20 to August 9. Internship sites were located at Rochester nonprofits that address social justice issues related to sex, gender, or sexual orientation. The community partner internship sites were also selected due to their ability to provide students with a feminist-identified internship supervisor. On Fridays, students met for the day and participated in group reflections, reading discussions, speaker series events, or field trips to historic sites. Throughout the summer, we encouraged students to keep a journal reflecting on their overall experiences in the community and in the cohort. The instructor received copies of all journal entries at the end of the semester. Students did not receive course credit or pay for the internship.

Developing the Rocxxy Curriculum

While designing the Rocxxy curriculum, six theoretical perspectives were woven into the core of its framework: (1) dialectic practices (Stanley, 1990),

(2) feminist praxis (Stanley, 1990; Williams & Ferber, 2008), (3) reflexivity (Nagar & Geiger, 2007), (4) the personal is political (Ginsberg, 2008), (5) positionality (Nagar & Geiger, 2007), and (6) that activism is integral to feminist pedagogy (Bubriski & Semaan, 2009). These six perspectives are connected across feminist pedagogies creating a critical lens for teachers and students to analyze their understandings and experiences of feminist theory and practice. Though these perspectives are not new to feminist pedagogy, little is written on similar programs. What literature that is available focuses on traditional classroom (versus co-curricular) spaces (Agha-Jaffar, 2000; Bricker-Jenkins & Hooyman, 1986; Bubriski & Semaan, 2009; Evans, Ozer, & Hill, 2006; Peet & Reed, 2002; Trigg & Balliet, 1997; Washington, 2000; Williams & Ferber, 2008). What we hoped to institute into the larger paradigm of engagement is the dialectical relationship (Stanley, 1990) between feminist scholarship and feminist activism. Professors and students use knowledge from the classroom to inform their activism outside of it. At the same time, students' and professors' experiences in the Women's Liberation Movement informed and facilitated learning within the classroom (Stanley, 1990). This relationship was vital in helping students understand the difference between altruistic service and the engaged citizenship of action.

Stanley (1990) describes feminist praxis as "unique in combining theoretical discussion of feminist methodology with detailed accounts of practical research processes" (p. 3). For the purposes of this summer program, students read feminist writings with the goal of understanding their implications for practice in feminist activism. SBAI hoped to move students toward a "radical consciousness of self in facing the political dimensions of fieldwork and construction of knowledge" (Nagar & Geiger, 2007, p. 268). If students could be more critical and reflexive about their place in this work, they may begin to move toward an activist consciousness. For us, the move toward an activist consciousness is potentially grounded in the students' recognition of self as an agent of social change.

The personal is political is a uniquely feminist concept and is important to students' agency through the authority of their experience, but we should not let it be the only thing. We must expand our thinking to see the perspectives of others (Ginsberg, 2008). Positionality has much to contribute to these frameworks. For students to truly be engaged feminist citizens they must understand their privileges, social identity, social situatedness, and insider/outsider status, or positionality in terms of gender, race, class, sexuality, and other axes of social difference (Nagar & Geiger, 2007, p. 268). Yet, how can we begin to teach students about feminist activism without creating a space for them to participate in it?

Williams and Ferber (2008) observe how important activism is to praxis as an example of connected learning. However, feminist teachers need to be wary that they do not just create service-oriented students, but social justice-oriented students (Bubriski & Semaan, 2008). Bubriski and Semaan (2008) offer five pedagogical guidelines to help teachers facilitate this process with their students. These include having direct contact with the agencies the students will be working at before they begin, teaching students the difference between service and social justice, working with students to help them come out of their comfort zone, meeting with students individually to guide them in their understanding of service versus social justice, and using writing assignments to help students to reflect (Bubriski & Semaan, 2008).

SBAI designed this model not only on existing research, but also from student interest. Students can be the driving force for the continuation of experiential learning and other "value added" programs (Trigg & Balliet, 1997). Meeting student needs is equally important to exposing them to the complexities of feminist activism. Throughout the Rocxxy program, we employed these and other feminist theoretical frameworks by maintaining a strong connection with our community partners and utilizing group reflections, journaling, readings on activism, historic field trips, guest speakers, and guided discussions. In the following sections, we will describe how we employed these frameworks in practice.

Internship Sites and Guest Speakers: Building Relationships with Community Partners

Current trends in experiential learning, such as service-learning, have been a contemporary way to legitimize feminist action in the women's studies classroom (Trigg & Ballet, 1997). Rocxxy frames feminism as a pedagogical tool for all students to learn about activism. Peet and Reed (2002) found that overall, students who participated in a feminist action project were more likely to embrace activism and political action. Partnerships with community organizations help to challenge the academic versus real-world divide in teaching activism and political action (Naples & Bojar, 2002). Cultivating good relationships with community partners, then, is a fundamental step in ensuring students' success in an engaged learning program.

Students who work with organizations doing feminist work have been shown to have a deeper understanding of social justice, activism, and feminist praxis (Bennett, 2002; Price, 2002). Price (2002) reflects on her own experience and asserts that her time spent at a feminist internship in DC inspired her to pursue a career as an activist scholar. Hill's (2002) work on campus partnerships, which she calls "sisterhood organizations" (p. 154), points out a different theme of community partnership, asserting that one of the greatest strengths of bringing campus feminist student groups, staff, and faculty together is the "kitchen-fights model of self disclosure" (p. 164). This model of self-disclosure creates a space to discuss critical issues in feminist work including race, gender, and class from a practical and theoretical perspective and helps keep lines of communication open.

In the Rocxxy program, we tried to foster community bonds through the site selection process, internships, and guest speakers. After the initial application and interview process, students who were accepted to the Rocxxy program were assigned their internships through a site selection process developed by Rochester AmeriCorps. Students, SBAI staff, and internship site supervisors met together for a lunch and informal conversation about expectations and goals for the internship component of Rocxxy. SBAI staff worked with the sites beforehand to develop position descriptions for students as well as with students to pass on their resumes to site supervisors. After lunch, site supervisors held brief one-on-one interviews with students. Supervisors and students got to rank their preference, and final decisions were made between SBAI staff and the community partners. This placement method was largely a success and was considered a very worthwhile process for all involved—especially our community partners.

Our community partners proved to be a valuable resource for our classroom-based learning by serving as guest speakers and workshops. Guest speaker workshops built on our model of action by offering students additional community role models. Speaker workshops ranged from resume-writing to a presentation on conflict resolution. Using guest speakers is an important pedagogical approach, providing an opportunity to connect theory to practice (Agha-Jaffar, 2000)—and in Rocxxy, from practice to theory.

Historic Fieldtrips: Place-Based Learning

Unique to the Rocxxy program is place, as Rochester lies in the region of upstate New York that was a hot bed of social, religious, and political reform from the mid-1800s through the early 1900s. Rocxxy took advantage of the opportunity to highlight the important feminist history in the greater Rochester area with historic field trips. These trips proved to be one of the most dynamic components of the Rocxxy program and included visits to the homes of Susan B. Anthony, Elizabeth Cady Stanton, Matilda Joslyn Gage, and Harriet Tubman. The value of place-based learning (Cravey & Petit, 2012) as it was implemented in Rocxxy lies in helping students contextualize their own activism. What was crucial about the historic field trips, however, was their ability to embed students within their real-world geographic location (Cravey & Petit, 2012). Activism was demonstrated as a practice that starts at home. In addition, students were able to have a shared experience. Shared experiences in experiential learning help students to bond as a group and introduce them to relationships with each other they might not have had outside this program (Gengler, 2011).

Readings and Reflection: Making Meaning of Student Experiences

Written reflection is another tool, which helps students to make meaning of their experience (Washington, 2000). Since all learners experience learning differently it is important to offer alternative ways for students to reflect and share. According to Collier and Driscoll (1999) "because of the rich variety of real-world learning experiences available to students participating in service-learning classes, the most sensible approach to promoting and supporting student reflection is multiple methods associated with different communication styles" (p. 291). Through the Rocxxy program we used four techniques to engage student reflection including: free writing, prompts for written reflection, dialogue with peers, and dialogue with site supervisors, guest speakers, and the instructor.

These techniques were integrated into the program through the cohort experience. On Fridays, Rocxxy students met as a group to discuss readings and reflect on their internship experiences. SBAI staff served as mentors—in addition to the site supervisors—to facilitate conversations and share their own experiences as activists and professionals in a nonprofit setting. Utilizing readings and group reflections helps students to process and make meaning of their experiences (Peet & Reed, 2002). Students were given the option to journal on their reflections. As stated previously, periodic prompts were given out during the 12-week session, but students were also encouraged to journal freely.

Meeting Student Needs: Engaging All Students in a Feminist Dialogue

During the construction of the Rocxxy curriculum, SBAI began to think about how best to ensure the program was suited for all undergraduate students interested in feminist activism and leadership. Unfortunately, the scholarship that uses feminist theory as a tool to teach citizenship, activism, or student engagement (Cravey & Petit, 2012; Gengler, 2011; Hill, 2002; Nagar & Geiger, 2007; Naples & Bojar, 2002; Price, 2002) tends not to extend outside of women's studies or the classroom. Most studies addressed classroom-based learning that contained an action component. Rocxxy's model of action-based learning with a classroom component offered an alternative to the dominant model. Even though women's studies is inherently interdisciplinary, Evans, Ozer, and Hill (2006) suggest that tailoring service projects to students' existing majors increases interest for students.

Bricker-Jenkins and Hooyman's (1986) research focuses on seven areas they believe feminism can add to the learning of social work students, including strategies for praxis and implementation in fieldwork. They outline the themes of ending patriarchy, empowerment, process, the personal is political, unity/diversity, the validation of the nonrational, and consciousness-raising (Bricker-Jenkins & Hooyman, 1986). Patriarchy, as an institutionalized system of male domination and privilege, has prevented women from this empowerment (Bricker-Jenkins & Hooyman, 1986). Bricker-Jenkins and Hooyman (1986) stress, "women must reclaim a lost and suppressed history, exposing the myths which distort our experiences and limit our vision of our capabilities" (p. 36). In Rocxxy, we open our program to male identified students as well in hopes that their involvement in this process will empower them to be allies. SBAI found these few studies helpful in preparing the curriculum to serve a wide range of students and in understanding the value of feminist theory and practice in student and community engagement.

Data Collection and Analysis

From the start of the Rocxxy pilot, SBAI wanted to collect feedback about the experiences of the students, community members, and the instructor. We wanted to not only ensure that the program was meeting our goals, but also to understand the processes by which these groups made meaning of their experience. We decided to conduct a formative evaluation of the program focusing on intrinsic and extrinsic value (Guba & Lincoln, 1989). Our guiding research questions included: (1) How do students make meaning of their time or experience in Rocxxy? and (2) Did students find value in the three main components of the program including internship sites, reading and reflections, and historical field trips?

We could not assume Rocxxy held inherent value in a feminist context solely because supervisors and interns felt positively about the program. Asking students about meaning making empowered them to define value, and whether they experienced value-added in a feminist context through Rocxxy. Student meaning making was understood as the process by which students synthesized different components of the Rocxxy program with previous learning to make sense of their experiences. Since students were from diverse backgrounds, we aimed to tailor the Rocxxy experience to help students become agents of social change.

To collect the data, we used qualitative methods. Rocxxy was in its first year and we were looking to evaluate the experience and curriculum to improve our practice as opposed to a summative program evaluation for empirical finding (Guba & Lincoln, 1989). A formative approach was the best selection for this case study analysis because it is focused on value and improvement of both the curriculum itself and the implementation. In order to collect the data needed to show the phenomena of Rocxxy, we collected information from multiple sources including: participant observations by the instructor of group reflections, student journals, and surveys upon completion of the program with students and community members.

In analyzing the data, we found memos were integral to the process because they helped the instructor to separate their perceptions from participant interactions and meaning. As feminists we believed it was important to not only observe as a researcher, but to clarify that our analysis was on the right track. We achieved this by asking questions, soliciting group feedback, and involving participants in the research—a process called member checking (Guba & Lincoln, 1989). As our goal was a joint construction of the meaning and value of the program, we did not want to apply the findings of current literature to Rocxxy. Instead we hoped to document what arose naturally during the Rocxxy experience as well as improve our practice.

In analyzing and interpreting the data, we focused on shared experiences, not only those explicit, but also those tacit moments that often go unexplained in scholarship. It is important to again note that we (the authors of this chapter) represent the instructor, a student, and a site supervisor of the Rocxxy program. According to our findings, the initial pilot achieved some, but not all, of its goals. Our data analysis revealed many strengths as well as challenges in the program which we describe in the next two sections. Overall Rocxxy reinforced the belief that feminism can be used as a tool to make students more engaged and aware as citizens.

Strengths

In this section we will discuss the three main strengths of the program including: (1) relationships with community partners, (2) historic field trips and place-based learning, and (3) the cohort experiences. We found in our strengths that students showed significant engagement in the community, connected with their supervisors and SBAI, and broadened their perspectives of feminist activism along with their own feminist identity. Going forward, we will describe the strengths of the program's first year as well as introduce some of the challenges we encountered. Finally, we will conclude with implications for both our practice and the practice of others.

Community Partnerships

The relationships forged with community partners were, by and large, one of the strengths of the program. Site supervisors from the community partner organizations were deeply invested in mentoring Rocxxy interns. One site supervisor described the value of mentoring young feminists within her own work.

> I enjoy working with feminist students and often seek out women and gender studies majors or feminist student activists to intern at our office. Part of doing professional feminist work is connecting with other feminists and playing an active role in their success. I have had many feminist mentors and inspirations in my career and continue to seek out meaningful relationships with diverse feminist leaders. (Personal communication, 2013)

Students were also invested in their relationships with their supervisors, turning to them for knowledge and insight. One Rocxxy intern put it best "[My supervisor]...always made time for me and gave me worthwhile projects to complete. She taught me a lot about how to lobby and rally around a good cause and it was truly inspiring" (personal communication, 2013). Throughout the summer SBAI stayed in communication with site supervisors to see how student interns were progressing. The engagement of explicitly feminist-identified supervisors proved to be a key component of success. The introduction to feminist community, through site supervisors and others at internship sites, provided relevant models for forging feminist identities as well as models of engaged political action. One student wrote:

> In the age of point and click politics going to rallies and lobbying was powerful. I didn't even know people still did that. This experience and my dialogues with my supervisor about feminist issues really helped me to think of myself as a feminist. (Personal communication, 2013)

Most importantly, however, relationships with feminist site supervisors became safe spaces for students to express a feminist identity. One student wrote, "Before the internship, my peers had always called me a feminist but I didn't feel like I was a feminist. When Rocxxy began and I was immersed with other like-minded individuals, I finally felt comfortable self-identifying as a feminist" (personal communication, 2013). Providing support for students outside of the classroom as they grow in feminism is an often critical and missing component of women's studies programs. A Rocxxy intern and junior at the University of Rochester expressed this well on one of her final reflections on the program:

> The best part about Rocxxy was becoming part of an activist community that exists in the "real world" and not just on a college campus. Communicating with the other interns in the program and their supervisors helped to integrate us into the network of Rochester feminists, and allowed us to be more involved and informed. In addition to being connected with like-minded students in Rocxxy, we all gained new role models and mentors. My supervisors both had day jobs but still spent hours upon hours working for their causes each week; it was inspiring to see their dedication and how they made feminist activism a major part of their lives despite other responsibilities. (Personal communication, 2013)

The site supervisors provided the bridge to close the gap between the University and the local surrounding community. It was apparent throughout the reflections that access to the community was one of the most effective resources students expressed finding through Rocxxy.

Historic Field Trips and Place-Based Learning

Belonging to a strong feminist network helped SBAI in setting up the historic field trip component of the program. SBAI staff's long-term relationships in the community enabled us to request personalized tours and workshops at the historic sites that intersected with Rocxxy's goals. The fieldtrips grounded concrete political action within a valued tradition of activism in the Rochester community. Rising junior and Rocxxy intern wrote, "I really enjoyed the historical field trips. I don't think I would have gotten to see the different sites (especially those outside of Rochester) had these trips and tours not been arranged through the program nor would I have learned local upstate-NY history" (personal communication, 2013). The Matilda Joslyn Gage house was the most popular field trip of the program and deeply impacted students. Gage's radical, progressive politics arguably echo many of the ideological stances of contemporary feminism. Because the museum includes contemporary issues in their exhibits, it gave students a chance to recognize the intellectual roots of contemporary feminism. The historic field trips helped to set a tone for a community beyond traditional education and time/ space borders.

The Cohort Experience

The community through Rocxxy did not end with student community relationships. Students also benefited from the cohort experience for the opportunity it provided for introspective reflection and peer group learning. One student noted, "[weekly meetings]...gave me something to really reflect upon and helped me grow as a feminist individual" (personal communication, 2013), another student expressed that weekly meeting were "meaningful and helpful throughout the program" (personal communication, 2013). Students had an opportunity to connect with, vent to, and validate one another.

Since the site placements were very different, weekly meetings also helped students learn more about other workplaces and models of activism. Discussion created a space for expressing emotions, anxieties, fears and frustrations that often are inappropriate in the workplace. Good relations between the students and the instructor also facilitated students' free expression. A Rocxxy student commented on this relationship saying, "[The instructor]...did a good job of facilitating discussions in terms of making sure everyone had time enough to speak and felt comfortable expressing themselves" (personal communication, 2013). The reflective sessions significantly added to the overall experience. Students in the cohort found Rocxxy to be a defining experience in the creation of a personal feminist identity. One student noted that weekly meetings and reflections "really sparked my inner feminist" (personal communication, 2013).

Challenges

Although pleased to see the success of the Rocxxy pilot, we realize that no program is without challenges—particularly in its pilot year. Students confronted difficulties largely with regards to lack of background in feminist theory, as well as a lack of preparation for certain aspects of the internship experience. In this section, we will discuss these challenges of the program organized into three main categories, including: (1) reading and feminist theory, (2) managing student expectations, and (3) access to the program.

Reading in Feminist Theory

At the end of the program students expressed a desire for more involved discussion of theories of feminism, leadership, and activism. This was one component of the weekly meetings that was not well received. One student wrote:

I was looking forward to learning more about feminist theory and discussing different types of feminism during these workshops. Aside from the first assigned reading which gave an overview of the history of feminism, we did not tackle feminist theory and the diversities within it and discussed only a few contemporary issues in feminism over the course of the summer. (Personal communication, 2013)

SBAI held a working assumption that students' interest in Rocxxy indicated a substantial enough theoretical background to keep the amount of readings light, focusing on the internship, trainings, and fieldtrips. It was assumed that previous classroom knowledge could be drawn on by students for insight. This was a misstep and represents an important piece of the curriculum to be reworked. As a result of the program's structure, the minimal academic materials made it difficult to construct a coherent student experience. At times, the instructor was left to force the point of these connections during reflection discussions at weekly meeting. A student pointed out that the primary text for the program was not overly useful to this end, stating, "What I did not enjoy about the Rocxxy internship was the book. It had great stories, but overall I didn't take a lot from it. I found that our discussions around the book were a lot more challenging" (personal communication, 2013).

Managing Student Expectations

Another area for improvement in the Rocxxy program is directly addressing student assumptions about the nature of feminist work, which can be in conflict with the realities of a feminist job. Student internship expectations became a stumbling block within the program due to the diverse backgrounds of students and the equally diverse range of internship sites. A Rocxxy student who was placed at a University internship site focusing on research wrote "As the only intern in a university setting, it made it hard to relate to my peers, but it also gave me a new understanding of how institution-based non-profit centers operate" (personal communication, 2013). One of the goals of the program was to help students realize that activism is itself a broad idea, and many different types of activism fall under the banner of feminist work. In addition to the student who worked at the University, one student in the cohort was placed in an internship that worked largely in ways that did not fit common student expectations of activism. For instance, their site was a feminist summer camp for girls and included extensive work with children. Dealing with student frustration, subsequent lack of motivation, and disappointment in relation to internship sites was a constant struggle in relation to these specific placements. Supervisors experienced similar discomfort with this situation. One site supervisor wrote, "Many college students envision graduating and automatically working in a big, shiny, office. But when starting your own non-profit organization there is a lot of grunt work that must be done in order to have a sustainable organization" (personal communication, 2013). A similarly governed internship site suggested a deeper student buy-in stating, "it only works if the intern self-selects the organization and this style of management" (personal communication, 2013). This is an important insight to the site selection process in the future.

Working in the nonprofit sector necessitates the realization that social justice organizations are not always ideal workplaces. Through Rocxxy, students were exposed to the inner workings of social justice organizations and witness to the friction that can, and often does, arise within the activist community as a whole, or even within a single organization. In one particular incident, two students, along with staff and site supervisors, had to negotiate sexism within the context of a nonprofit, feminist workplace. Methods of conflict resolution within an activist environment were taught implicitly. However, it was a sobering reminder that nonprofit work, while valuable, must not be construed as completely idyllic. The strong relationship between students, community partners, and SBAI staff kept lines of communication open from all sides to resolve this conflict.

Access

Finally, an interesting discussion among the students and SBAI developed around access to the program. Though Rocxxy was open to all undergraduate students at the University, it was not as accessible as it could be because the program was not for credit and required car transportation thus limiting access for students who may have fiscal limitations. Students did not receive pay nor were they provided credit, housing, or transportation for their participation. Transportation for historic field trips and some meals on meeting days was provided. Also, if students sought credit for their internship, they could arrange an independent study. Though these efforts are promising, they do not address the financial constraints that truly limits access. In the future, we hope to provide housing, meals, and bus passes so the Rocxxy program is not only available to students who live locally or can afford to stay on campus – or who have access to transportation for historic fieldtrips and have familial or financial support for their education.

Implications

In this section we will discuss the lessons learned from this analysis and the implications they provide for practice. The challenges we faced during the Rocxxy program were critical to a formative evaluation because they helped identify areas for improvement. By examining the strengths and the challenges, we believe the implications include (1) building upon the value of the cohort experience, (2) expanding community partnerships, (3) the importance of feminism to embracing activist identities, (4) using feminism as a tool for student engagement.

The Cohort Experience

With respect to the cohort experience, we believe better-selected readings—which include feminist theory and history—will forge a stronger tie between Rochester's own history, feminist practice, and feminist theory. In addition, more than one weekly meeting or the separation of trips and workshops from group reflection time will help to slow the fast pace of the program. In our view, program administrators should not be afraid to challenge students to commit more time to do more readings or to dig deeper. Asking for deeper engagement from students will ultimately improve the overall program experience as well as facilitate student learning. These shortfalls of the Rocxxy program were brought up by the students and remind us that the strength of the cohort experience was how the students made meaning of their internships. If this is the case, then all internship programs should consider incorporating peer group meeting and reflection to enhance the internship experience. As students often intern at sites in geographically disparate locations, it may not always be possible to do this. We would like to suggest that colleges and universities should consider privileging internships for students in their own local communities. This is a uniquely feminist standpoint that may improve the practice of experiential learning as a whole. Local internships are not dependent on historic sites for reaping the benefits of place-based learning. Engagement across local communities as well as peer group reflective experiences create value for students that cannot be replicated without such components.

Expanding Community Partnerships

Despite obstacles to student engagement and motivation in relation to internship sites, by the end of the program all four students in the cohort reported both in their journals and through surveys their satisfaction with their experience in the program. This suggests that modeling different strategies of activism can have an impact on student learning. Reflecting back on these challenges, we are confident that including various styles of nonprofit organizations can give valuable shared experience to students. Incorporating models from the grassroots organization with no office space to the corporate model with shiny offices and complex hierarchy gives students a chance to think specifically about where they see themselves making change in their future careers. Given the tendency of women's studies service-learning programs to interact with only one or two sites, the breadth Rocxxy provides students is unique. Working with multiple sites has been shown through Rocxxy to give students a broader understanding of activist work, potentially making them more aware of themselves as change agents. This model is an important implication for other colleges and universities on the need for expanded community networks in student engagement efforts.

Feminism and Identity

It is relevant to note that only one internship site placement through Rocxxy included a student-intern and site supervisor who shared similar racial and gender identities. At the rest of the placements, students and site supervisors connected through shared political goals across (and sometimes because of) lines of race, gender, and age. Supervisors and students often shared conceptions of feminism oriented toward the ideas and practices of what is known as feminism's Third Wave. The Third Wave refers to the modern era of the feminist movement starting in the 1990s in contrast to the First Wave and Second Wave of feminism. Constructed with the objective of expanding "what 'feminist' means" (Moraga & Anzaldua, 1983, p. xxiii), Third Wave feminism has allowed for the inclusion of diverse voices within the movement.

The popularity of certain theories of the Third Wave, specifically intersectionality, created common theoretical ground for student interns and supervisors to analyze systems of power and social inequities (Hill-Collins, 2010). In particular, intersectionality has allowed feminists of color and non-middle-class feminists a space for critique of the mainstream feminist movement, as well as for productive dialogue (Carbin & Edenheim, 2013). We believe this understanding accounted for the success of student-interns working in organizations of differing social demographics. It also has implications for the relevance of feminism to models of inclusive leadership. The specifically feminist nature of the Rocxxy program allowed a summer internship to become a powerful platform for student identity development. The Rocxxy interns, coming from a number of distinct backgrounds, used

Rocxxy as a catalyst for personal growth. Establishing feminist frameworks as necessary components of service-learning programs expands the concept of experiential learning to include identity development. The use of theoretical frameworks like feminism not only facilitates student learning and engagement, but can also grow students' commitment to social justice. We encourage all service-learning programs to look to social justice movements like feminism to create programs of experiential learning that foster active citizenship.

Feminism as a Tool for Student Engagement

The Rocxxy program was explicitly constructed to be open to all students at the University. Initially, SBAI thought the target audience for Rocxxy would be women's studies majors and minors. As news of the pilot program spread on campus, it became clear that students outside of the major or minor were interested in the Rocxxy program. Meeting this demand required expanding and opening the program application to all University of Rochester undergraduate students. SBAI's position as an institute at the University fortunately provided a high level of flexibility in the construction of the program curriculum, allowing us to meet that need.

While SBAI understands that one does not need to be a women's studies major to be a feminist, what we failed to understand in the initial planning was the important contributions of feminism to student and community engagement. Feminist epistemologies demand we challenge inequities of sexism, racism, colonialism, class, and all other forms of oppression (Naples, 2003). The expansion of feminist thought throughout the academy—outside the silo of gender and women's studies—is one realization of the role of women's studies departments in the fulfillment of that activist goal. Naples (2003) points to the cross-disciplinary and cross-community mission of feminism: "Feminist theoretical perspectives were developed in the context of diverse struggles for social justice inside and outside the academy" (p. 13). If consciousness-raising fosters this feminist political agency (Naples & Bojar, 2002), then we must include students across disciplines, as well as members of the community, when teaching the value of feminist activism, leadership, and organizing.

Conclusion

Having completed the pilot of the *Rocxxy: Summer Internship in Feminist Leadership and Activism*, we are more deeply committed than ever as an Institute within a university setting to providing our students with a bridge between feminist theory and practice. The program provides vital professional skills and insights to students inside and outside of the discipline of women's studies, which empower them to serve as agents of social change within their lives past their undergraduate years. However, most important to us when looking over the reflections of students and engaging with them in dialogue over the course of the summer was the role of Rocxxy, as a program, on the path to the development of a confident feminist identity for all students. Though room exists for restructuring to maximize the experience and minimize challenges, overall we believe that the pilot was a success. This novel program at the University of Rochester created a space for the lived practice of feminism to be worked out by students in a way that was safe and challenging. We are proud that Rocxxy permitted students from diverse backgrounds to grow and find a voice by way of feminist action. By forging and strengthening the bonds between students and the community, the program facilitated an internal process of growth and learning that strikes at the heart of the mission of feminist scholarship—to transform those it touches.

References

Agha-Jaffar, T. (2000). From theory to praxis in women's studies: Guest speakers and service-learning as pedagogy. *Feminist Teacher, 13*(1), 1–11.

Bennett, N. M. (2002). Ms. Smith goes to Washington: Feminist internships in the nation's capital. *Feminist Teacher, 14*(2), 146–160.

Bricker-Jenkins, M., & Hooyman, N. (1986). Feminist pedagogy in education for social change. *Feminist Teacher, 2*(2), 36–42.

Bubriski, A., & Semaan, I. (2009). Activist learning vs. service learning in women's studies classroom. *Human Architecture: Journal of the Sociology of Self-Knowledge, 7*(3) 91–98.

Carbin, M., & Edenheim, S. (2013). The intersectional turn in feminist theory: A dream of a common language? *European Journal of Women's Studies, 20*(3) 233–248.

Collier, P. J., & Driscoll, A. (1999). Multiple methods of student reflection in service-learning classes. *The Journal of General Education, 48*(4), 280–292.

Cravey, A. J., & Petit, M. (2012). A critical pedagogy of place learning through the body. *Feminist Formations, 24*(2), 100–119.

Evans, S. Y., Ozer, J., & Hill, H. (2006). Major service: Combining academic disciplines and service-learning in women's studies. *Feminist Teacher, 17*(1), 1–14.

Gengler, A. M. (2011). That's when it hit home: Creating interactive, collective, and transformative learning experiences through the traveling classroom. *Feminist Teacher, 20*(3), 249–257.

Ginsberg, A. E. (2008). *The evolution of American women's studies: Reflections on triumphs, controversies, and change.* New York: Palgrave Macmillan.
Guba, E. G., & Lincoln, Y. S. (1989). *Fourth generation evaluation.* Newbury Park, CA: Sage.
Hill, S. A. (2002). Activism and alliance within campus sisterhood organizations. In N. A. Naples & K. Bojar (Eds.), *Teaching feminist activism: Strategies from the field* (154–165). New York: Routledge.
Hill-Collins, P. (2010). The new politics of community. *American Sociological Review, 75*(1), 3–70.
Nagar, R., & Geiger, S. (2007). Reflexivity and positionality in feminist fieldwork revisited. In A.Tickell, E. Sheppard, J. Peck, & T. Barnes (Eds.), *Politics and practice in economic geography* (pp. 267–278). London: Sage.
Naples, N. A. (2003). *Feminism and method.* New York: Routledge.
Naples, N. A., & Bojar, K. (2002). *Teaching feminist activism.* New York: Routledge.
Moraga, C., & Anzaldua, G. (1983). *This bridge called my back.* New York: Kitchen Table: Women of Color Press.
Peet, M. R., & Reed, B. G. (2002). The development of political consciousness and agency: The role of activism and race/ethnicity in an introductory women's studies course. *Feminist Teacher, 14*(2), 106–122.
Price, K. (2002). The making of an activist-scholar, or my year as a congressional fellow. *Feminist Teacher, 14*(2), 134–145.
Stanley, L. (1990). *Feminist praxis.* London: Routledge.
Trigg, M. K., & Balliet, B. J. (1997). Finding community across boundaries: Service learning in women's studies. In R. Guarasci & G. Cornwell (Eds.), *Democratic education in an age of difference* (pp. 51–72). San Francisco: Jossey-Bass.
Washington, P. A. (2000). From college classroom to community action. *Feminist Teacher, 13*(1), 12–34.
Williams, R. L., & Ferber, A. L. (2008). Facilitating smart-girl: Feminist pedagogy in service learning in action. *Feminist Teacher, 19*(1), 47–67.

CHAPTER 10

Developing Sustainable Community Engagement by Repositioning Programs into Communities

Jana Noel

Community engagement has long been valued as a philosophical framework for education (Benson, Puckett, & Harkavy, 2007) and in recent years has been identified as a high impact practice for university students by the American Association of Colleges and Universities (Kuh, 2008). Community engagement work is so valued as a means of fostering students' civic learning, in fact, that institutions of higher education can now receive national recognition for their commitment to community engagement through programs such as the Carnegie Community Engagement Classification and the President's Higher Education Community Service Honor Roll.

However, when courses that include community engagement are located on a university campus, set apart from communities, they run the risk of overlooking or misunderstanding the challenges communities face as they struggle toward social, economic, cultural, and racial justice (Noel, 2013a). In this chapter, I argue for repositioning community engagement courses, and entire programs if possible, into the communities they are designed to impact. Repositioning programs in this way prioritizes relationship-building, the examination of issues of power, race and class, and a commitment to community-based social justice efforts. This approach is based in part on feminist theory that "insist[s] on being active in the community rather than simply observing it from behind the walls of the university" (Webb, Cole, & Skeen, 2007, p. 251).

The Problem

Community engagement efforts have been criticized for being dominated by a university-agenda, attending superficially to issues impacting communities, and lacking in sustainability. Too often, an inequality of roles, with university programs and faculty, sets the tone for interactions (Kahne & Westheimer, 1996). As Zeichner (2010) points out, "colleges and universities continue to maintain hegemony over the construction and dissemination of knowledge" (p. 90). Harkavy and Hartley (2009) urge institutions of higher education toward "rejecting the unidirectional, top-down approaches that all too often have characterized university-community interaction" (p. 12).

Implicit in the top-down approach is the privilege associated with the university in a university-community relationship. As King (2004) suggests, "to be in a position to 'provide service' to another party may itself be a mark of privilege" (p. 123). There are both real and perceived differences in authority and voice between community and university, and community members may not readily accept efforts from outside institutions to enter their lives. As Reed (2004) describes:

> Low-income neighborhoods are jaded [and]...weary of seeing new initiatives come and go. They are tired of the disruptions caused by those who live outside the neighborhood who try to offer solutions that, no matter how well intentioned, are not grounded in the realities of the street. (p. 81)

Mathieu (2005) cautions that "an academic entitled by race and cultural capital, who launches thoughtlessly into unfamiliar streets and buildings" and who is "focused solely on *her* work, damn the consequences," has no understanding of a community partner's "mistrust and apprehension or a sense of why people might be suspicious of working with universities" (p. x, italics in original).

Finally, such university-driven practices tend to have the needs of the university structure and schedule first in mind. Due to the often one-semester length of service-learning courses and the lack of flexibility that such a framework engenders, it can be difficult to develop sustainable partnerships. As Gilbert and Masucci (2004) describe, the sustainability of university-community partnership activities... [are] threatened due to the lack of continuity presented by relying solely on service learning courses as the means of implementing partnership programs... tension... is presented by the differences between community needs for sustainability and long-term involvement versus the schedule and shorter-term orientation of students enrolled in specific classes... (pp. 150–151)

As Kahne and Westheimer (1996) famously ask of service-learning, "In the Service of What?" In many cases, professors set the goals and purposes of a service-learning course ahead of time, at the beginning of the semester, sometimes concreted into a syllabus. For sustainable and impactful community engagement, there is a need to remain flexible, ready for inevitable changes in the life of a community, "where goals and purposes of a 'service' effort are not established beforehand' (Webb et al., 2007, p. 241).

Developing Relationships and Repositioning Ourselves in Our Local Communities

Developing relationships has been identified as a key to sustainable community engagement (Noel, 2011; Porfilio & Hickman, 2011). As Madsen-Camacho (2004) explains, "The experience must focus on relationship building first before service begins" (p. 10). Theories of *presence* in community engagement point out that becoming accepted and integrated into a community requires time spent in that community (Noel, 2010). Murrell (2001) discusses the idea of *being there*, of being physically present in communities in order to learn, to show commitment, and to build trust with community members. Rosenberg's (1997) concept of *dwelling* means that "We need to think about what it means for us to 'dwell' in the institution [the k-12 school]... to fasten our attention, to tarry, to look again. We take root, day after day" (p. 88). This is the beginning of developing more authentic, sustainable relationships.

Authentic relationships between partners "recognize privilege, power, and positionality" (Noel, 2013b, p. 220). Those from the university "must consistently consider how people in the neighborhoods may take a racially, economically, and educationally marked view of [them], marking [them] as 'other'" (Noel, 2010, p. 212). Giroux (1988) elaborates that roles are not to be set in stone; that educators "cross over into realms of meaning, maps of knowledge, social relations, and values that are increasingly being negotiated"

(Hill-Jackson & Lewis, 2011, pp. 29–30). Acting with these considerations in mind moves us toward Daniel's (2007) conception of community as "a group of persons wherein the members remain aware of the intersections of oppressions, the multiple relational dynamics inherent in that space, and are continually working at making the community a comprehensive learning space for all of its members" (p. 32). This brings all involved into the community, recognizing layers of power dynamics, and consistently negotiating action toward social justice.

Building Trust

Clearly, a key feature of such partnerships is the presence of trust. Hoy and Tschannen-Moran (1999) have identified five facets of trust involved in establishing trust between people and organizations: benevolence, honesty, openness, reliability, and competence. Weaving through these facets of trust is the confidence that one person or organization has in the partner's intentions toward the people and project. As Tschannen-Moran writes, "Perhaps the most essential ingredient and commonly recognized facet of trust is a sense of caring or benevolence; the confidence that one's well-being or something one cares about will be protected and not harmed by the trusted party" (p. 19).

Collaborative relationships, however, do not begin with all five facets of trust already in place. Rather, trust builds over time (Noel, 2011). Trust, according to Tschannen-Moran and Hoy (2000), is a "dynamic phenomenon that takes on a different character at different stages of a relationship" (p. 570). Trust "thickens," they add, "as a relationship develops" (p. 570; see also Gambetta, 1988). To this point, Noel (2011) proposes three stages in developing trust between institutional partners. At the first stage, when partners do not have a professional or personal relationship, they will make a calculation about the worthiness of a potential collaborative partner based on factors such as the amount of risk connected with the collaboration, or whether the activities and partners can be monitored (Gambetta, 1988). This calculation may be based in part on a potential partner organization's reputation.

The second stage occurs when the collaboration begins and activities commence, during which time partners can gauge the level of commitment of their partners based on repeated activities. At this stage, trust moves beyond a speculative calculation, and reaches a new level based on knowledge of practice in a common realm (Bottery, 2003; Tschannen-Moran, & Hoy, 2000). This signifies a developing knowledge of individuals' work, commitment, and trustworthiness.

The third stage occurs when partners spend time working together, and repeated collaborative activities have been effective. Partners come to recognize, first, that they have developed relationships based on shared goals, procedures, and beliefs (Stefkovich & Shapiro, 2002); and second, that they can act on behalf of each other, comfortable and confident in the decisions, activities, and outcomes of the partnership.

Once these stages of partnership development have been reached, a sustainable partnership can be realized. Flexibility is a hallmark of a mature partnership that has gone through this three-step process of trust development (Hands, 2005). A sustainable partnership, built on trust, allows for flexibility by enacting change and incorporating new community needs and institutional demands when needed.

Toward Sustainability

The three-pronged approach proposed by Noel (2011) can be utilized to develop such a sustainable community engagement program based on trust. First, a program must physically "be there" (Murrell, 2001) in the community, aware of issues of power and "otherness," becoming integrated into the life of that community. Second, the university needs to work with the community to collaboratively develop "community studies" that allow for a deeper understanding of the community—the lives of its members, the community's needs, and the strengths of that community. The purpose will be to not impose a plan for service from the university, but rather to co-determine, with the community, the activities that would be most beneficial. Murrell (2001) explains that

> our program development must be loosely linked to the everyday practical activities of school and community development. This means the elimination of "helperism" in our relationship to our partners in urban communities and working with them on *their* enterprises of change. (pp. 32–33)

It is only after becoming integrated into the community's life, and collaboratively studying the community, that the third step should be undertaken—actually engaging in service-learning or other community engagement activities. This approach to community engagement reverses a common pattern of deciding which community service activities should be conducted before engaging with community. If community engagement programs attempt to begin without the first two steps of physically becoming a part of and learning with the community, then those programs risk promoting and perpetuating the community's feeling of disconnect from the university. By locating ourselves in the community, developing relationships and trust, we can minimize feelings and beliefs held by some community members that universities come and go and do not have a strong base within the community itself (Noel, 2011).

Exemplary Community Engagement Programs Repositioned into Communities

Three community engagement programs from California State University, Sacramento (Sacramento State) exemplify sustainable community engagement, demonstrating this three-pronged approach to developing sustainable university-community relationships. Sacramento State is a regional comprehensive university with 28,000 students, offering Bachelor's and Master's degrees, as well as doctorates in education and physical therapy. The students are diverse (40% White, 21% Asian/Pacific Islanders, 19% Latino, 6% African American, and the remainder a mix of "other" demographic categories). The university has been designated an Asian American and Native American Pacific Islander-Serving Institution (AANAPISI). Sacramento State received the 2010 Carnegie Community Engagement Classification, signifying its commitment "to become more deeply engaged, to improve teaching and learning and to generate socially responsive knowledge to benefit communities" ("Carnegie Selects," 2011, ¶ 3). It has also been selected for the President's Higher Education Community Service Honor Roll for five consecutive years, an honor given by the Corporation for National and Community Service. The city of Sacramento was identified as "America's Most Diverse City" in 2002 by the Civil Rights Project (Stodghill & Bower, 2002). It is not so much that Sacramento is the most diverse city, but that it is the "most integrated city," with a diversity of residents in all neighborhoods. The demographic mix is quite similar today than in 2002, with no racial or ethnic group constituting over 50 percent of the total population. The high level of racial integration does not mean a lack of racism or ethnic intolerance; it does mean, however, that children and adults who have grown-up in Sacramento have spent significant time with a wide diversity of people and ideas. Socioeconomic distinctions can clearly be seen within the city's schools, with the most economically advantaged schools being identified by test scores as very high-achieving, while schools in the lowest income neighborhoods are currently on "watch lists" for possible takeover or closure due to low test scores. It is within this context that Sacramento State engages with its community.

Science for Social Responsibility/Community Health Fair Program

The Science for Social Responsibility Program exemplifies university-community partnerships developed through relationship-building (Lum, Aguirre, Martinez, Campa-Rodriguez, & Ultreras, 2009). Initiated by teachers in the K-12 school, and joined by a Sacramento State professor, the group undertook community studies prior to developing a new service-learning curriculum. With community in mind, this university-school partnership group created a new curriculum and program, and only then were Sacramento State students invited to engage in service-learning as part of this new, community-based program. This program carefully avoids the university-driven approach, and the resulting sustainability is evident as the program is now in its ninth year as a partnership.

The Science for Social Responsibility and Community Health Fair Programs developed as a result of the school-community-university collaborative of the Spanish-English Developmental Bilingual Department at Bowling Green Charter Complex (elementary school) and the Sacramento State Bilingual/Multicultural Education Department (BMED) (Lum et al., 2009). BMED utilizes a social justice framework to prepare future teachers to teach in low-income, culturally and linguistically diverse schools and communities. The majority of students enrolled in BMED programs are what the university calls "Underrepresented Minorities." To best prepare future teachers with an eye to social justice, all field experiences, community engagement, and even some coursework are offered within very low-income, very demographically diverse schools and communities.

Bowling Green Charter School is located within just such a community. The school's charter calls for the school "to create a social action plan that involves our students in helping their neighborhood community" (Lum et al., p. 75). Demographics of Bowling Green Charter Complex students are as follows:

- 85% eligible for free-or-reduced lunch
- 96% students of color
  - 58% Hispanic
  - 18% Asian
  - 16% Black
  - 4% White
- 56% English Language Learners
  - Home languages of ELL students—68% Spanish
  - Home languages of ELL students—21% Hmong

As of 2004, Bowling Green teachers had been discussing for several years the possible development of a social justice, community-oriented science curriculum. They had also received a technology grant to support their work. These conceptual frameworks were in place before the school was contacted by Professor Hugo Chacón, from the Sacramento State BMED program, asking if the school would be willing to partner with him to prepare pre-service teachers on site at the school. Bowling Green saw this as a perfect opportunity to further develop their curriculum.

In order to develop a curriculum that directly reflected local neighborhood issues, Bowling Green and BMED faculty studied the health of community members and learned that nearly 90 percent of the Latino families within the school had one or more family member with diabetes. Thus began the partnership to address an important need within the community.

Bowling Green invited BMED to bring students into the school to strengthen the developing partnership. BMED repositioned its "Methods of Teaching Science" course onsite at Bowling Green School. Professor Chacón was the professor of record, but the course included frequent co-teaching by Bowling Green teachers. Thus, BMED pre-service teachers learned from both university faculty and classroom teachers in this school-community-based setting.

The result was both a new school science curriculum addressing the health needs of the community and a community-wide health fair. The health fair is a collaboration among teachers, elementary school students, university professors, university students, community members, and various community agencies and organizations. Held at Bowling Green Charter Complex, a number of learning and screening stations are available for community members to get health information. Some of the learning stations are staffed by community health groups, in multiple languages represented within the community. During the health fair, university students, sixth-grade students, and community members, supervised by a community medical doctor, screen for cholesterol, blood pressure, and diabetes. Community members learn about heart disease from fifth-graders' PowerPoint presentations, and about diabetes from the fourth-graders' brochures. Participants also watch a drug awareness play presented by the sixth-graders, and watch K-3 students singing and dancing to tunes about health and nutrition. Additional activities include nutrition and physical fitness games, a tour of an ambulance, and enjoying nutritious snacks.

The Bowling Green Charter Complex has now been reorganized, into two Academies, one which flowed directly out of the work of this university-school-community partnership. The Bowling Green Carter Chacón Language & Science Academy, named after the first University professor involved in the partnership, recognizes the history of this community engagement partnership. The Community Health Fair continues today, 9 years after the formation of the university-school-community partnership, with 300–400 attendees each year gaining invaluable health information developed through this university-school-community partnership.

65th Street Corridor Community Collaborative

A second example of sustained community engagement is the 65th Street Corridor Community Collaborative Project ("The Collaborative") (Sobredo, Kim-Ju, Figueroa, Mark, & Fabionar, 2008). Differing from the previous example, in which the idea for the program began in the K-12 school, the Collaborative began as an effort in the Sacramento State Ethnic Studies Department. Similar to the previous example, though, the university and school faculty engaged in community studies to determine the needs and strengths of the community before assigning Sacramento State students to service-learning work in this community. The faculty chose to develop their program in a diverse community that had already developed a trusting relationship with the university, a nearby high school that already had several other partnership programs established with Sacramento State, and the resulting service-learning projects have been sustained over a decade.

The Collaborative is a multi-component community mobilization effort aimed at increasing student academic achievement, fostering student leadership, and improving parent participation for children living in neighborhoods where gang violence, a lack of access to resources and low civic engagement create a need for innovative, culturally competent strategies (Sobredo et al., 2008). The overall goal is to build a more healthy, engaged, and vibrant community.

Founded in 1969, Sacramento State's Ethnic Studies Department offers interdisciplinary Bachelor's Degrees, with options in Asian American, Chicano, Native American, and Pan African Studies. Courses focus on the histories, cultures, and issues that shape ethnic groups' experiences in the United States. The Ethnic Studies Department has a well-developed undergraduate service-learning program, aided by the university's Community Engagement Center. The Collaborative serves the students and families of Hiram Johnson High School and Will C. Wood Middle School, along Sacramento's 65th Street Corridor, a low-income, culturally, linguistically, and racially diverse community adjacent to the University campus. The demographics of the 65th Street Corridor community are as follows:

65th Street Corridor Community
- 25% below poverty
- 50% of adults received less than a high school diploma

Hiram Johnson High School
- 70% eligible for free-or-reduced lunch
- 95% students of color
  - 40% Hispanic
  - 30% Asian
  - 13% Black
  - 9% White
- 30% English Language Learners
  - Home languages of ELL students—45% Spanish
  - Home languages of ELL students—22% Hmong

Once the Ethnic Studies faculty had developed an initial relationship with Hiram Johnson High School,

> Key faculty members and administrators brought the proposed community partnership to their respective institutions for formal approval. A meeting between the two programs was then held, allowing administrators and faculty from both campuses to meet, establish social bonds, and share ideas about the direction and scope of the partnership. (Sobredo et al., p. S83)

Upon hearing the concerns voiced by the principal and faculty at Hiram Johnson about behavioral and violence issues, the partnership conducted a community study to identify both the needs and strengths of this high school and its community.

[A] "walk-the-block" community survey was conducted by CSUS students (many of whom are multilingual), Healthy Start staff, and volunteers from VISTA, Ameri-Corps, and the National Civilian Community Corps. Supervised by Department faculty and Healthy Start staff, 57 volunteers worked in groups of two or three to conduct surveys, and took advantage of community events occurring that day (e.g., a community health fair, a neighborhood association pancake breakfast, and a Southeast Asian community resident forum). (Sobredo et al., p. S86)

The community study identified a need for tutoring, mentoring, parent education, and a greater focus on transitioning to higher education.

The Collaborative has established four programmatic components in partnership with Hiram Johnson High and Will C. Wood Middle Schools, both within the 65th Street Corridor: (a) Tutoring and Mentoring, (b) Student Bridge, (c) Parent Partnership, and (d) Action Research. The Tutoring and Mentoring Program allows university tutors/mentors to serve as a resource in classrooms to increase the standardized test scores of 7th–12th grade students in Math and English classes. The Student Bridge Program is a series of individual field trips for 7th–12th grade students to build a "college-going culture" at each school and conduct workshops that provide them with college information and skills (e.g., financial aid, application process, student life, and academic expectations). The Parent Partnership Program consists of field trips and workshops that provide opportunities for parents to not only learn about college preparation and higher education, but also to assist their children to have greater academic success. An Action Research Program involves university service-learners who gather basic information about Hiram Johnson and Will C. Wood Schools and the Collaborative and disseminate this information to various individual and organizational stakeholders. These students serve as advocates on behalf of the schools and the Collaborative to individuals outside of the specific target groups, for example, community members, businesses, and politicians residing or serving in those areas. They are also able to more directly link their actions to public issues such as those that impact underrepresented and disadvantaged schools and groups.

The Collaborative focuses on creating educational pathways, developing student leadership, and building communities, and this mission is evident today with the tutoring and mentoring program, student bridge programs, and parent participation programs. A long-term outcome is the development of community celebrations, hosted at Will C. Wood Middle School but sponsored by Sacramento State. In a recent community celebration, hundreds of families attended a Reading Fair to celebrate students' reading efforts, with live music, a talent show, and a book give-away. The Collaborative, through its many programs, has developed into a comprehensive model of change for local residents and students in the 65th Street Corridor. The trusting, sustained relationships among community members, members of K-12 schools, and university faculty are the direct result of the time, intentional efforts, and shared commitments of school and university to develop community-based programs.

Urban Teacher Education Center (UTEC)

The Urban Teacher Education Center (UTEC) represents another model of repositioned community engagement, yet ends with a different result. UTEC as a program no longer exists, but the social transformation begun by the partnership is still strong and gaining even more momentum within the community and the school. The strength of this program was its "presence" (Noel, 2010) and "being there" (Murrell, 2001) in the community. The trusting relationships took a while to build, but those relationships outlasted the actual program and have allowed a deep relationship between university and community that is open to multiple different types of work for social justice within this community.

In 2004, a Sacramento State faculty member approached the Sacramento City Unified School District to ask for permission to develop a school-community-based teacher education program. The Assistant Superintendent immediately agreed, but only if UTEC were to be located with what was then Jedediah Smith School. So the program began from the outside, with the university and the school district administration determining where the partnership would exist.

UTEC was a community-oriented, field-based program designed to prepare future educators for urban schools and communities. A key principle driving the creation of UTEC was that by moving teacher education into urban schools and communities, pre-service teachers and faculty would better understand the realities of urban education, including the social, political, and economic conditions impacting the lives and education of urban children and their families. A key goal of UTEC was to become part of the daily fabric of Jedediah Smith Elementary School and its community. To this end, all courses were taught at Jedediah Smith, where university students learned in collaboration with community members, groups, and agencies, and took part in neighborhood efforts to provide support for their children and their families. The school has now been re-named Leataata Floyd Elementary School (more on that later in this chapter).

Eighty percent of the university students and faculty in UTEC were White, middle-class, monolingual English speakers, none of whom lived in the Jedediah Smith/Leataata Floyd community. On the other hand, Leataata Floyd is a very low income, diverse elementary school that serves children from two neighborhood public housing projects.

Demographics of Leataata Floyd students are as follows:

- 97% eligible for free-or-reduced lunch
- 97% students of color
  - 55% Black
  - 21% Hispanic
  - 9% Asian
  - 3% White
- 18% English Language Learners
  - Home languages of ELL students—33% Spanish
  - Home languages of ELL students—16% Vietnamese

After moving all courses into the school, UTEC spent two years building trust by "dwelling" and "being there"—spending time daily among others in the school and the neighboring community. Over the first two years, the UTEC coordinator and her students attended community barbecues and back-to-school events, sometimes volunteering and sometimes just enjoying the events. Through seeing UTEC faculty members and students at the school every weekday during the university school year, the school's principal and teachers began to trust university faculty's intentions. Perhaps more importantly, UTEC eventually gained the trust of the matriarch of the neighborhood housing projects. Teachers demonstrated trust in the program by inviting the university students to take part in more and more school-wide activities. Over time, the K-6 students began to tell their parents and guardians about the "university people" at their school. Parents and community members no longer saw UTEC faculty members and students as strangers; rather, they began to trust the intentions of these "university people."

Drawing on the relationships developed over this time period, the UTEC faculty leader made arrangements for UTEC students to interview community members and talk with the children and their families about both their needs and their strengths. The community engagement activities that emerged from these studies were collaboratively developed by the university, school, and community, and varied based on the needs identified during each subsequent set of UTEC community studies.

- The Panthers. The longest-term relationship was developed with the Panthers community organization, which operated an after school tutoring/mentoring program within one of the housing projects. The Panthers program was created and is operated by two men who grew up in the neighborhood, moved out to get their college degrees, and

now give back to their former community by running this program. After gaining the community's trust, UTEC students and faculty were invited to serve as tutors and mentors for the program, which serves approximately 100 children per year.
- Family Resource Center. UTEC students and faculty, with the school's Assistant Principal, created a Family Resource Center in 2006. UTEC students served coffee to parents, assisted with computer access, and operated the children's book give-away section and the parent book exchange.
- School Library. Jedediah Smith did not have a librarian in 2005–2006, so the library officially closed. UTEC students re-opened and operated the library during three lunchtime periods each week for that year. Eighty children took advantage of the opportunity to go to the library during their lunch recess, where UTEC students read with them, helped them to locate books, and created bulletin boards with the children.
- Family Literacy Nights. UTEC students helped the school's Reading Coach and classroom teachers plan, prepare, and facilitate a Family Literacy Night in the spring of 2007. Approximately 30 children and their families attend this first offering of the event. The Family Literacy Night has continued to this day, although it is now solely offered by the school and its community partners.

In 2010, in the attempt to "turnaround" a history of low academic achievement, a new superintendent declared Jedediah Smith a "turnaround school" replacing all administrators, most teachers, and many programs. Like several other university-school-community organization partnership programs, UTEC was not invited back to the school; therefore UTEC moved back to the university campus. However, the partnership with the Panthers community organization has lasted over time. The UTEC Coordinator nominated the Panthers for a Community Partnership Award from Sacramento State, which it received in the spring of 2006. In the several years following, the Panthers applied for and received nonprofit status, based in part on the additional hours of tutoring and mentoring provided by UTEC students. With UTEC students helping to operate the program, one of the founders of the Panthers felt it was "in good hands" and was able to go back to school to earn a Special Education teaching credential. He is now a teacher at one of the community's high schools, and has expanded the tutoring/mentoring program to that setting. And finally, with all of this expanding capability to provide services to the children of the community, the former Jedediah Smith School has now been re-named in honor of the matriarch of the community, Leataata Floyd, the community partner for UTEC. This is an honor for which UTEC, through its university-school-community partnership, is proud to have played a part.

Conclusion and Some Reflections

Community engagement is a valued practice within higher education today. However, critics of this work point out its inherent hierarchical, paternalistic attitude toward the communities served. A feminist approach to community engagement recognizes the dangers of such an attitude, and instead approaches community engagement with an orientation "toward social transformation, consciousness-raising, and social activism that is the translation of thought into action..." (Ward, 2007, p. 104). The critical community engagement described here seeks to address inequitable power relationships in a university-community partnership by beginning with the community's needs and strengths, and "dwelling" in a community over time in order to develop trusting relationships between university and community. The three programs described in this chapter are vivid examples of the theory, practice, and long-term outcomes of repositioning either entire programs or individual university courses into the schools and communities. By becoming trusted partners, integrating into, and learning with our communities, we may develop service-learning programs that become stable, sustainable, and transformative forces that serve to strengthen ourselves, our programs, and our communities.

References

Benson, L., Puckett, J. L., & Harkavy, I. (2007). *Dewey's dream: Universities and democracies in an age of education reform, civil society, public schools, and democratic citizenship*. Philadelphia: Temple University Press.

Bottery, M. (2003). The management and mismanagement of trust. *Educational Management & Administration, 32*(3), 245–261.

Carnegie selects colleges and universities for 2010 community engagement classification. (2011, January). Carnegie Foundation for the Advance of Teaching. Retrieved from http://www.carnegiefoundation.org/newsroom/press-releases/carnegie-selects-colleges-and-universities-2010-community-engagement-classification

Daniel, B. J. (2007). Developing educational collectives and networks: Moving beyond the boundaries of "community" in urban education. In R. P. Solomon & D. N. R. Sekayi (Eds.), *Urban teacher education and teaching: Innovative practices for diversity and social justice* (pp. 31–47). Mahwah, NJ: Lawrence Erlbaum Associates.

Gambetta, D. (1988). Can we trust trust? In D. Gambetta (Ed.), *Trust: Making and breaking cooperative relations* (pp. 213–219). Oxford, UK: Basil Blackwell.

Gilbert, M., & Masucci, M. (2004). Feminist praxis in university-community partnerships. In D. Fuller & R. Kitchin (Eds.), *Radical theory/critical praxis: Making a difference beyond the academy?* (pp. 147–158). Victoria, BC: Praxis (e)Press.

Giroux, H. (1988). *Teachers as intellectuals: Toward a critical pedagogy of learning.* Westport, CT: Bergin & Garvey Publications, Inc.

Hands, C. (2005). It's who you know and what you know: The process of creating partnerships between schools and communities. *The School Community Journal, 15*(2), 63–84.

Harkavy, I., & Hartley, M. (2009). University–school–community partnerships for youth development and democratic renewal. *New Directions for Youth Development, 122,* 7–18.

Hill-Jackson, V., & Lewis, C. W. (2011). Service *loitering*: White pre-service teachers preparing for diversity in an underserved community. In T. Stewart & N. Webster (Eds.), *Problematizing service-learning: Critical reflections for development and action* (pp. 295–321). Charlotte, NC: Information Age Publishing.

Hoy, W. K., & Tschannen-Moran, M. (1999). Five facets of trust: An empirical confirmation in urban elementary schools. *Journal of School Leadership, 9,* 184–208.

Kahne, J., & Westheimer, J. (1996). In the service of what? The politics of service learning. *Phi Delta Kappan, 77,* 593–599.

King, J. T. (2004). Service-learning as a site for critical pedagogy: A case of collaboration, caring, and defamiliarization across borders. *The Journal of Experiential Education, 26*(3), 121–137.

Kuh, G. D. (2008). *High-impact educational practices: What they are, who has access to them, and why they matter.* Washington, DC: Association of American Colleges and Universities.

Lum, C. A., Aguirre, E. M., Martinez, R., Campa-Rodriguez, M., & Ultreras, R. (2009). Science for social responsibility. In P. L. Wong & R. D. Glass (Eds.), *Prioritizing urban children, teachers and schools through Professional Development Schools* (pp. 69–85). Albany, NY: SUNY Press.

Madsen-Camacho, M. (2004). Power and privilege: Community service learning in Tijuana. *Michigan Journal of Community Service Learning, 10*(3), 31–42.

Mathieu, P. (2005). *Tactics of hope: The public turn in English composition.* Portsmouth, NH: Boynton/Cook Publishers, Inc.

Murrell, P. C., Jr. (2001). *The community teacher: A new framework for effective urban teaching.* New York: Teachers College Press.

Noel, J. (2010). A critical interrogation of privilege, race, class, and power in a university faculty—urban community relationship. *The Urban Review, 42*(3), 210–220. DOI: 10.1007/s11256-009-0131-4

────── (2011). Striving for authentic community engagement: A process model from urban teacher education. *Journal of Higher Education Outreach and Engagement, 15*(1), 31–52.

────── (Ed.) (2013a). *Moving teacher education into urban schools and communities: Prioritizing community strengths.* New York: Routledge.

——— (2013b). Conclusion: Prioritizing community strengths in urban teacher education. In J. Noel (Ed.), *Moving teacher education into urban schools and communities: Prioritizing community strengths* (pp. 217–223). New York: Routledge.
Porfilio, B. J., & Hickman, H. (Eds.). (2011). Introduction. In B. J. Porfilio & H. Hickman (Eds.), *Critical service-learning as revolutionary pedagogy: A project of study agency in action* (pp. ix–xx). Charlotte, NC: Information Age Publishing.
Reed, W. A. (2004). A tree grows in Brooklyn: Schools of education as brokers of social capital in low-income neighborhoods. In J. L. Kincheloe, A. Bursztyn, & S. R. Steinberg (Eds.), *Teaching teachers: Building a quality school of urban education* (pp. 65–90). New York: Peter Lang.
Rosenberg, P. M. (1997). Underground discourses: Exploring Whiteness in teacher education. In M. Fine, L. Weis, L. C. Powell, & L. M. Wong (Eds.), *Off White: Readings on race, power, and society* (pp. 79–89). New York: Routledge.
Sobredo, J., Kim-Ju, G., Figueroa, J., Mark, G., & Fabionar, J. (2008). An ethnic studies model of community mobilization: Collaborative partnership with a high risk public high school. *American Journal of Preventive Medicine, 34*(Suppl. 2), S82–S88.
Stefkovich, J., & Shapiro, J. P. (2002). Deconstructing communities: Educational leaders and their ethical decision-making processes. In P. T. Begley & O. Johansson (Eds.), *The ethical dimensions of school leadership* (pp. 77–87). Dordrecht, The Netherlands: Kluwer Academic Publishers.
Stodghill, R., & Bower, A. (2002, August 25). Welcome to America's most diverse city. *Time*. Retrieved from http://www.time.com/time/nation/article/0,8599,340694-1,00.html
Tschannen-Moran, M. (2004). *Trust matters: Leadership for successful schools*. San Francisco, CA: Jossey-Bass.
Tschannen-Moran, M., & Hoy, W. K. (2000). A multidisciplinary analysis of the nature, meaning, and measurement of trust. *Review of Educational Research, 71*, 547–593.
Ward, V. E. (2007). Women as social warriors: A framework for community service learning combining Amazonian feminist thinking and social justice education theories. In G. B. Stahly (Ed.), *Gender identity, equity, and violence: Multidisciplinary perspectives through service learning* (pp. 103–120). Sterling, VA: Stylus.
Webb, P., Cole, K., & Skeen, T. (2007). Feminist social projects: Building bridges between communities and universities. *College English, 69*(3), 238–259.
Zeichner, K. (2010). Rethinking the connections between campus courses and field experiences in college and university-based teacher education. *Journal of Teacher Education, 61*(1–2), 89–99.

CHAPTER 11

Conclusions: Re-visioning Community Engagement as Feminist Praxis

Jennifer Hauver James and
Susan Van Deventer Iverson

We began this volume by asking the question, "What might be gained by bringing a feminist lens to the work of community engagement?" Though action is central to feminist thought and practice, many feminist pedagogues have resisted aligning themselves with the discourses of community engagement. Why? Because, as Westheimer and Kahne (2004) assert, the vast majority of classroom-based community engagement efforts have as their aim charity-oriented service that reinforces the notion of engagement as "feel good" participation. Students participate in book drives, they tutor "under privileged" children, they collect trash along the side of the road, they may even lend their skills to refurbish homes for *Habitat for Humanity*. But once the service is complete, as Poppendieck (1999) notes, the volunteer rests comfortably in her familiar space, she is affirmed of her "goodness" for having given herself to the less fortunate, and the underlying social issues remain untouched. The student who says (upon completing her shift at the soup kitchen) that she hopes her grandchildren will someday have an equally rewarding opportunity to serve their community, emphasizes the benefits of service for herself. But if the issue of hunger were addressed in her community and her grandchildren were denied the opportunity to serve soup at the local shelter, would that not be better? Volunteer work plays an important role in society toward attending to the *symptoms* of social ills, but many feminists argue that being truly engaged with one's community demands attention to the *causes* of those ills.

The contributors to this book share a commitment to reimagining community engagement with an eye to feminist aims of dismantling of the institutional, discursive, sociopolitical contexts that perpetuate inequality—particularly inequalities hinging on gender, sex, and sexual orientation. Each is committed to extending the conversation of community engagement in ways that acknowledge, unpack, and address the barriers to equality and access that exist in their communities. Because they bring their unique experiences and perspectives to bear on the question posed, the book offers a wide variety of possibilities for re-visioning CE as feminist pedagogy.

Re-visioning Purpose

First and foremost, the women in this book complicate our understanding of the purposes and possibilities of CE when considered through a feminist lens. The contributors push us to think deeply about what CE might aspire to achieve if reimagined with feminist goals in mind. Like other scholars critical of traditional CE, the authors argue for examination of social issues that perpetuate inequities in our communities. They maintain that CE must aim to be collective and collaborative if it is to be powerful and sustainable. Beyond these important goals, however, the women in this volume suggest that bringing a feminist lens to their work means striving toward political activism, authenticity and reciprocity of relationships, and attending specifically to social issues facing women today.

Inviting Students to "Try On" Feminist, Activist Identities

Central to the aims contributors ascribe to their work is providing students with opportunities to experience feminist activism first-hand. Clark-Taylor, Mitchell, and Rich write of the Rocxxy Summer Internship Program: "This combination of academic, experiential, and professional experience was meant to inspire students to become stronger, more resilient agents of social change upon graduation as well as equip them with the necessary skills for realizing feminist ideals in their post-college lives" (p. 157). Student participants reported growing more comfortable with their feminist, activist identities because they were paired with positive role models and mentors in the community. As one student reflected, "My supervisors both had day jobs but still spent hours upon hours working for their causes each week; it was inspiring to see their dedication and how they made feminist activism a major part of their lives despite other responsibilities" (p. 165).

Similarly, Dana Bisignani speaks about her efforts to engage students in "activist-apprentice pedagogy." Here, students are paired with community organizers from local nonprofits who serve as activist role models. Bisignani writes, "This *apprenticeship* with an experienced activist prioritizes students' learning practical grassroots organizing tools and also provides an affirmation of the real possibility of change—in effect, local organizers train a new generation of practitioners in a set of skills that they are then be able to practice on their own" (p. 102). She reports that, at the close of the experience, many students "claimed 'activist' as part of their identities" (p. 105). The intergenerational nature of this apprenticeship allowed students to see themselves as part of a long tradition of activists working to address issues facing women in their communities.

Though CE is typically lauded for its impact on students' evolving sense of efficacy as citizens, the question often asked is *what kind of citizenship?* Here that question is answered: justice-oriented, activist citizenship. The contributors to this volume hold high expectations for their students that they will come to understand and appreciate the power of collective action for attending to persistent societal inequities. Whether students choose to embrace the aims and practices of feminist activism is not a requirement— such an expectation would run counter to the freedom to name ourselves that feminists hold dear. Making the choice possible—helping students to envision themselves as members of this larger feminist community and providing them opportunities to try it on—this is the goal.

Fostering Authentic Relationships among Students and Others

Developing students' identities as feminist activists is closely tied to the goal of helping students develop authentic relationships with community partners—relationships that are reciprocal and sustaining and serve as spaces for risk taking and exploration. Jana Noel, in Chapter 10, "Developing Sustainable Community Engagement by Re-positioning Programs into Communities," argues for "repositioning" CE into the communities we aim to serve in ways that emphasize "relationship-building, the examination of issues of power, race and class, and a commitment to community-based social justice efforts" (p. 176). Such a relocation of CE outside of the university aims to shift the balance of power between those doing the service and those being served. CE designed with this shift in mind engages students in reciprocal relationships with others who together take up the issues facing their communities. The aims here are trust, understanding, and shared responsibility over time—a powerful counter-narrative to traditional "top-down" programs that maintain the privileged position of university faculty and students as knowers and doers.

Likewise, Mena and Vaccaro call for authentic engagement with others to ensure "group survival" through collective resistance to the many manifestations of institutional oppression. They write, "It was not a form of traditional service-learning...for 'others' done out of guilt or to fulfill a requirement. Instead CE was a 'do with' form of authentic CE (Marullo & Edwards, 2000) that was a crucial aspect of their identities and life work as women of color" (p. 64).

As contributors show us, this "do with" approach to CE helps students come to see themselves as part of something larger (both now and throughout time), it introduces them to role models so they can see feminist activism as it is lived, and it teaches them powerful lessons about what is made possible when people work together to bring about change.

Understanding Persistent Social Issues Impacting Our Communities

Finally, there is a resounding call for us to pay attention to the role power and privilege play inside and outside of the institutions in which we work, examination of the taken-for-granted, and specifically, interrogation of inequities related to gender and sexuality. The goals of feminist CE, then, go far beyond helping students to "feel good" about what they've given to others, but to critically reflect on their positionality with respect to the issues and people in their communities.

Magaña and Miller's *Young Men's Leadership Program*, in which a group of ten to twelve male undergraduate students to serve as mentors to fifth-grade boys from a local elementary school, for instance, aims to facilitate examination of dominant constructs of gender and masculinity in the lives of young boys. They describe their use of film as a means to

> examine how media outlets endorse a guise, or performance, of a violent masculinity as an arbitrary concept of manhood that can and should be challenged...reflect on their own gender socialization and complicity or engagement along a continuum of harm of sexist behavior, and the personal and societal costs of this...examine limitations placed on boys and men to perform a traditionally celebrated masculinity that emphasizes physical strength, constrained emotional expression, competition over collaboration, and narrow understandings of "successful manhood" marked by sexual prowess and financial success. (p. 142)

Cunningham and Crandall similarly outline the study of larger social issues as a central aim of their work: "We designed the course to have both online and face-to-face opportunities for students to examine the social, economic and political forces influencing the use of communication technologies." And Seher, in her efforts to re-vision her course through a feminist lens, explains,

> My aim, therefore, by (re)positioning PIF as the *possibility* of feminist student philanthropy is to draw explicit attention to the artificial and conflated distinction between the "politics" of activism and the safety of "service"...I argue feminist educators can (and should) reclaim student philanthropy for what it already is—an inherently political teaching strategy that presents the opportunity to teach activism—in that the underlying social issues often at the center of philanthropic initiatives (e.g., hunger, access to health care, health disparities, violence against women) are some of the most pressing social concerns of our time affecting women. (p. 120)

Re-visioning CE through a feminist lens reshapes our purposes—pushing us to strive for individual and group transformation through more critical, authentic engagement with the world around us. We are encouraged to consider new identities, new relationships, and new understandings as outcomes of feminist CE.

Re-visioning Practice

Reaching new goals requires new methods, of course. And so the authors in this volume introduce us to new ways of imagining the practical aspects of CE. Among these are role modeling and apprenticeship models of engagement, embracing new contexts for CE work, engaging in collaborative critical examination of the contexts in which we work, and extending the boundaries of our work to include new partners.

CE as Role Modeling and Mentoring

Traditional CE involves placing students with local community organizations where they spend time over the course of a semester providing service and reflecting on the intersections of their experience and course content. Students may or may not be supervised in these experiences and their "service" may or may not be well connected to the academic goals of the courses in which they're enrolled. Often the fact that students are giving time to their communities and practicing a "personally responsible" form of citizenship is sufficient justification for the experience. The contributors to this volume are not satisfied with volunteerism and loosely tied connections to the community as characteristics of CE. Because they aim to foster students' growth toward a feminist, activist form of citizenship, they create and implement experiences that provide ample exposure to and opportunities to engage in community activism.

Mena and Vaccaro, for instance, speak to the power of role modeling and mentorship for "group survival." They offer examples of women faculty and staff of color joining groups and assuming mentorship of junior colleagues. They celebrate their participants' shared sense of responsibility for "paying it forward" to future generations, creating safe spaces where dialogue and action to resist institutional and sociopolitical oppression can thrive. Bisignani's *activist-apprenticeship pedagogy* ascribes to similar aims, pairing students with experienced activists in their communities. These intergenerational partnerships allow for up-close and personal experience of feminist activism through which students gain appreciation for and understanding of the aims and practices of feminist engagement. In both instances, students grow more comfortable with their evolving identities as feminists and as activists because they have traversed the theoretical space of feminist practice to a lived experience of it. In this way, the pedagogy of CE moves from methods aimed at merely enhancing course content toward *praxis*—where students come to see themselves as potential members of a collective committed to feminist causes.

Embracing New Contexts and New Partners

Because the authors want to grow relationships that are authentic, mutual, and sustaining, they seek to relocate their work within communities, crossing the physical boundaries of the institutions where they work and embracing new partners in their efforts. Noel underscores the importance of stepping outside of the academy, "'dwelling' in a community over time in order to develop trusting relationships between university and community" (p. 189). She attributes the success of the *Science for Social Responsibility/Community Health Fair, 65th Street Corridor Collaborative,* and the *Urban Teacher Education Center* to the joint decision-making, shared responsibility for implementation and continued dialogue, which marked these university-community relationships. Like Bisignani and others, Noel asserts that feminist CE requires new ways of imagining ourselves in relation with our communities, shifting the existing balance of power, learning and acting alongside those around us.

Other authors emphasize the importance of extending our definition of community—not only redefining the roles of traditional partners, but inviting *new* partners to take up the work. Magaña and Miller reflect on their experience of creating a program implemented by male partners for adolescent boys at the local elementary school. In their efforts to extend the domain of feminist CE to include men as equal partners, they recognize their own suspicion difficulties in trusting men to carry the load. Honest reflections like these help us to see the barriers of our own imagination and the promise of what can come when we have the courage to overcome them.

Of course, we need not always look outside of our institutions and immediate spaces for new partners. Sometimes the most powerful relationships we establish are with those around us who share our commitments. Because CE work is so often isolated, it is important, as Mena and Vaccaro (Chapter 4) and Verjee and Butterwick (Chapter 3) remind us, to call on each other as partners for shared reflection and collective action.

Deepening and Extending Our Reflection

Though reflection has long been heralded as a crucial element of CE, the reflection touted here moves beyond classroom-based discussion and student journals. The authors speak to the importance of ongoing, collaborative, *critical* examination of the institutional, sociopolitical and discursive contexts of our CE work inside and outside of the academy.

Of course, many critical CE scholars advocate the interrogation of underlying social issues impacting the communities in which we work. The authors here echo that call. Cunningham and Crandall write, "We designed the course to have both online and face-to-face opportunities for students to examine the social, economic and political forces influencing the use of communication technologies" (p. 75). Similarly, Seher argues that feminist educators must "reclaim student philanthropy...[as] an inherently political teaching strategy" in an effort to explore and act upon "the underlying social issues often at the center of philanthropic initiatives" (p. 120). Attention to the causes—not simply the symptoms—of social ills is central to the work of those who share their stories here. But the authors call us to do more. They ask us to interrogate our own positionality within the spaces we inhabit and the ways we may be complicit in their maintenance.

Verjee and Butterwick, for example, suggest that together we should attend to "the ways in which universities disenfranchise and marginalize women of color...highlighting the inequities and injustices that women of color face in the academy, and therefore in CE organizing... to foreground how racism is a key dimension of oppressive societal, social and institutional structures" (p. 33). Their autobiographical method is a powerful example of collaborative examination of taken-for-granted. The collaborative nature pushed these women from their comfort zones as they articulated their experience for one another. This is difficult yet important work if we are to recognize the ways that we are complicit in the very structures we wish to disrupt and disempower.

As the authors here demonstrate, reflection can take place in small groups with one another as we reflect on our practice, it might occur individually as we push ourselves to be activist role models for our students, alongside community partners who share our commitments to social justice, and with our students. What is essential is that we push ourselves into unfamiliar spaces— by making the familiar strange, feminist CE is made possible.

Challenges to Feminist CE

In our view, an important contribution of this volume—made possible by bringing a feminist lens to the work of CE—is that we come to see more clearly the barriers to our work. Taking a close look at our efforts to enact feminist praxis in CE settings, we see not only what is made possible, but also what gets in our way. To move forward, we must know the obstacles that stand before us.

To begin with, CE takes time. We need time to develop partnerships with those in our communities. As Noel notes, we must "dwell" in community, be present, so that we might begin to understand the contexts in which we hope to participate. We need time to collaboratively design and implement field-based experiences for our students if they are to have any meaningful, lasting impact. We need time to read and reflect, to re-vision our work. Time is a valuable source that many who engage CE work do not have. Rather, we work over and above our assigned teaching, research, and service loads. The feminist educators who tell their stories here worked "over time." Recall Seher, who in her first year at the University of Akron took it upon herself to reflect upon and re-vision the PIF program with feminist aims in mind. No one asked her or expected her to do this re-visioning. It is our shared call to prepare students for activist, critical engagement with society, and our commitment to the causes harnessed by feminist thinkers that drive us.

There is also quite often a lack of resources to support the CE work we do. It should not come as a surprise that the research reported here was conducted by the instructors themselves, on their own teaching, typically one semester at a time. Building and sustaining research programs around key aspects of CE work is made difficult by the lack of funding to support it—funding that provides release time and research assistantships. If CE work, in general, is undervalued and underresourced, then critical approaches to CE are even less so. Again, the work of CE—this time the documentation of it, the inquiry into it, so that we might grow ever more competent in our efforts to implement it—requires "over time." As with the work described in the pages of this book, CE is often done *in spite of* the institutions in which it occurs.

Buttressing these structural barriers are prevailing discourses and narratives that privilege particular ways of being. Verjee reflects on her experience at a service-learning conference where "the charity model of service learning dominated the discussions, with much attention given to getting as many students as possible involved with 'doing good' and helping those less fortunate..." (p. 37). The faculty Verjee encountered made every effort to resist a more critical stance. Charity work somehow seems less political—more neutral, perhaps, than other forms of CE—particularly CE that is overtly feminist in its aims. But of course, it is not. A charity discourse is dangerous because its politics are masked by this discourses of neutrality. Those who oppose it are quickly identified as rabble-rousers, likely to inappropriately use their positions of power to push an agenda on their students. "Feminist" and "activist" are "dirty words" simply because they are honest and transparent about their politics.

Neutrality and objectivity, are of course, gendered discourses that relegate feeling, intuition, and relationship to the margins. So too is the narrative of "service" gendered. Narratives about who should do the work of CE are powerful in their taken-for-grantedness. We think it is no accident that the authors who responded to our call for chapters were all women. As Verjee and Butterwick remind us, women (and often women of color) typically shoulder the brunt of the service work for the academy—individuals whose voices fail to reach the level of policy and persuasion of their male counterparts because they have been "relegated to the kitchen." The service conducted goes largely unrecognized and unrewarded because it is not valued in the same ways other contributions are.

Dominant notions about *who* is best suited to conduct service work in the academy are tied up in gendered discourses about *what* counts as knowledge and who ought to be in the business of constructing it. Research on teaching, research that emphasizes voice and experience, research that is autobiographical and narrative rather than quantitative in its rendering is harder to fund, less likely to be published in top tier journals, and—because it is women's work—is less valued.

In the face of these challenges, it is helpful to have the concrete examples of success described in the preceding chapters. The contributors inspire us with the big and small steps they take toward realizing the goals of feminist praxis. Though there are of course voices missing from the conversation captured here, a strength of this volume is the varied positions of contributors—with respect to their evolving identities and work as feminist educators. We look to them for some closing thoughts about how to move forward in our efforts to realize the potential of CE as feminist praxis.

Where to Go from Here?

The chapters in this book contain any number of wonderful examples and reflections on the difficult, yet important work of feminist CE. Here, we cull what we think are four helpful lessons we can take with us as we push forward.

First, the authors remind us to *start with ourselves*. They remind us that becoming the feminist pedagogues we wish to become is an ongoing process, enhanced by deep reflection, extensive reading, and critical engagement with the world around us. We ought not to be afraid to ask difficult questions of ourselves as we ask them of others, so that we may begin to name the places we wish to occupy in the contexts that work to shape us. We are also reminded to continuously strive to articulate our experiences, our understandings, and our aims. Stories are worth sharing—not only for ourselves, but for others engaged in the work; our lived experience is a powerful site for meaning making.

Second, we are encouraged to *connect with others* in order to deepen our reflection, grow in our understanding and have a larger impact on our world. Whether those connections are within our institutions, across generational lines, in our local communities, with practicing activists, or with men, the authors here push us to step outside of traditional partnerships in order to grow the work. Role modeling and mentoring, in particular, are highlighted as valuable means of growing our capacity as we learn from more knowledgeable others.

Third, the women who share pieces of themselves in this volume challenge us to *imagine and hope*. Their stories of resistance, the small and large successes they meet as a result of their courage and commitment, are powerful reminders of the possibility of CE as feminist praxis. Revisioning CE as role modeling, mentoring, as apprenticeship, as occurring in cyberspace, with new partners, as authentic and sustained relationship, and as work that is transformative for those who take it up...are not the outer limits of what we can imagine. They are only the beginning.

And finally, despite the devaluing of research on practice, we see the collection of studies and reflections captured in this volume as essential for *combating the discursive, institutional, sociopolitical barriers* we encounter as those committed to feminist CE. Research on CE which examines its impact on students and communities, which extends across time and space to understand the reach of our efforts, which critically examines the contexts in which CE work is done and keeps the dialogue alive—we believe—is desperately needed for growing our work and speaking back, in hopes of shifting the institutional climate.

Putting this volume together has been an important part of our journey as feminist pedagogues—one that has challenged us to broaden our conceptions, question our assumptions, re-vision our work, and dream of new possibilities. We hope that it has done the same for you. Mostly we hope that it will be one of many volumes of its kind, a call to carry on and grow the conversation.

References

Marullo, S., & Edwards, B. (2000). From charity to justice: The potential of university-community collaboration for social change. *American Behavioral Scientist, 43*(5), 895–912.

Poppendieck, J. (1999). *Sweet charity? Emergency food and the end of entitlement.* New York, NY: Penguin Books.

Westheimer, J., & Kahne, J. (2004). What kind of citizen? The politics of educating for democracy. *American Educational Research Journal, 41*(2), 237–269.

Contributors

Dana Bisignani teaches in the Women's, Gender, and Sexuality Studies Program at Purdue University and is currently a doctoral candidate in Literature. Her research examines the labor of poet-activists in the antiwar movement during the Vietnam era, and gendered discourses surrounding the role of the poet in wartime more broadly. In 2013, she received the Berenice A. Carroll Award for Feminism, Peace, and Social Justice for the service-learning project she writes about in this volume.

Shauna Butterwick is Associate Professor in the Department of Educational Studies at the University of British Columbia, Vancouver, Canada. She has served as the President of the Canadian Association for the Study of Adult Education. She teaches in the Adult Learning and Education program and also instructs courses on research methodology and community engagement. Most of her research is community-based and conducted in partnership with various community groups focusing mainly on women's learning in various contexts including: the workplace, social movements, and welfare-based programs.

Angela Clark-Taylor has a MA in Women's Studies from SUNY Brockport and a MS in Educational Administration from the University of Rochester. She has been with the Susan B. Anthony Institute for Gender & Women's Studies at the University of Rochester since 2008. Through her work at the Institute, she coordinates local, national, and international conferences and events. She also serves as an undergraduate adviser and coordinates the Institute's experiential learning programs. Her research and teaching focus on issues of sex, gender, and sexuality in higher education. She is currently working on her PhD in Educational Leadership at the University of Rochester.

Heather M. Crandall is Associate Professor in the Masters Program in Communication and Leadership Studies at Gonzaga University where she teaches rhetorical criticism, media literacy, and interpersonal and small group communication. Her research interests include social change through visual rhetoric, communication and instruction, and media literacy. Her published works include articles in *Communication Teacher*, and *The Journal of Leadership Studies*, and reviews in *Communication Research Trends*, and a chapter in *Misbehaviors in Higher Education*. Currently she edits *The Northwest Journal of Communication*.

Carolyn M. Cunningham is Assistant Professor in the Masters Program in Communication and Leadership Studies at Gonzaga University where she teaches courses on communication theory and research, communication technology, and communication pedagogy. Her research looks at the intersections of gender and technology and her work has been published in *New Media & Society* and the *Journal of Children and Media*. She is also the editor of *Social Networking and Impression Management: Identity in the Digital Age* published in 2012 by Lexington Books.

Susan Van Deventer Iverson is Associate Professor of Higher Education Administration & Student Personnel at Kent State University where she is also an affiliated faculty member with both the Women's Studies and LGBT Studies Programs. Prior to becoming faculty, Iverson worked in student affairs administration for more than ten years, and was most recently active in a federally grant-funded project to combat violence against women. Iverson's scholarly interests include women and leadership, multicultural competence, feminist pedagogy, and the use of feminist poststructural research; she has coedited a volume published by Routledge (2010), *Reconstructing policy analysis in higher education: Feminist poststructural perspectives*.

Jennifer Hauver James is Associate Professor in the Department of Educational Theory & Practice at the University of Georgia. Her scholarship explores various dimensions of teachers' identity and lived experience as they influence their relationships with formal and hidden curricula, students, families, and communities. She is particularly interested in the gendered nature of discursive, institutional, and sociopolitical contexts that shape the possibilities we imagine as educators. Her work has been published in leading national and international journals, including *Gender & Education, Teaching & Teacher Education,* and *Theory & Research in Social Education.*

Lamea "Elle" Shaaban-Magaña serves as Director for The University of Alabama Women's Resource Center. She has worked to expand services to reach marginalized groups and provide more comprehensive, inclusive programs addressing gender issues on campus. Elle brings to the center experience in the area of coalition building and outreach program development. With an educational background in the areas of communications, women's studies, and human development and family studies, she has previously worked in the fields of social services, child welfare, and the judicial system. She is currently completing a PhD in social and cultural studies of education.

Jasmine A. Mena, PhD, is Assistant Professor of Clinical Psychology at the University of Rhode Island (URI). Her research examines the experiences of marginalization and oppression and subsequent impact on physical and mental health and wellbeing. Recent research includes the experiences of women of color in higher education; LGBTQ students of color; and academic perseverance among Latino students. The goal of this research is translation to clinical service delivery to culturally diverse vulnerable and underserved populations. Her work also encompasses the practice of Spanish language psychotherapy services and clinical supervision through a cultural lens.

Melanie L. Miller holds a Bachelor's in Social Welfare, Master of Arts in Community Counseling, and an EdD in Higher Education Administration. Prior to coming to the University of Alabama (UA) in 1995, as Director of the Women's Resource Center, her work experience included work with community nonprofit agencies. During her tenure at UA, Dr. Miller has served in several positions, including Associate Dean of Students. She is currently Director of Student and Community Engagement in the Center for Community-Based Partnerships. Her research interests include interpersonal violence, student development, and social justice ally development.

Quinlan Mitchell is a current undergraduate student at the University of Rochester. His majors include Comparative Literature and Linguistics. His studies have taken him abroad to Beijing, China, and Buenos Aires, Argentina, studying literature, film, and culture. Quinlan was accepted into the Take 5 Scholars program—a tuition-free fifth year of undergraduate study—and is engaging in academic investigation within the departments of Visual and Cultural Studies and Women's Studies. His coursework looks at the representation of women in recent and contemporary American film and photography through a variety of feminist lenses. Quinlan participated in *Rocxxy: Summer Internship in Feminist Activism and Leadership* in Summer 2013.

Jana Noel is Special Assistant to the President and Professor of Education at California State University, Sacramento. Her areas of scholarship are teacher education, multicultural education, and community engagement. Her 2013 book *Moving Teacher Education into Urban Schools and Communities: Prioritizing Community Strengths* (Routledge, 2013) received a 2013 Critics Choice Award for outstanding book from the American Educational Studies Association. Noel also created and coordinated the Sacramento State Urban Teacher Education Center, which received a 2008 California Quality Education Partnership Award for Distinguished Service to Children and the Preparation of Teachers, awarded by the California Council on Teacher Education.

KaeLyn Rich has been the Genesee Valley Chapter Director of the New York Civil Liberties Union since 2011. Rich specializes in direct action organizing, nonprofit administration and young adult engagement. Formerly, Rich was the community affairs coordinator at Planned Parenthood of the Rochester/Syracuse Region, where she was responsible for legislative advocacy, government relations, coalition building, and the regional campus organizing program. Rich holds BA degrees in Women's Studies and English from SUNY Oswego and a graduate certificate in nonprofit management from SUNY Brockport.

Christin L. Seher, MS, RDN, LD, is a doctoral candidate in Higher Education Administration at Kent State University and an instructor of nutrition/dietetics at the University of Akron. Her research interests include: dietetics curriculum/professionalization practices; public health practice/policy; issues/trends in higher education; cultural competence/diversity education; academic motherhood; and the scholarship of teaching and learning—including service-learning and critical pedagogy. She has presented her research internationally, nationally, and regionally and authored/coauthored over a dozen publications. She lives near Cleveland with her partner and son who keep life exciting, and who remind her daily why she wants—no needs—to be an academic.

Annemarie Vaccaro, PhD is Associate Professor at the University of Rhode Island (URI). Her research interests focus on the intersections between college student development and gender, race, class, and sexual orientation.

Her work is inspired by critical and feminist perspectives which call attention to underlying inequalities embedded in society and social structures such as higher education. Dr. Vaccaro primarily uses qualitative inquiry to delve deeply into the lived experiences of students, faculty, and staff in higher education.

Begum Verjee graduated with an MEd in Counseling Psychology and an EdD in Educational Leadership & Policy, both from the University of British Columbia. As a higher education professional, community psychology practitioner, and social change agent, she has a strong record in adult, global, and continuing education; program planning and development; and student development, retention, engagement and success, particularly with regard to students of color. She has an interest in exploring post-secondary mental health issues from social determinants of health lens, and in institutional transformation through creating inclusive and equitable communities.

Index

activism, 2, 6, 10, 15, 20, 22, 32, 35, 41, 54, 57, 64, 66, 70, 97–9, 104, 109, 116, 119, 136, 140, 158–9, 161, 194–5, 198
activist-apprentice pedagogy, 4, 94, 101–2, 105, 109, 195, 198
  pro-feminist men's, 139
ally, allies, 31, 44, 135, 139, 140, 141, 150, 162
anarchist, 100
  educators, 96, 99, 100, 101
  theories of education, 94
Anzaldua, Gloria, 61, 135, 137, 143, 151, 170
authentic relationships, 5, 54, 71, 118, 177, 194, 195–6, 198, 202
autobiographical method, 200

border crossing, 20, 108, 135, 137, 151
boundary crossing, 5, 6
boundary spanner, 42
Butin, Dan, 9, 14, 18–20, 120

Carnegie Community Engagement Classification, 175, 180
Carnegie Foundation for the Advancement of Teaching, 15
change agents; agents of (social) change, 15, 157, 158, 162, 170, 172, 194

Childers, Sara, 138, 139
citizens; citizenship, 14, 18, 20, 94, 102, 126, 158, 171, 195, 198
  justice-oriented, 18, 20, 195
  participatory, 18
  personally responsible, 18, 128–9, 198
civic, 16, 42
  consciousness, 1
  discourse, 20–1
  education, educators, 18, 20, 53
  engagement, 1, 14, 18–9, 22, 56, 77, 97, 98, 99, 117, 183
  identity, 1
  knowledge, 2
  learning, 2, 18, 175
  maturity, 18
  minded, 19
  participation, 18
  responsibility, 1, 16, 54, 123
classism, 3, 31, 32, 33, 38, 39, 43, 62, 66, 149
code switching, 145
Collins, Patricia Hill, 12, 39, 57
colonialism, 37, 40, 41, 45, 46, 17137, 40, 46, 171
  cnticolonial, 31, 32, 40, 45
  colonial relationships, 41
color blind, 36, 41, 45

community, 4, 5, 16–17, 18, 37, 45, 53, 57, 58, 60–1, 64, 69, 71, 149–50, 189
  of color, 70
  deficit, 37, 42, 43
  strengths based model, 150
community engagement, 1, 6, 14, 15–16, 18, 20, 22, 53, 54–7, 61–4
  as charity, 5, 6, 17, 22, 31
  feminist, 3, 5, 6, 9, 17, 32–4, 40
  as justice, 22, 32, 53, 56, 63, 71
  partners, 6, 15, 22, 32, 34, 43, 150, 159–60, 164–5, 169–70, 176–7, 181–3, 186, 188, 199, 200
  reciprocal, 22, 42, 149
competence, 19, 59, 69, 115, 117, 178, 183, 201
  multicultural/intercultural, 19
  relational, 59
consciousness, 4, 5, 11, 14–15, 41, 94, 119, 121, 129, 137, 139, 158, 162, 171
  lack of consciousness, 34, 41
Corporation for National and Community Service, 180
counter-stories, 3, 12, 31
  counter-narrative, 33, 34, 36, 149, 151, 196
counter-sites, 94, 99
critical analysis, 21, 150
cyber
  bullying, 88
  civics, 14
  pedagogies, 14, 78
  space, 5, 14, 76, 77, 202

decolonizing, 41, 42, 43, 45
democracy, 2, 19, 95, 104
demographic, 123, 149, 170, 180, 181, 184, 187
disruption, 20, 136, 176
diversity, 3, 19, 45, 70, 162, 180
"doing the university's housework" (Masse & Hogan), 17, 36

educate, 43, 66, 68, 94, 127, 137
empower/ment, 6, 53, 57, 58, 62, 64, 66, 69, 70, 76, 95, 149, 151, 162, 172
  empowerment as tool, 14, 87
  disempower, 94, 200
engaged learning, 16, 54, 159
experiential, 1, 21, 115, 157, 194
  learning, 6, 15, 116, 117, 119, 121, 155, 159, 161, 169, 171

face-to-face, 75, 84, 197, 199
feminist, 2, 4, 5, 6, 9, 10–15, 21, 31, 40, 53, 57, 61, 70, 77, 88, 95, 98, 99, 100, 105, 106, 109, 116, 119, 121, 127, 129, 130, 137, 138, 139, 146, 149, 151, 156, 158, 170–1, 176, 189, 194, 200, 202
  civic engagement, 10
  critical race feminism, 12, 32–4, 40, 41, 42, 46, 137
  cyberfeminism, 4, 14, 75, 76–7, 78, 79, 84, 85, 88
  free market feminism, 95–6
  liberal feminism, 10–11, 20–1
  multicultural feminism, 12–13, 53
  pedagogy, 4, 13, 14, 21, 22, 78, 80, 96, 121, 123, 141, 156, 158, 159, 194, 202
  philanthropy, 4, 116, 119, 120, 123, 124–30, 197, 199
  post-structural feminism, 13, 19–20, 136
  radical feminism, 11–12, 56, 99, 100, 108
  standpoint, 169
  technofeminism, 76–7, 86, 87
  third Wave, 95
Foucault, Michel, 13, 139
Freire, 19, 45, 96, 119

grassroots, 39, 70, 90, 102, 103, 105, 170, 195

heterosexism, 11
hooks, 17, 19, 21, 33, 39, 40, 53, 97

identity, 4, 13, 20, 34, 53, 54, 55,
  57, 59, 60, 61, 62, 64, 66, 69, 70,
  71, 100, 105, 116, 127, 129–30,
  130, 137, 140, 146, 150, 158,
  163, 164, 166, 169, 195, 196,
  198, 202
  boundaries, 5
  discourses, 13
  feminist, 116, 146, 163, 164, 166,
    170–1, 194
  positionality, 13, 59, 158, 177, 196
  standpoint, 12, 33, 56, 169
insider, 3, 63, 68, 135, 139, 158
institutional structures, 11, 33, 44,
  200
institutional transformation, 32, 33,
  38, 209
internship, 155, 160, 169

Katz, Jackson, 139, 141
Kaufman, Michael, 139
Kimmel, Michael, 139
Kivel, Paul, 139, 142
knowledge, 5, 6, 12, 13, 15, 18, 20, 37,
  40, 70, 79, 80, 85, 87, 93, 94, 101,
  102, 103, 139, 141, 142, 164, 176,
  178, 180
  about women, 156
  antithetical, 34
  brokers, 42
  civic, 2
  classroom, 158, 167
  of communities, 35, 45, 63
  construction/Production, 21, 96, 98,
    99, 119, 138, 158
  cultural, 43
  exchange of, 100
  maps of knowledge, 177
  pedagogical, 151
  technologies, 77
  what counts as, 201

Lather, Patti, 13, 136, 138
leadership, 34, 65, 138, 143–4, 145,
  157, 170, 183
  feminist, 6
  young men's, 5, 140–2
learning, 2, 4, 5, 13, 15, 16, 18, 32,
  54, 84, 85, 95, 96, 99, 101, 102,
  105, 106, 107, 115, 116, 117, 118,
  119, 121, 122, 130, 143, 145, 150,
  157, 158, 159, 160, 161, 162, 167,
  169, 170, 171, 172, 175, 178, 179,
  180, 182, 189, 195, 198. *See also*
  service-learning
  active, 115, 162
  civic, 2, 18, 175
  classroom, 101, 121, 160, 161
  community-based, 77, 189
  connected, 159
  engaged, 16, 54, 159
  group, 166
  objectives, 6, 122
  outcomes, 2, 4, 19, 22, 117
  paradigms, 119
  participatory, 78, 81
  passive, 96
  place-based learning, 160, 163, 165,
    169
  teaching and, 13, 15, 19, 180
  theoretical, 106
  transformative, 150
Lorde, Audre, 11

masculinity, 140, 143, 196
  Man box, 142
  boy code, 141, 142
  traditionally celebrated, 142, 196
  normative, 6, 12, 19, 37, 88, 141,
    142, 147
  violent, 141, 144, 196
  successful, 142, 146, 147, 196
  unsuccessful, 147, 148
mentoring, 5, 56, 65, 66, 68, 69, 70,
  136, 137, 140, 142, 145, 147, 150,
  151, 164, 185, 187, 188, 202

micro-aggressions, 39, 40
mission, 38, 80, 82, 103, 118, 122, 138, 156, 185
　of feminism, 171, 172
mutuality, 34, 42

Naples, Nancy, 109, 171
nonprofit, 4, 5, 75, 77–8, 80, 85, 86, 103, 116, 117, 118, 125, 128, 157, 161, 167, 168, 188, 195

online, 75, 76, 77, 79, 86, 197, 199
　education, 14
　courses, 14
　discussions, 82
　education, 14
　experience, 76
　platforms, 86
　presence, 75
outsider, 63, 135, 139, 158

patriarchy, 11, 33, 95, 120, 138, 139, 162
pedagogy, 4, 6, 13, 14, 15, 19, 21, 22, 78, 80, 94, 95, 96, 98, 102, 105, 109, 115, 119, 123, 150, 156, 158, 194, 195, 198
　active learning, 115
　activist-apprentice, 94, 101–2, 109, 195, 198
　critical, 94
　cyber, 14, 78
　disruptive, 6
　feminist, 4, 13, 14, 21, 22, 78, 80, 96, 121, 123, 141, 156, 158, 159, 194, 202
　liberatory, 95, 108
　is political, 98
　service-learning, 13, 15, 22, 105, 116
people of color, 36, 42, 53, 55, 56, 60, 61, 62, 67, 70, 71, 116, 157
　boys of color, 146
　communities of, 62, 67, 70
　scholars of color, 53

staff of color, 57, 58, 69, 70, 198
students of color, 43, 54, 65, 67, 68, 69, 70, 181, 184, 187
writers of color, 60, 64
philanthropy, 6, 98, 104, 109n5, 116, 117, 118, 119, 120, 121, 127, 128, 129, 149
　feminist, 4, 116, 119, 120, 123, 124–30, 197, 199
place-based, 160, 163, 169
political, 1, 10, 14, 17–21, 33–4, 36, 39, 45, 57, 64, 70, 75, 83–5, 93, 97–9, 102, 108, 109n1, 116, 120, 128–9, 136, 158, 164, 197, 201
　personal is political, 4, 17, 135, 158, 162
power, 6, 11, 12, 13, 14, 17, 34, 35, 36, 37, 39, 42, 59, 60, 71, 75, 76, 82, 84, 85, 93, 96, 98, 100, 106, 116, 119, 121, 123, 128, 136, 139, 151, 170, 175, 177, 178, 179, 195
　of community engagement, 18, 69
　imbalance, 19, 85, 189
　powerless, 37
　and technology, 85, 86
praxis, 5, 21–2, 34, 36, 40, 43, 45, 46, 70, 78, 94, 98, 130, 151, 158–9, 162, 198, 200, 202
President's Higher Education Community Service Honor Roll, 175, 180
privilege, 5, 11, 18, 20, 31, 32, 33, 34, 35, 36, 38, 39, 40, 41, 54, 57, 60, 63, 67, 69, 83, 84, 88, 93, 98, 104, 121, 127, 130, 140, 142, 145, 149, 158, 162, 176, 177, 193, 196, 201

racial dysconsciousness, 41, 45
racism, 3, 32, 33, 34, 35, 36, 39, 41, 43, 44, 46, 60, 62, 64, 65, 68, 107, 149, 171, 180, 200
　antiracist, 31, 32, 40, 42, 45
　normative assumptions, 37

reciprocity, 6, 15, 22, 34, 42, 98, 100, 121, 127, 149, 194, 195
recognition, 2, 12, 22, 32, 33, 37, 45, 124, 135, 147, 158, 175
redistribution, 42, 45
reflection, 15, 21, 54, 57, 100, 101, 105–8, 123, 124, 127, 130, 140, 141, 143, 157, 161, 166, 169, 199–200, 202
   reflective writing, 123, 124, 128
   self-reflection, 101, 127, 140, 143
reflexivity, 5, 21, 59, 69, 100, 121, 123, 128, 130, 158
relational, 5, 59, 178
relationship, 57, 58, 67, 70, 94, 98, 99, 101, 102, 104, 106, 107, 119, 140, 143, 145, 168, 177, 178, 183, 186, 198, 201
   authentic, 5, 71, 177, 195, 198
   Black women's, 12, 66
   building, 102, 105, 140, 159, 175, 177–8, 181
   collaborative, 58, 101, 118, 144, 150
   colonial, 41
   community, 22, 54, 163, 164–5, 166, 176, 180, 185, 198
   dialectical, 158
   gender and technology, 76
   harmful, 54
   long-term, 33, 165, 187
   mentor/mentee, 144
   one-way, 42, 98
   power, 14, 59, 60, 151, 189, 199
   reciprocal, 98, 194
resistance, 13, 36, 94, 102, 136, 143, 151, 196
risk taking, 44, 46, 195
role model/ing, 5, 53, 54, 57, 64–6, 68, 69, 70, 160, 165, 194, 195, 196, 197–8, 202
   male, 144
   women of color, 4, 71

service-learning, 6, 15, 16, 18–20, 22, 34, 54, 71, 97–9, 108, 115, 117, 129, 159, 177, 181
   as charity, 17, 35, 37, 42, 44, 45, 63–4, 71, 116, 118, 121, 193, 201
   feminist, 108
   justice-oriented (also termed change-oriented or activist), 18, 20, 22, 35, 40, 54–5, 99, 102, 116, 130, 195
   pedagogy, 13, 15, 22, 105, 116
sexism, 3, 11, 21, 31, 32, 36, 38, 39, 43, 60, 65, 66, 76, 136, 137, 140, 141, 149, 168, 171, 196
social justice, 4, 5, 14, 18, 20, 31, 32, 33, 35, 41, 42, 45, 54, 55, 56, 63, 71, 88, 97, 102, 103, 108, 109, 129, 130, 136, 140, 150, 157, 159, 168, 171, 175, 178, 181, 186, 195, 200
social media, 4, 5, 14, 75, 76, 77, 78, 81, 85, 86, 117
sustainability, 179–80
   of partnerships, 176–7, 179
   of programs, 5, 144, 168, 179–81, 201
stratification (Gender, race & class), 33, 35, 37, 40, 147
structural & systemic change, 33
structural change, 15, 56
systemic change, 126, 151

teaching and learning, 13, 15, 19, 122, 180, 208
   engaged, 69
technology/ies, 14, 75, 76, 77, 78, 79, 80, 83, 84, 85, 86, 87, 88, 199
   for social change, 79
traditional, 102, 149
   classrooms, 5, 9, 105, 121, 158
   community engagement, 55, 66, 69, 71, 194, 197
   education, 54, 165
   feminism, 151

traditional—*Continued*
  hierarchical structures, 19, 119, 196
  leadership, 140, 143
  masculinity, 136, 142, 150, 196
  partners, 199, 202
  service-learning, 53, 61, 64, 66, 69, 94, 116, 118, 122, 196
transformation, 18, 19, 32, 33, 34, 35, 38, 42, 43, 45, 94, 96, 99, 129, 143, 149, 151, 186, 189, 197, 209
  of learning, 35, 86, 189
trust, 145, 148, 178–9, 186, 187, 189, 196

volunteer/ism, 2, 6, 18, 41, 77, 94, 98, 101, 103, 116, 117, 118, 126, 128–9, 155, 193, 198

Westheimer & Kahne, 2, 18, 20, 32, 128, 176, 177, 193
white supremacy, 39–41, 44

Whiteness Studies, 32, 34, 41, 42, 43, 46
  hegemonic whiteness, 37
  institutionalizing Whiteness, 39
  of universities, 41
women of color, 3, 4, 5, 12, 13, 31, 33, 36, 37, 39, 40, 44, 45, 53, 55, 56–7, 58–9, 60–4, 65–9, 70–2, 196, 199, 201
  feminists of color, 54, 56, 69, 70, 170
  working class, 60
women's center, 4, 5, 62, 135, 136, 137–8, 144, 150
Women's Studies, 2, 3, 4, 6, 9, 11, 14, 18, 21, 94, 97, 99, 102, 155, 156–7, 159, 161, 162, 165, 170, 171, 172
  National Women's Studies Association, 2

Young Men's Leadership Program, 137, 140, 196